Praise for *C# 2.0: Practical Guide for Programmers*!

Great book for any C# developer! It describes the basic programming language with EBNF notation and provides a number of practical programming tips and best practices on program design that enable you to utilize the C# language features effectively.
– **Adarsh Khare**, Software Design Engineer, Microsoft

C# 2.0: A Practical Guide provides an amazing breadth of information in a compact and efficient format, with clear and concise writing and useful code examples. It cuts right to the core of what you need to know, covering every aspect of the C# language, an introduction to the .NET API, and an overview of pertinent object-oriented concepts. This book tops my recommendation list for any developer learning C#.
– **David Makofske**, Principal Consultant/Architect, Akamai Technologies

This book is essential for programmers who are considering system development using C#. The two authors have masterfully created a programming guide that is current, complete, and useful immediately. The writing style is crisp, concise, and engaging. This book is a valuable addition to a C# programmer's library.
– **Edward L. Lamie**, PhD, Director of Educational Services, Express Logic, Inc.

At last, a programming language book that provides complete coverage with a top-down approach and clear, simple examples! Another welcome feature of this book is that it is concise, in the tradition of classics such as Kernighan and Ritchie. The new book by De Champlain and Patrick is the best introduction to C# that I've seen so far.
– **Peter Grogono**, Professor and Associate Chair of Computer Science, Concordia University

The book covers the basic and the advanced features of a relatively new and well established programming language, C#. A truly Object Oriented style is used throughout the book in a consistent manner. C# and Object Oriented concepts are well illustrated through simple and concise examples to hold the reader's attention. A very well-written book.
– **Ferhat Khendek**, PhD, Research Chair in Telecommunications Software Engineering, Concordia University

C# 2.0: Practical Guide
for Programmers

The Morgan Kaufmann Practical Guides Series
Series Editor: Michael J. Donahoo

TCP/IP Sockets in C#: Practical Guide for Programmers
David Makofske, Michael J. Donahoo, and Kenneth L. Calvert

Java Cryptography Extensions: Practical Guide for Programmers
Jason Weiss

JSP: Practical Guide for Java Programmers
Robert J. Brunner

JSTL: Practical Guide for JSP Programmers
Sue Spielman

Java: Practical Guide for Programmers
Zbigniew M. Sikora

The Struts Framework: Practical Guide for Java Programmers
Sue Spielman

Multicast Sockets: Practical Guide for Programmers
David Makofske and Kevin Almeroth

TCP/IP Sockets in Java: Practical Guide for Programmers
Kenneth L. Calvert and Michael J. Donahoo

TCP/IP Sockets in C: Practical Guide for Programmers
Michael J. Donahoo and Kenneth L. Calvert

JDBC: Practical Guide for Java Programmers
Gregory D. Speegle

For further information on these books and for a list of forthcoming titles,
please visit our website at *http://www.mkp.com/practical*

C# 2.0: Practical Guide for Programmers

Michel de Champlain

DeepObjectKnowledge

Brian G. Patrick

Trent University

ELSEVIER

AMSTERDAM • BOSTON • HEIDELBERG
LONDON • NEW YORK • OXFORD
PARIS • SAN DIEGO • SAN FRANCISCO
SINGAPORE • SYDNEY • TOKYO

Morgan Kaufmann is an imprint of Elsevier

MORGAN KAUFMANN PUBLISHERS

Senior Editor	Rick Adams
Associate Editor	Karyn Johnson
Publishing Services Manager	Simon Crump
Project Manager	Brandy Lilly
Cover Design	Yvo Riezebos Design
Cover Image	Photo by Steve Cole, Photodisc Green, Getty Images
Composition	Cepha Imaging Pvt. Ltd.
Copyeditor	Kolam Inc.
Proofreader	Kolam Inc.
Indexer	Kolam Inc.
Interior printer	Maple Press
Cover printer	Phoenix Color

Morgan Kaufmann Publishers is an imprint of Elsevier.
500 Sansome Street, Suite 400, San Francisco, CA 94111

This book is printed on acid-free paper.

Library of Congress Cataloging-in-Publication Data
Application submitted.

ISBN: 0-12-167451-7

For information on all Morgan Kaufmann publications, visit our Web site at *www.mkp.com*

Transferred to Digital Printing 2009

To Hélène, the air that I breathe
— Michel

With love to my parents, Lionel and Chrissie
— Brian

Contents

Preface

Writing a short book on a comprehensive programming language was most definitely a challenge. But such was our mandate and such is C#.

The C# programming language was first released in 2000 and has quickly established itself as the language *de rigueur* for application development at Microsoft Corporation and other software houses. It is a powerful language based on the paradigm of object-orientation and fully integrated with the Microsoft .NET Framework. Hence, C# is architecturally neutral and supported by a vast library of reusable software.

To describe all minutiae of the C# language or to indulge in all facets of the .NET Framework would require a tome or two. Yet the authors realize that experienced software programmers are not looking to plough through extraneous detail but are focused on extracting the essentials of a language, which allow them to commence development quickly and confidently. That is our primary objective.

To realize this objective, we followed the ABCs of writing: accuracy, brevity, and completeness. First and foremost, care has been taken to ensure that the terminology and the discussion on the syntax and semantics of C# are consistent with the latest language specifications, namely C# 2.0. For easy reference, those features that are new to C# 2.0 are identified in the margins.

Second, for the sake of brevity, we strike at the heart of most features of C# with little digression, historical reflection, or comparative analysis. Although the book is not intended as a tutorial on object-oriented design, a few tips on good programming practice are scattered throughout the text and identified in the margins as well.

Finally, all principal features of the C# programming language are covered, from basic classes to attributes. The numerous examples throughout the text, however, focus on the most natural and most common applications of these features. It is simply not possible within the confines of two hundred pages to examine all permutations of C#.

This practical guide emerged from the experiences of the first author in teaching, training, and mentoring professional developers in industry and graduate students at university on the use of the C# language. Its organization is therefore rooted in several C# jump-start courses and one-day tutorials with an intended audience of experienced programmers. Although some background in object-oriented technology is ideal, all object-oriented features are reviewed in the broader context before they are described with respect to their implementation in C#.

In short, *C# 2.0: Practical Guide for Programmers* rests its hat on three hooks:

- Provide a concise yet comprehensive explanation of the basic, advanced, and latest features of the C# language. Each feature is illustrated with short, uncluttered examples. To ensure that code is error-free, the large majority of examples have been automatically and directly extracted from source code that has been verified and successfully compiled.

- Cover the essentials of the .NET Framework. Modern programming languages like Java and C# are supported by huge application programming interfaces (APIs) or frameworks in order to tackle the flexibility and complexity of today's applications. Although the focus of this book is on the C# language and *not* on the .NET Framework, we would be remiss to omit a basic discussion on the core functionalities of the .NET libraries. Any greater depth, however, would far exceed our mandate.

- Include a refresher on object-oriented concepts. The C# language is fully object-oriented, replete with a unified type system that encapsulates the full spectrum of types, from integers to interfaces. In addition to classes, the concepts of inheritance and polymorphism are given their share of proportional representation as two of the three tenets of object-oriented technology.

Organization of the Book

The book is organized into ten concise chapters and two appendices. Chapter 1 introduces the C# programming language and the .NET Framework. It also outlines a small project that is used as the basis for the exercises at the end of most chapters. This project is designed to gradually meld the features of the C# language into a comprehensive solution for a practical problem.

Unlike in books that present a programming language from the bottom up, Chapters 2, 3, and 4 immediately delve into what we consider the most fundamental, though higher-level, concepts of C#. Chapter 2 begins our discussion with classes and objects, the first of the three tenets of object-oriented technology. We demonstrate how classes are defined as an amalgam of behavior and state, how objects are created, and how access to classes and to class members is controlled. Namespaces are also described as an important aspect of "programming in the large" and how they are used to organize classes into logical groups, to control name conflicts, and to ease the integration and reuse of other classes within applications.

A fuller exposé on the basic class members of C# follows in Chapter 3: methods that define behavior and data members that define state. Constructors, destructors, and parameter passing by value and by reference are also covered. Chapter 3 concludes with an important discussion on class reuse and how classes derive, refine, and redefine their behavior and state via inheritance, the second tenet of object-oriented programming. We compare inheritance with aggregation (composition) and offer a few guidelines on their appropriate use.

The unified type system of C# is presented in Chapter 4, showing how value and reference types are derived from the same root class called Object. All value types, including nullable types, are fully described, along with a brief introduction to the basic notion of a reference type. The Object class itself provides an excellent vehicle to introduce polymorphism (the third tenet of object-oriented programming), virtual methods, and cloning using deep and shallow copying. The chapter ends with a presentation of two predefined but common classes for arrays and strings.

In Chapters 5 and 6, the rudiments of C# expressions and statements are reviewed with numerous short examples to illustrate their behavior. Expressions are built from arithmetic, logical, relational, and assignment operators and are largely inspired by the lexicon of C/C++. Because selection and iterative statements, too, are drawn from C/C++, our presentation is terse but comprehensive. However, whenever warranted, more time is devoted to those features, such as exceptions and the exception-handling mechanism of C#, that bolster its reliability and robustness.

Chapter 7 extends our discussion on the reference types that were first introduced in Chapter 4. These advanced reference types include delegates, events, abstract classes, and interfaces. New features such as delegate inferences and anonymous methods are also covered. In this chapter, we carefully distinguish between the single inheritance of classes and the multiple implementation of interfaces. Polymorphism, first mentioned with respect to the Object root class, is illustrated once again with a comprehensive example based on a hierarchy of counter-classes and interfaces. The two accessors in C#, namely properties and indexers, are also presented, noting the latest specifications for property access modifiers.

The last three chapters (8, 9, and 10) shift their focus away from the programming language concepts of C# and examine some of the basic but indispensable features of the .NET Framework. Chapter 8 extends the notion of class reuse with a look at the different types of predefined collections and their constructors and iterators. Although not associated with the .NET Framework itself, one of the newest features of C# is generic classes (or templates) and is presented as a natural counterpart to collections.

Our discussion on resource disposal begun in Chapter 3 is rounded out in Chapter 9 along with input/output and threads. Input/output is a broad topic and is limited here to representative I/O for binary, bytes, and character streams. Threads, on the other hand, is a challenging topic, and the synchronization mechanisms required to support concurrent programming are carefully explained with several supporting examples. Finally, Chapter 10 examines the use and collection of metadata using reflection and attributes, both pre- and user-defined.

The first of the two appendices summarizes the grammatical rules of the C# language using EBNF notation. The second appendix provides an abridged list of the common XML tags used for the automatic generation of web documentation.

Source Code Availability

The code for most examples and all exercises of each chapter is available and maintained at the website www.DeepObjectKnowledge.com.

Acknowledgments

Any book goes through a number of incarnations, but none is more important than that based on the constructive and objective feedback of its reviewers. Much improvement on the organization and technical content of the book is due to their invaluable input, and our sincere thanks are extended to Gerald Baugartner (Ohio State University), Eric Gunnerson (Microsoft Corporation), Keith Hill (Agilent Technologies), Adarsh Khare (Microsoft Corporation), David Makofske (Akamai Technologies), and Mauro Ottaviani (Microsoft Corporation). Over the past year, we have also received timely advice and ongoing encouragement from the kind staff at Morgan Kaufmann and Kolam. We acknowledge their support with a special "tip of the cap" to Rick Adams, Mona Buehler, Karyn Johnson, and Cara Salvatore.

Finally, we warn all potential authors that writing a book is a wonderful way to while away the weeks and weekends. Unfortunately, these precious hours are spent apart from our families, and it is to them that we extend our deepest appreciation for their understanding, patience, and unconditional love.

We hope in the end that you enjoy the book. We hope that it reads well and provides a solid introduction to the C# language. Of course, full responsibility for its organization and content rests with the authors. And with that in mind, we defer to you, our reader, as our ultimate source for both improvement and encouragement.

Michel de Champlain
mdec@DeepObjectKnowledge.com

Brian G. Patrick
bpatrick@trentu.ca

About the Authors

Michel de Champlain is the President and Principal Architect of DeepObjectKnowledge Inc., a firm that provides industry with mentoring and training support in object technologies. Michel holds a Ph.D. in Software Engineering from the École Polytechnique de Montréal and has held university appointments at the Collège Militaire Royal de Saint-Jean, the University of Canterbury in New Zealand, and Concordia University in Montréal. He has also been a regular invited speaker at the Embedded Systems Conference for the last fourteen years. Working in close collaboration with industry as well as academia, Michel has trained thousands of people throughout Canada, the United States, Europe, and down under in object-oriented analysis, design, and implementation. His current research interests include object-oriented languages, frameworks, design patterns, compilers, virtual machines, and real-time microkernels.

Brian G. Patrick is an Associate Professor of Computer Science/Studies at Trent University in Peterborough, Ontario. He first met Michel as a colleague at the Collège Militaire Royal de Saint-Jean and has developed a close working relationship with Michel over the years. Brian earned his Ph.D. in Computer Science from McGill University in Montréal, where he later completed an M.B.A. in Finance and International Business. His research interests have included heuristic search, parallel algorithms, and software reuse. He is currently investigating job scheduling schemes for parallel applications.

chapter 1

Introducing C# and .NET

In the late 1990s, Microsoft created Visual J++ in an attempt to use Java in a Windows context and to improve the interface of its Component Object Model (COM). Unable to extend Java due to proprietary rights held by Sun, Microsoft embarked on a project to replace and improve Visual J++, its compiler, and its virtual machine with a general-purpose, object-oriented language. To head up this project, Microsoft engaged the talents of Anders Hejlsberg, formerly of Borland and the principal author of Windows Foundation Classes (WFC), Turbo Pascal, and Delphi. As a result of this effort, C# was first introduced in July 2000 as a thoroughly modern object-oriented language that would ultimately serve as the main development language of the Microsoft .NET platform.

In this short introductory chapter, we lay out the fundamental features of the C# programming language and the .NET Framework. We also outline the requirements of a small project that will serve as an ongoing exercise throughout the text. The chapter ends with a few words on syntactic notation.

1.1 What Is C#?

As part of the lineage of C-based languages, C# has incorporated and exploited programming language features with a proven record of success and familiarity. To that end, most syntactic features of C# are borrowed from C/C++, and most of its object-oriented concepts, such as garbage collection, reflection, the root class, and the multiple inheritance of interfaces, are inspired by Java. Improvements in C# over Java, often with syntax simplification, have been applied to iteration, properties, events, metadata, versioning, and the conversion between simple types and objects.

In addition to being syntactically familiar, C# is strongly typed, architecturally neutral, portable, safe, and multi-threaded. Type security in C# is supported in a number of ways, including initializing variables before their use, eliminating dangerous explicit type conversions, controlling the limits in arrays, and checking the overflow of type limits during arithmetic operations. Its architecturally neutral intermediate format, implemented as the Common Intermediate Language (CIL) and executed on a virtual machine, makes C# portable and independent of its running environment.

C# is also safe. It controls access to hardware and memory resources, checks classes at runtime, and does not allow the implicit usage and manipulation of pointers (as C/C++ do). The explicit use of pointers, on the other hand, is restricted to sections of code that have been designated as unsafe. With the support of a garbage collector, frustrating memory leaks and dangling pointers are a non-issue. The C# language also supports multi-threading in order to promote efficient interactive applications such as graphics, input/output, and so on. Other modern features in C# include Just-in-Time (JIT) compilation from bytecode to native code, exceptions for error handling, namespaces for preventing type collisions, and documentation comments.

In order to promote the widespread use and acceptance of C#, Microsoft relinquished its proprietary rights. With the support of Hewlett-Packard and Intel, Microsoft quickly pushed for a standardized version of C#. In December 2001, the first standard was accepted by the European Computer Manufacturer Association (ECMA). The following December, a second standard was adopted by the ECMA, and it was accepted 3 months later by the International Organization for Standardization (ISO). The standardization of C# has three principal benefits:

1. To support the portability of C# applications across different hardware architectures,

2. To foster the development of C# compilers among different manufacturers, and

3. To encourage the emergence of high-quality software tools to support the development of C# applications.

In this text, C# 2.0 is used as the final arbiter of the language.

1.2   What Is the .NET Framework?

The .NET Framework provides a new platform for building applications that are easily deployed and executed across multiple architectures and operating systems. This portability is achievable only because of ongoing standardization through the ECMA and ISO organizations. In this way, the framework offers independence to languages by supplying an international standard called the Common Language Infrastructure (CLI).

The framework was designed to be installed on top of an operating system and is divided into two main layers, as shown in Figure 1.1: a runtime environment called the **Common Language Runtime** (CLR), similar to the Java Virtual Machine, and a large library of classes called the **Framework Class Library** (FCL), which provides the required services for modern applications.

Applications	Development Tools for C#, J#, C++, VB, ...
Framework Class Library	
Common Language Runtime	
Operating System	

Figure 1.1: Overview of the .NET Framework.

The bottom layer of the .NET Framework contains the CLR. The CLR provides the runtime services to execute C# programs that have been translated into the CIL. The top layer encapsulates all services in the FCL for user interface, control, security, data access, Extensible Markup Language (XML), input/output, threading, and so on. User interface (UI) services—both Window and Web Forms—support graphic interfaces and server-side controls, respectively. ASP.NET provides control, security, sessioning, and configuration for dynamic web pages. Data access by ADO.NET adds XML as an intermediate format for data and supports connections to datasets using XML caches. The FCL also contains system classes to manage I/O, execution threads, serialization, reflection, networking, collections, diagnostics, debugging, and so on.

Applications and development tools are typically layered on top of the .NET Framework. Visual Studio .NET, in particular, is a good example. It provides an integrated development environment (IDE) that standardizes support for many programming languages, including C#, J#, C++, and Visual Basic.

After the standardization of the C# and CLI specifications in December 2001, Microsoft released the CLR as both a commercial implementation of the CLI runtime virtual machine and a subset of the FCL. Since then, C# has become the programming language of choice for developing applications in the .NET Framework. CLR, FCL, and the C# compiler are all released as part of the .NET Framework Software Development Kit (SDK), which is freely available from Microsoft at http://msdn.microsoft.com. At the time of this writing, there are other .NET implementations in progress, such as the open-source Mono and DotGNU projects. All these implementations include a C# compiler that extends language availability to platforms other than Windows.

The C# code executed on this framework follows object-oriented development practices defined by the Common Language Specification (CLS). The CLS defines a collaboration standard between languages and object development practices. Obviously, some older traditional programming languages, such as COBOL and Fortran, cannot exploit the full characteristics offered by the CLS. The Common Type System (CTS) of the .NET Framework represents a standardized set of basic data types that permit language interoperability. In other words, the CTS defines the rules implemented in the CLR. The CLS supports a (common) subset of the CTS in order to allow cross-language integration. Therefore, a CLS-compliant component can be used by applications written in other languages.

The following subsections highlight the relationships between a number of important features of the .NET Framework and the C# programming language, including the .NET virtual machine, .NET virtual code, and .NET assemblies.

1.2.1   The .NET Virtual Machine: Common Language Runtime

The CLR is the .NET virtual machine. It handles the compiling, loading, and execution of a C# application. The compiling process employs a JIT approach that translates the CIL into machine code as required. In addition to a traditional runtime system, it also provides debugging and profiling functionalities. The CLR implements the CTS, which defines types and data. Moreover, C# applications contain a complete description of their types, called metadata, providing code visibility to other applications or tools. With this metadata, the CLR uses reflection in order to resolve library references, link components, and resolve types at runtime. The garbage collector is a subsystem of the CLR that cleans up memory that is no longer needed. It frees developers of the tedious and error-prone responsibility of recovering (deleting or deallocating) memory space allocated during object creation.

1.2.2   The .NET Virtual Code: Intermediate Language

The applications written in C# are not traditional Windows programs compiled into machine code. Rather, the C# compiler generates CIL code, often referred to as managed code. This code is dedicated to run safely within the .NET environment. In fact, the CLR takes care of the back-end part of the compilation before execution, allowing the possibility of JIT translation from CIL code into native machine code without compromising security. On the other hand, unmanaged code, such as that generated by C/C++ compilers in the Windows environment, uses native and potentially dangerous instructions (for example, pointers). Like Java bytecode, CIL is also virtual machine code and is therefore completely independent of any underlying processor architecture. It is fully cross-language compatible on the .NET platform, offering at the time of this writing support for many different programming languages. Therefore, all programs implemented in any of these languages and compiled into CIL may share components without any extra effort.

1.2.3   The .NET Assemblies: Applications and/or Components

An assembly is the logical unit of deployment in .NET and encompasses two kinds of implementation units: applications (.exe) and components (.dll[1]). Whereas applications represent fully executable C# programs, components represent core reusable objects that provide basic services to build up applications. Indeed, Microsoft prefers to call C# a component-oriented rather than an object-oriented programming language.

    Each assembly is either private or public and contains a manifest (a set of metadata) that provides information about its implementation units, such as name, owner, version, security permissions, culture, processor, operating system, public key signature, and all other needed resources (such as bitmaps). Private assemblies are used only by the application that installed them, but public (shared) assemblies are stored in a repository maintained by the .NET Framework called the Global Assembly Cache (GAC).

---

[1]DLL stands for Dynamic-Link Library and refers to a class library in Visual Studio .NET.

Finally, because every assembly contains version information, the CLR is able to handle multiple versions of the same component on the same platform.

1.3 Project Exercise

Throughout this text, the exercises at the end of most chapters are based on a small project. The project was chosen to offer a nice continuity among the exercises and to provide the reader with a practical application that can be used, reused, and modified. All the source code for the exercises is available and maintained on the web site of DeepObjectKnowledge (http://www.DeepObjectKnowledge.com).

The project consists of two distinct applications, each of which will be presented incrementally throughout the text. The first application allows a user to enter, modify, or delete an organization, its domain, and its e-mail format. Using the keywords First(F) and Last(L), e-mail formats can be represented in any number of ways, as shown below for the contact name John Smith.

```
Email Format        Resulting Name

First.Last          John.Smith
Last.First          Smith.John
F.Last              J.Smith
First+Last          JohnSmith
Last+First          SmithJohn
...
```

The second application allows a user to enter, modify, or delete a contact's name, organization, and e-mail address. However, using a property file generated by the first application, the e-mail address of the contact may also be deduced from the corresponding e-mail format of an existing organization. The latter approach generates contact information (in this case, the e-mail address) quickly and accurately.

Using a three-tier design approach, the application is divided into three distinct subsystems (Figure 1.2). Each subsystem is a layer that has been decoupled as much as possible to promote the reusability of classes. These subsystems are as follows:

- **Presentation**, which isolates user inputs and outputs,

- **Business**, which represents domain objects that perform specific processing tasks, and

- **Data**, which loads information from files or databases to domain objects, and also saves information from domain objects to files or databases.

Later on, each subsystem is represented by a namespace.

In order to remain focused on the features of the C# language and on the principles of good design, the project is built on the simplicity of a text user interface (TUI) for a console application. But as shown in Figure 1.2, the three-tier design easily allows one

Presentation	TUI	GUI
Business	Domain Objects	
Data	Files	Database

Figure 1.2: Three-tier design of our project exercise.

to reuse the business and data layers with a different presentation subsystem, such as a graphical user interface (GUI). Although files are used in this text as the internal persistent medium to save and store information, one can also reuse the presentation and business layers with a database instead of files in the data layer. Whether we are dealing with TUIs or GUIs, or databases or files, we are reusing the same domain objects in the business layer. The three-tier design therefore provides a flexible structure for this application that can be customized for other projects. It avoids a monolithic application where the replacement of one layer has a domino effect on all other classes in the project.

1.4 Syntax Notation

In this text, the Extended Backus–Naur Form (EBNF) notation, which is summarized in Table 1.1, is used to define the syntax rules (or **productions**) of the C# programming language. The EBNF notation was chosen for its conciseness and readability. On rare occasion, an EBNF definition in the text may be simplified and noted as such for expository purposes. However, the full EBNF definition of C# given in Appendix A is well over half the length of the equivalent BNF definition provided by the language specification itself.

Each production describes a valid sequence of tokens called lexical elements. Nonterminals represent a production and begin with an uppercase letter. Terminals are either keywords or quoted operators. Each production is terminated by a period, and parentheses are used for grouping.

Notation	Meaning
A*	Repetition—zero or more occurrences of A
A+	Repetition—one or more occurrences of A
A?	Option—zero or one occurrence of A
A B	Sequence—A followed by B
A | B	Alternative—A or B
"0".."9"	Alternative—one character between 0 and 9, inclusive
(A B)	Grouping—of an A B sequence

Table 1.1: Notation for Extended Backus–Naur Form.

For example, identifiers and numbers are defined in most programming languages by the following four productions:

```
Identifier = Letter (Letter | Digit)* .
Number     = ("-" | "+")? Digit+ .
Letter     = "a".."z" | "A".."Z" .
Digit      = "0".."9" .
```

According to these rules, an `Identifier` must begin with a `Letter` and is followed by zero or more `Letter`(s) or `Digit`(s). Hence, the following identifiers are valid:

```
Pentium    SuperH    x86
```

A `Number`, on the other hand, is preceded by an optional plus or minus sign followed by at least one digit.

The EBNF notation can also be used to express command-line syntax. For example,

```
CsharpCompilerCommand = "csc" Option* File+ .
Option = "/help" | "/target:<file>" | "/nowarn:<level>" | "/doc".
```

Here, the C# compilation command `csc` may have an empty sequence of options followed by at least one source file.

In order to simplify the EBNF rules in such a large grammar as C#, we assume that:

```
<non-terminal>s = <non-terminal>+
```

is equivalent to:

```
<non-terminal>s
```

and that:

```
<non-terminal>List = <non-terminal> ( "," <non-terminal> )*
```

is equivalent to:

```
<non-terminal>List
```

Based on the preceding simplifications, the following productions:

```
Block      = "{" Statements? "}" .
Statements = Statement+ .
Statement  = ExprList ";" .
ExprList   = Expr ( "," Expr )* .
```

can be reduced to:

```
Block      = "{" Statements? "}" .
Statement  = ExprList ";" .
```

chapter 2

Classes, Objects, and Namespaces

Software development is a non-trivial activity; even simple software systems have inherent complexity. To tackle this complexity, two paradigms have dominated the software development landscape. The first and older paradigm is based on the notion of procedural abstraction and divides developmental work into two distinct parts. First, real-world entities are identified and mapped as structures or records (data) and second, subprograms are written to act upon this data (behavior). The primary drawback of the procedural approach is the separation of data and behavior. Because data may be shared among several subprograms using global variables or parameters, responsibility for its behavior is scattered and open ended. For this reason, applications using the procedural approach can be difficult to test, debug, and maintain.

The second paradigm, otherwise known as the object-oriented approach, is based on the notion of data abstraction and divides developmental work into two very different tasks. First, the data *and* behavior of each real-world entity of the problem domain are identified and encapsulated into a single structure called a class. Second, objects created from the different classes work together to provide a solution to the given problem. Importantly, each object is ideally responsible for the behavior of its own data.

The C# programming language is based on the object-oriented paradigm. This chapter, therefore, begins with a discussion on classes and objects. It describes how objects are created based on classes and how access to data and methods is controlled. It also covers how classes are logically grouped into namespaces. The last two sections describe the composition of a compilation unit and how a C# program is implemented, compiled, and executed as a collection of compilation units.

2.1   Classes and Objects

A **class** is an abstraction that represents the common data and behavior of a real-world entity or domain object. Software objects that are created or instantiated from a class, therefore, mimic their real-world counterparts. Each **object** of a given class evolves with its own version of the common data but shares the same behavior among all objects of the same class. In this respect, a class can be thought of as the cookie cutter and the objects of that class as the cookies.

Classes are synonymous with types and are the fundamental building blocks of object-oriented applications, much as subprograms are the fundamental building blocks of procedural programming. As a modern abstraction, classes reduce complexity by:

- Hiding away details (implementation),

- Highlighting essential behavior (interface), and

- Separating interface from implementation.

Because the class encapsulates both data and behavior, each object is responsible for the manipulation and protection of its own data. At its core, **object-oriented** (OO) technology is not concerned primarily with programming, but rather with program organization and responsibilities. Based on the concept of an object where each object has a clear and well-defined responsibility, program organization is achieved by finding the right objects for a given task.

Designing a class itself is also a skill that shifts the focus of the designer to the user's point of view in order to satisfy the functional requirements of the domain expert. The domain expert is not necessarily a software developer but one who is familiar with the entities of the real-world domain. Of course, a software developer who gains experience in a particular domain can become a domain expert as well.

2.1.1   Declaring Classes

As mentioned previously, a class declaration encapsulates two kinds of class members:

- **Data**, otherwise known as a field, attribute, or variable, and

- **Behavior**, otherwise known as a method, operation, or service.

In this text, fields and methods, respectively, are used to represent the data and behavior members of a class. By way of example, consider the Id class given below. This class defines an abstraction that represents a personal identification and is composed of two fields and four methods. The two fields, firstName and lastName, are both of type string; the four methods simply retrieve and set the values of the two data fields.

```
class Id {
    // Methods (behavior)
    string GetFirstName()          { return firstName;  }
    string GetLastName()           { return lastName;   }
```

```
    void    SetFirstName(string value) { firstName = value; }
    void    SetLastName(string value)  { lastName = value;  }

    // Fields (data)
    string firstName = "<first name>";
    string lastName  = "<last name>";
}
```

Experienced C++ and Java programmers will notice the absence of constructors. Without an explicit declaration of a constructor, a default constructor is automatically generated by the C# compiler. A complete discussion on constructors, however, is deferred until Chapter 3.

2.1.2   Creating Objects

An **instantiation** is the creation or construction of an object based on a class declaration. This process involves two steps. First, a variable is declared in order to hold a reference to an object of a particular class. In the following example, a reference called id is declared for the class Id:

```
    Id  id;
```

Once a variable is declared, an instance of the class is explicitly created using the new operator. This operator returns a reference to an object whereupon it is assigned to the reference variable. As shown here, an object of the Id class is created and a reference to that object is assigned to id:

```
    id = new Id();
```

The previous two steps, declaring a variable and creating an object, can also be coalesced into a single line of code:

```
    Id id = new Id();
```

In any case, once an instance of the class Id is created, the fields firstName and lastName are assigned to the literal strings "<first name>" and "<last name>", respectively.

The variable id provides a reference to the accessible fields and methods of the Id object. Although an object can only be manipulated via references, it can have more than one reference. For example, id and idAlias handle (and refer to) the same object:

```
    Id id       = new Id();
    Id idAlias = id;
```

A constant is declared by adding the const keyword as a prefix to a field class member. The constant value is obtained from a constant expression that must be evaluated at compile-time. For example, the constants K and BufferSize are defined by 1024 and 4 * K, respectively, as shown:

```
const int K = 1024;
const int BufferSize = 4 * K;
```

It is worth noting that only built-in types, such as int, are allowed in a constant declaration.

2.2 Access Modifiers

To uphold the principle of information hiding, access to classes and class members may be controlled using modifiers that prefix the class name, method, or data field. In this section, we first examine those modifiers that control access to classes, followed by a discussion on the modifiers that control access to methods and data fields.

2.2.1 Controlling Access to Classes

In C#, each class has one of two access modifiers: public or internal. If a class is public as it is for the Id class here, then it is also visible from all other classes.

```
public class Id {
    ...
}
```

On the other hand, if a class is internal then it is only visible among classes that are part of the same compiled unit. It is important to point out that one or more compilation units may be compiled together to generate a single compiled unit.[1]

```
internal class Id {
    ...
}
```

Classes are, by default, internal; therefore, the internal modifier is optional.

2.2.2 Controlling Access to Class Members

The C# language is equipped with five access modifiers for methods and data fields: public, private, protected, internal, and protected internal. The semantics of these modifiers depends on their context, that is, whether or not the class itself is public or internal.

If a class is public, its public methods and data fields are visible and, hence, accessible both inside and outside the class. Private methods and data fields, however, are only

---

[1]A full discussion on compilation units and compilation is found in Sections 2.4 and 2.5.

visible within the class itself. The visibility of its protected methods and data fields is restricted to the class itself and to its subclasses. Internal methods and data fields are only visible among classes that are part of the same compiled unit. And finally, methods or data fields that are protected internal have the combined visibility of internal and protected members. By default, if no modifier is specified for a method or data field then accessibility is private.

On the other hand, if a class is internal, the semantics of the access modifiers is identical to those of a public class *except* for one key restriction: Access is limited to those classes within the same compiled unit. Otherwise, no method or data field of an internal class is directly accessible among classes that are compiled separately.

When used in conjunction with the data fields and methods of a class, access modifiers dually support the notions of **information hiding** and **encapsulation**. By making data fields private, data contained in an object is hidden from other objects in the system. Hence, data integrity is preserved. Furthermore, by making methods public, access and modification to data is controlled via the methods of the class. Hence, no direct external access by other objects ensures that data behavior is also preserved.

As a rule of thumb, good class design declares data fields as private and methods as public. It is also suggested that methods to retrieve data members (called getters) and methods to change data members (called setters) be public and protected, respectively. Making a setter method public has the same effect as making the data field public, which violates the notion of information hiding. This violation, however, is unavoidable for components, which, by definition, are objects that must be capable of updating their data fields at runtime. For example, a user may need to update the lastName of an Id object to reflect a change in marital status.

| Tip |

Sometimes, developers believe that going through a method to update a data field is inefficient. In other words, why not make the data field protected instead of the method? The main justification in defining a protected method is twofold:

- A protected method, unlike a data field, can be overridden. This is very important if a change of behavior is required in subclasses.

- A protected method is normally generated inline as a macro and therefore eliminates the overhead of the call/return.

It is also important to remember that, in software development, it is always possible to add public methods, but impossible to remove them or make them private once they have been used by the client. Assuming that the class Id instantiates components, we add public modifiers for all methods and private modifiers for all data fields, as shown:

```
public class Id {
    // Methods (behavior)
    public  string GetFirstName()           { return firstName; }
    public  string GetLastName()            { return lastName;  }
    public  void   SetFirstName(string value) { firstName = value; }
    public  void   SetLastName(string value)  { lastName = value;  }
```

```
    // Fields (data)
    private string firstName = "<first name>";
    private string lastName  = "<last name>";
}
```

2.3 Namespaces

A **namespace** is a mechanism used to organize classes (even namespaces) into groups
and to control the proliferation of names. This control is absolutely necessary to avoid any
future name conflicts with the integration (or reuse) of other classes that may be included
in an application.

   If a class is not explicitly included in a namespace, then it is placed into the default
namespace, otherwise known as the global namespace. Using the default namespace,
however, is not a good software engineering strategy. It demonstrates a lack of program
design and makes code reuse more difficult. Therefore, when developing large applications, the use of namespaces is indispensable for the complete definition of classes.

2.3.1 Declaring Namespaces

The following example presents a namespace declaration for the Presentation subsystem in Figure 1.2 that includes two public classes, which define the TUI and the GUI,
respectively.

```
namespace Presentation {
    public class TUI { ... }
    public class GUI { ... }
}
```

This Presentation namespace can also be nested into a Project namespace containing all
three distinct subsystems as shown here:

```
namespace Project {
    namespace Presentation {
        public class TUI { ... }
        public class GUI { ... }
    }
    namespace Business {
        // Domain classes ...
    }
    namespace Data {
        public class Files { ... }
        public class Database { ... }
    }
}
```

Access to classes and nested namespaces is made via a qualified identifier. For example, Project.Presentation provides an access path to the classes TUI and GUI. This mechanism allows two or more namespaces to contain classes of the same name without any conflict. For example, two front-end namespaces shown below, one for C (Compilers.C) and another for C# (Compilers.Csharp), can own (and access) different classes with the same name. Therefore, Lexer and Parser for the C compiler are accessed without ambiguity using the qualified identifier Compiler.C.

```
namespace Compilers {
    namespace C {
        class Lexer  { ... }
        class Parser { ... }
    }
    namespace Csharp {
        class Lexer  { ... }
        class Parser { ... }
    }
}
```

Furthermore, the classes Lexer and Parser can be included together in separate files as long as they are associated with the namespaces Compilers.C and Compilers.Csharp, respectively:

```
namespace Compilers.C {
    class Lexer { ... }
    class Parser { ... }
}
namespace Compilers.Csharp {
    class Lexer { ... }
    class Parser { ... }
}
```

A graphical representation of these qualifications is shown in Figure 2.1.

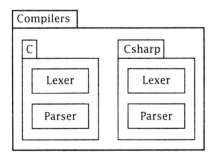

Figure 2.1: Namespaces for compilers.

EBNF The formal EBNF definition of a namespace declaration is given here:

```
NamespaceDecl       = "namespace" QualifiedIdentifier NamespaceBody ";"? .
QualifiedIdentifier = Identifier ( "." Identifier )* .
```

The namespace body may contain using directives as described in the next section and
EBNF namespace member declarations:

```
NamespaceBody = "{" UsingDirectives? NamespaceMemberDecls? "}" .
```

A namespace member declaration is either a (nested) namespace declaration or a type
declaration where the latter is a class, a structure, an interface, an enumeration, or a
EBNF delegate.

```
NamespaceMemberDecl = NamespaceDecl | TypeDecl .
TypeDecl            = ClassDecl | StructDecl | InterfaceDecl | EnumDecl |
                      DelegateDecl .
```

So far, only class declarations have been presented. Other type declarations, however, will
follow throughout the text.

A Digression on Namespace Organization

Tip A common industry practice is to use an organization's internet domain name (reversed)
to package classes and other subnamespaces. For example, the source files for the project
were developed under the namespace Project:

```
namespace com.DeepObjectKnowledge.PracticalGuideForCsharp {
    namespace Project {
        ...
    }
}
```

This again is equivalent to:

```
namespace com.DeepObjectKnowledge.PracticalGuideForCsharp.Project {
    ...
}
```

2.3.2 Importing Namespaces

The using directive allows one namespace to access the types (classes) of another without
EBNF specifying their full qualification.

```
UsingDirective = "using" ( UsingAliasDirective | NamespaceName ) ";" .
```

For example, the WriteLine method may be invoked using its full qualification,
System.Console.WriteLine. With the using directive, we can specify the use of the

System namespace to access the WriteLine method via its class Console:

```
using System;

public class Welcome {
    public static void Main() {
        Console.WriteLine("Welcome to the practical guide for C#!");
    }
}
```

If the qualification is particularly long then an alias can be used instead:

EBNF

```
UsingAliasDirective = Identifier "=" NamespaceOrTypeName .
```

For example, PGCS on line 1 below is defined as an alias for the lengthy namespace qualification on the right-hand side. Suppose that PGCS also encapsulates a class called Id. In order for the User class within namespace N to create an instance of the Id class of PGCS, class Id is qualified with the alias PGCS as was done on line 10. Otherwise, if the User class refers to Id without qualification as shown on line 11, it refers instead to the Id class within its own namespace N.

```
1      using PGCS = com.DeepObjectKnowledge.PracticalGuideForCsharp;
2
3      namespace N {
4          public class Id {
5              // ...
6          }
7
8          public class User {
9              public static void Main() {
10                 PGCS.Id a = new PGCS.Id(); // use PGCS.Id
11                     Id b = new      Id(); // use    N.Id or Id by default
12                 // ...
13             }
14         }
15     }
```

2.3.3 Controlling the Global Namespace

C# takes special care to avoid namespace conflicts and to promote the absence of global variables or methods. In other words, more control over the global namespace is available for the following reasons:

- Every variable and method is declared within a class;
- Every class is (eventually) part of a namespace; and
- Every variable or method may be referred to by its fully qualified name.

Tip Resolving name conflicts is certainly advantageous, but not referring to global entities directly decreases the coupling factor between software components. This is an important software engineering requirement that supports reuse code, improves readability, and facilitates maintainability. We will discuss decoupling components more when we introduce abstract classes and interfaces in Chapter 7.

2.3.4 Resolving Namespace Conflicts

A nested namespace may have an identifier name that conflicts with the global namespace. For example, a company, Co, has developed several in-house classes, such as OurList, that are logically grouped under its own System.Collections namespace. An application App (lines 11–15) would like to use the ArrayList class from the .NET System.Collections namespace and the OurList class from the nested Systems.Collections namespace. Unfortunately, the Co.System.Collections namespace hides access to the .NET System.Collections and generates a compilation error at line 13 as shown here:

```
1          using SC = System.Collections;  // To access ArrayList class.
2
3          namespace Co {
4              namespace System {
5                  namespace Collections {
6                      public class OurList { /* ... */ }
7                      // ...
8                  }
9              }
10             namespace Project {
11                 public class App {
12                     // ...
13                     private System.Collections.ArrayList a; // Compilation error.
14                     private System.Collections.OurList   o;
15                 }
16             }
17         }
```

C# 2.0 The error in this example can be removed if the global namespace qualifier :: is used instead. This qualifier tells the compiler to begin its search at the global namespace. Since the .NET System is rooted at the global namespace, replacing System.Collections at line 13 by its alias SC:: enables access to the ArrayList class in the .NET namespace System.Collections:

```
    private SC::ArrayList  a;
```

2.4 Compilation Units

A C# program is composed of one or more compilation units where each compilation unit is a source file that may contain using directives for importing public classes, global attributes for reflection (see Chapter 10), and namespace member declarations:

EBNF

CompilationUnit = UsingDirectives? GlobalAttributes? NamespaceMemberDecls?.

For the most part, each **compilation unit** is a plain text file with a .cs extension that contains the source code of one or more classes and/or namespaces. In this section, we first present a relatively simple but complete C# program that is made up of two compilation units. Second, we show how a single class can be divided across several compilation units.

2.4.1 Presenting a Complete C# Program

Although a compilation unit in C# may contain more than one class, it remains a good programming practice to include only one class (or interface) per compilation unit. By editing a file that contains several classes, one of two problems can arise. First, other classes may be unintentionally modified and second, massive recompilation may be triggered on dependents of the file.

Tip

   Our program, therefore, contains two compilation units called Id.cs and TestId.cs. Each compilation unit contains a single class, namely the Id class in Id.cs (already implemented on p. 13) and the TestId class in TestId.cs given here. Together, these classes define a complete program in C#.

```
1     using System;
2     using com.DeepObjectKnowledge.PracticalGuideForCsharp;
3
4     public class TestId {
5         public static void Main() {
6             const int  NumberOfEntries = 5;
7             const char NameSeparator = '/';
8
9             Id id = new Id();
10
11            for (int n = 0; n < NumberOfEntries; n++) {
12                Console.Write("First: ");
13                string firstName = System.Console.ReadLine();
14                id.SetFirstName(firstName);
15
16                Console.Write("Last: ");
17                string lastName = System.Console.ReadLine();
18                id.SetLastName(lastName);
19
```

```
20                    Console.WriteLine( id.GetLastName()+
21                                       NameSeparator+id.GetFirstName() );
22               }
23          }
24     }
```

To produce an executable program in C#, one of the classes, in this case TestId, must define a static method called Main from where the program starts to run and to where we focus our attention. On lines 6 and 7, two constant values, NumberOfEntries and NameSeparator, are initialized, respectively, to the integer literal 5 and the character literal '/'. An instance of the class Id is created on line 9 and assigned to an object reference called id where its fields, firstName and lastName, are assigned to literal strings "<first name>" and "<last name>". The for loop, which begins on line 11 and encompasses statements from line 12 to line 21, is then executed five times. For each iteration, the string variables firstName and lastName are assigned values that are read from the console (keyboard) and then passed as parameters to the methods SetFirstName and SetLastName of the object id. Finally, the last and first names of the object id are retrieved using the methods GetLastName and GetFirstName, concatenated with a forward slash using the '+' operator and written back to the console (monitor).

A Digression on Naming Conventions

At this point, we pause to discuss the naming conventions of identifiers used for class names, method names, field names, and other constructs in C#. An identifier is a case-sensitive sequence of Unicode characters that begins with a letter or an underscore and excludes keywords, such as for and static, unless preceded by an @. Using keywords as identifiers is typically restricted to facilitate the interface between a program in C# and a program in another language where a C# keyword appears as an identifier. The following identifiers, therefore, are all legal:

        _123   Café   @this

Tip

In C#, many identifiers such as get, set, partial, yield, and so on have contextual meanings but are not keywords. Although these identifiers can be used for class names, method names, and other constructs, it is not recommended.

Tip

    Today, modern programming languages are augmented with huge class libraries that have been developed with consistent naming guidelines. As developers, it is very important to adhere to these guidelines in order to promote homogeneity and to facilitate the maintenance of applications. The C# standard proposes two main capitalization styles for identifiers:

- **Pascal casing**, which capitalizes the first character of each word, such as Analyzer and LexicalAnalyzer.

- **Camel casing**, which capitalizes the first character of each word except the first word, such as total and subTotal.

The standard, which is closely followed throughout the text, strongly suggests the use of Pascal casing for classes, attribute classes, exception classes, constants, enumeration types, enumeration values, events, interfaces, methods, namespaces, properties, and public instance fields. Camel casing, on the other hand, is encouraged for local variables, protected instance fields, private instance fields, and parameters. Finally, nouns are associated with class identifiers and verbs are associated with method identifiers.

2.4.2 Declaring Partial Classes

Although declaring one class per source file is the best-practice policy in the software industry, a class declaration may grow so large that it becomes unwieldy to store it in a single file. In that case, the class is better divided among more than one file to ease development, testing, and maintenance. Using the prefix partial before the class name, different parts of a class can be distributed across different files. Two key restrictions, however, must be satisfied. First, all parts of a partial type must be compiled together in order to be merged at compile-time and second, already compiled types are not allowed to be extended to include other partial types. As an example, the partial class Parser is implemented in three separate files (parts) as shown here:

```Tip```

```C# 2.0```

ParserCompilationUnit.cs file (Part 1):

```
public partial class Parser {
    private ILexer        lexer;
    private IReportable   errorReporter;
    private ISymbolTable  symbolTable;
    // ...

    // Compilation Unit productions
    void ParseCompilationUnit() { ... }
    void ParseNamespace()       { ... }
    // ...
}
```

ParserClass.cs file (Part 2):

```
public partial class Parser {
    // Class productions
    void ParseClassDecl()       { ... }
    void ParseClassMemberDecl() { ... }
    // ...
}
```

`ParserExpr.cs` file (Part 3):

```
public partial class Parser {
    // Expression productions
    void ParseExpr() { ... }
    void ParseExprList() { ... }
    // ...
}
```

When the preceding files are compiled together, the resulting code is the same as if the class had been written as a single source file `Parser.cs`:

```
public class Parser {
    private ILexer        lexer;
    private IReportable    errorReporter;
    private ISymbolTable  symbolTable;
    // ...

    // Compilation Unit productions
    void ParseCompilationUnit() { ... }
    void ParseNamespace()       { ... }
    // ...

    // Class productions
    void ParseClassDecl()        { ... }
    void ParseClassMemberDecl() { ... }
    // ...

    // Expression productions
    void ParseExpr() { ... }
    void ParseExprList() { ... }
    // ...
}
```

The notion of partial classes also applies to other types, such as structures and interfaces.

2.5 Compilation and Execution

Compiling and running C# programs is easily done with a Microsoft development tool such as Visual Studio .NET. However, it is still important to know how to compile programs at the command line. These compilation commands can be integrated and completely automated by the rule-based, dependency-management utility called nmake.[2] This utility as well as compilers, assemblers, linkers, and so on are part of the .NET Framework SDK.

---

[2] The equivalent of the make utility on Unix boxes.

Suppose now that our classes Id and TestId are part of the same compilation unit called IdWithTest.cs. The command:

```
csc IdWithTest.cs
```

invokes the C# compiler csc and generates an executable binary file called IdWithTest.exe. If our classes remain separate in compilation units Id.cs and TestId.cs, respectively, the command:

```
csc TestId.cs Id.cs
```

compiles both files together and generates a single executable file called TestId.exe. To execute an .exe file, only the name of the file is entered. For example:

```
TestId
```

Within the .NET Framework, the C# source code is first compiled into CIL code to produce the assembly file. The CLR then loads the assembly that contains the main method entry point. From there, each method to be executed is translated "just-in-time" into machine code. In order to improve performance, this translation takes place only once for each method that is invoked. During execution, the CLR also monitors the application's memory use and may (in the background) ask the garbage collector to free up unused memory.

2.5.1 Using Assemblies for Separate Compilation

Individual files, such as Id.cs and TestId.cs, can also be compiled into separate .NET object modules using the option /target:module[3] as shown here:

```
csc /target:module Id.cs
```

In this case, the file Id.cs is compiled into a .NET object module called Id.netmodule. To generate the same TestId.exe file as before, the object file Id.netmodule is then linked using the option /addmodule:Id.netmodule when TestId.cs is compiled:

```
csc TestId.cs /addmodule:Id.netmodule
```

An executable (or .exe) file represents one kind of assembly. As mentioned in Chapter 1, the second kind of assembly is a component (or class library), which is stored in a dynamic library (or .dll). Using this command, the component class Id is added to the library Business.dll:

```
csc /target:library /out:Business.dll /addmodule:Id.netmodule
```

In our project, the Business.dll library contains all business (domain) classes.

---

[3]The default option for a target is /target:exe.

2.5.2   Revisiting Access Modifiers

In this section, we present an example with two compilation units to clarify the behavior of access modifiers for both classes and class members, casting a particular eye on internal access. The first compilation unit called NA.cs contains three classes, one each for public, internal, and internal default. Each of the three classes in turn contains six methods, one each for public, private, protected, internal, internal protected, and private default. Each method is also designated as static and is, therefore, associated with the class itself and not with a particular instance of the class as described in Chapter 3.

```
1   namespace NA {
2       public class PublicClass {
3           public              static void pubM() {}
4           protected           static void proM() {}
5           protected internal static void proIntM() {}
6           internal            static void intM() {}
7           private             static void priM() {}
8         /* private    */      static void defM() {}
9       }
10
11      internal class InternalClass {
12          public              static void pubM() {}
13          protected           static void proM() {}
14          protected internal static void proIntM() {}
15          internal            static void intM() {}
16          private             static void priM() {}
17        /* private    */      static void defM() {}
18      }
19
20      /* internal */ class InternalClassByDefault {
21          public              static void pubM() {}
22          protected           static void proM() {}
23          protected internal static void proIntM() {}
24          internal            static void intM() {}
25          private             static void priM() {}
26        /* private    */      static void defM() {}
27      }
28  }
```

The second compilation unit is called NB.cs. It contains a single class called Usage with only a single method called Main. Within Main, all methods for each class in NA.cs are invoked.

```
1   namespace NB {
2       using NA;
```

```
3
4       class Usage {
5           public void Main() {
6               PublicClass.pubM();
7               PublicClass.proM();                  // Error: Inaccessible
8               PublicClass.proIntM();
9               PublicClass.intM();
10              PublicClass.priM();                  // Error: Inaccessible
11              PublicClass.defM();                  // Error: Inaccessible
12
13              InternalClass.pubM();
14              InternalClass.proM();                // Error: Inaccessible
15              InternalClass.proIntM();
16              InternalClass.intM();
17              InternalClass.priM();                // Error: Inaccessible
18              InternalClass.defM();                // Error: Inaccessible
19
20              InternalClassByDefault.pubM();
21              InternalClassByDefault.proM();       // Error: Inaccessible
22              InternalClassByDefault.proIntM();
23              InternalClassByDefault.intM();
24              InternalClassByDefault.priM();       // Error: Inaccessible
25              InternalClassByDefault.defM();       // Error: Inaccessible
26          }
27      }
28  }
```

If both files—NA.cs and NB.cs—are compiled together using:

```
csc /target:exe NA.cs NB.cs
```

then all classes share access to their internal members; that is, no error is generated with the usage of the internal access modifier. Other errors on lines 7, 10, 11, 14, 17, 18, 21, 24, and 25 are generated due to the protection level of the methods, either private, protected, or internal protected. Of course, public methods are available to all classes within the same compiled unit. It is important to point out that internal access is enabled *not* because classes share a namespace but because the classes are compiled together. In other words, if two classes that share a namespace are compiled separately, they no longer have access to the internal methods and data fields of the other class. By first compiling NA.cs to generate a dynamic library (NA.dll) and then compiling and linking NB.cs as follows:

```
csc /target:library NA.cs
csc /target:exe NB.cs /reference:NA.dll
```

additional errors are generated on lines 8, 9, 13, 15, 16, 20, 22, and 23. In fact, all lines from 7 to 25, inclusively, no longer have access to the internal methods of NA.cs and NB.cs.

2.5.3   Adding XML Documentation

In an industry where there is always pressure to get software products out the door, it is sometimes tempting to regard source code documentation as a pesky afterthought. Fortunately, the C# compiler automatically generates well-formatted documentation in XML using doc comments (///) and XML tags (<...>) that have been entered by the developers at their proper places in the source code. Although there are many predefined XML tags (see Appendix B), only the minimum have been introduced in the Id.cs file here to produce reasonable documentation. Such minimal documentation provides a concise declaration of the class and its public methods, including their parameters and return values.

Tip

```
/// <summary>
/// The Id class represents the first and the last name of a contact person.
/// </summary>
public class Id {
    /// <summary>Gets the first name.</summary>
    /// <returns>The first name.</returns>
    public string GetFirstName() { return first; }

    /// <summary>Gets the last name.</summary>
    /// <returns>The last name.</returns>
    public string GetLastName()  { return last; }

    /// <summary>Sets the first name to <c>value</c>.</summary>
    public void SetFirstName(string value) { first = value; }

    /// <summary>Sets the last name to <c>value</c>.</summary>
    public void SetLastName(string value)  { last = value;  }

    private string first;
    private string last;
}
```

By adding the doc option, the compilation command:

```
csc /target:module /doc:Id.xml Id.cs
```

generates the following XML file Id.xml:

```
<?xml version="1.0"?>
```

```
<doc>
    <members>
        <member name="T:Id">
            <summary>
                The Id class represents the first and the last name of a
                contact person.
            </summary>
        </member>
        <member name="M:Id.GetFirstName">
            <summary>Gets the first name.</summary>
            <returns>The first name.</returns>
        </member>
        <member name="M:Id.GetLastName">
            <summary>Gets the last name.</summary>
            <returns>The last name.</returns>
        </member>
        <member name="M:Id.SetFirstName(System.String)">
            <summary>Sets the first name to <c>value</c>.</summary>
        </member>
        <member name="M:Id.SetLastName(System.String)">
            <summary>Sets the last name to <c>value</c>.</summary>
        </member>
    </members>
</doc>
```

Apart from the doc comments, the source code should use // for short one-line comments and /* ... */ for longer multi-line comments. Because of the size of this book and its mandate to be as concise as possible, XML documentation comments are not applied to our examples.

Exercises

Exercise 2-1. Write a class Id in the namespace Project.Business and compile it to generate an object file Id.netmodule. This Id class encapsulates both first and last names of type string. Instantiate this class by another class TestId containing a Main method in a different namespace, such as Project.Tests.

Exercise 2-2. Write a class Email in the namespace Project.Business and compile it to generate an object file Email.netmodule. This Email class encapsulates an address of type string. Instantiate this class by another class TestEmail containing a Main method in a different namespace, such as Project.Tests.

chapter **3**

Class Members and Class Reuse

How a class limits access to its members (fields and methods) defines, in a sense, its private and public persona. On one hand, data fields that define the state of a class or object are typically hidden away. Allowing outside classes or objects to unwittingly change the state of another class or object undermines the notion of responsibility. On the other hand, the behavior of a class or object is generally defined by its public methods. All other classes, therefore, are only able to invoke behavior that is well-defined and consistent. In this chapter, we distinguish between static and instance members and describe how to access fields and invoke methods of both C# classes and objects. Particular attention is paid to two special methods, constructors and destructors, as well as passing parameters by value and by reference.

We also present the mechanisms of inheritance and aggregation that are used to build new classes from those that already exist. Reuse of classes in these ways is one of the hallmarks of object-oriented technology, and one of its most powerful features. Because each class encapsulates both data and behavior, it is relatively easy and economical to define new classes in terms of others. Issues related to inheritance, such as constructor/destructor chaining and protected data members, are also discussed.

3.1 Fields and Methods

The fields and methods of a C# class may be associated with either the class itself or with particular objects of the class. In the former case, these members are called **static fields** and **static methods** and are not part of any object instantiated from the class. Members that are associated with a particular object or instance of a class are called **instance fields** or **instance methods**. From a syntactic point of view, static members are declared

29

and preceded by the keyword static as shown here in the class Id. This class is responsible for generating a unique identification number, idNumber, for each object that is created.

```
1    class Id {
2        public              Id()        { number++; idNumber = number; }
3              static  Id()                { number = 0;       }
4        public      int GetIdNumber()        { return idNumber; }
5        public  static int GetNumberOfIdsCreated() { return number;    }
6
7        private         int idNumber;
8        private static int number;
9    }
```

The field number and the method GetNumberOfIdsCreated are static members, and the field idNumber and the method GetIdNumber are instance members. The two Id methods are special methods called constructors and are discussed later in Section 3.1.3. Static fields are initialized when the class is loaded into memory. Hence, number is initialized to 0 before any instance of Id is created. Instance fields, on the other hand, are initialized when an object is created. If a static or instance field is not explicitly initialized, it is assigned a default value generated by the compiler. A class that is also prefixed by the static modifier is called a static class and must satisfy the following constraint: All class members including the constructor are static. The ubiquitous System.Console is a typical example of a static class.

C# 2.0

3.1.1 Invoking Methods

Methods in C# define the behavior of a class and are analogous to functions in procedural languages such as C. The complete method declaration within a class, otherwise referred to as its signature or prototype, is composed of optional modifiers, a return type, a specification of its formal parameter(s), and a method body as defined by its EBNF definition:

EBNF

```
MethodDecl = Modifiers? ReturnType MethodName "(" Parameters? ")" MethodBody.
```

Modifiers that can be used include the access modifiers described in Chapter 2. The return (or result) type of a method defines the value or reference type that must be returned to the calling method. A full description of value and reference types is given in Chapter 4 but for the moment, it suffices to think of a value type as a simple numeric value and a reference type as a class. If no value is returned then void is used as the return type. If an array is returned then square brackets ([ ]s) are used. For example:

```
int    value() { ... } // Returns an integer value (like a C function).
void   print() { ... } // Returns no value (like a procedure).
int[] vec()   { ... } // Returns the reference of an array of integers.
```

In the preceding Id class, the method GetIdNumber has a return type of int and no parameters.

To invoke a method from within a given class, the MethodName is followed by its appropriate number of arguments:

EBNF

```
MethodInvocation = MethodName "(" Arguments? ")" .
```

However, methods are far more likely to be invoked from outside the class itself and therefore, must be preceded by a class or object reference:

EBNF

```
( ClassReference | ObjectReference ) "." MethodInvocation
```

Once a method is invoked, the execution of the caller is suspended until the method is processed by the class or object. Naturally, the sender of the method must ensure that the arguments of the invocation are compatible with the parameters of the method.

Invoking Instance Methods

To invoke an instance method, such as GetIdNumber, an instance of Id must first be created:

```
Id id = new Id();
```

Once created, the method is invoked using the reference variable to the object, as follows:

```
id.GetIdNumber()
```

An instance method cannot be invoked with its class name, in this case Id. As an instance method, GetIdNumber, therefore, is only accessible through its reference variable id. Hence,

```
Id.GetIdNumber()
```

would generate a compilation error.

Invoking Static Methods

The number of Ids created so far is obtained by calling the static method GetNumberOfIdsCreated using the class name as a prefix:

```
Id.GetNumberOfIdsCreated()
```

Unlike Java, no reference variable can invoke a static method. Therefore, the static method GetNumberOfIdsCreated is only accessible through its class name Id. Hence,

```
id.GetNumberOfIdsCreated()
```

generates a compilation error as well. It is worthwhile to note that a static method is always accessible and callable without necessarily having any instance of that class available. Therefore, a client can invoke the GetNumberOfIdsCreated method without first creating an instance of the class Id. By way of example, all methods in the Math class within the System namespace of C# are defined as static methods. Therefore, if a call is made to Math.Sqrt, it appears as a "global method" similar to a C function and must be referred to by the class name Math.

3.1.2   Accessing Fields

EBNF

For a field to be accessed from outside the class itself, it must be preceded by a class or object reference:

```
( ClassReference | ObjectReference ) "." FieldName
```

Because both fields are private, neither the static field number nor the instance field idNumber in the example is accessible from outside the class itself.

Accessing Instance Fields

If an instance field, such as idNumber in the class Id, is public rather than private then access is made via the reference variable to the object:

```
id.idNumber
```

Like instance methods, instance fields can only be accessed via objects of the class.

Accessing Static Fields

If a static field, in this case number, is also public rather than private then access is made via the class name:

```
Id.number;    // Returns 24 (if 24 objects exist)
```

Like static methods, static fields can only be accessed via the class name.

3.1.3   Declaring Constructors

A constructor in C# is a special method that shares the same name of its class and is responsible for the initialization of the class itself or any object that is instantiated from the class. A constructor that is responsible for the initialization of an object is called an **instance constructor**, and a constructor that is responsible for the initialization of the class itself is called a **static constructor**. Our example on page 30 illustrates an instance constructor Id (line 2) and a static constructor Id (line 3).

A static constructor is invoked automatically when a class is loaded into memory. Therefore, a static constructor initializes static, and only static data fields before any instance of that class is instantiated. For example, the static Id constructor initializes the static field number to 0 on line 3. A static constructor is also unique, cannot have access modifiers or parameters, and cannot be invoked directly.

An instance constructor on the other hand creates and initializes an instance of a class (or object) at runtime. Unlike a static constructor, it must be invoked explicitly as shown previously in Chapter 2 and here:

```
Id id = new Id( );
```

A class may have more than one instance constructor as long as the signature of each constructor is unique as shown here:

```
class Id {
    public Id()           { ... } // Constructor with no parameters.
    public Id(int number) { ... } // Constructor with a single parameter.
}
```

A constructor with no parameters is called a **parameterless** constructor. If no constructor is provided with a public or internal class then a **default** constructor with public access is automatically generated by the compiler. This implicitly defined constructor is parameterless and initializes all instance data members to their default values as shown by the equivalent Id classes here:

```
class Id {
    private int number;
}

class Id {
    public Id () { number = 0; }
    private int number;
}
```

Whether a class is public or internal, any explicitly defined constructor without an access modifier is private as shown by the equivalent Id classes:

```
class Id {
    Id () { number = 0; }
    private int number;
}

class Id {
    private Id () { number = 0; }
    private int number;
}
```

In one important application, the well-known design pattern called the **singleton** uses the notion of a private constructor to ensure that only one instance of a class is created. This is achieved by giving the responsibility of instantiation to the class itself via a static method often called GetInstance. The first user to invoke the GetInstance method receives the object reference. All subsequent users receive the same reference. The following is a complete implementation of an Id singleton and its test harness:

```
public class Id {
    public static Id  GetInstance() {
        if (instance == null) { instance = new Id(); }
```

```
        return instance;
    }
    public int GetIdNumber() {
        int number = idNumber;
        idNumber++;
        return number;
    }
    private Id() { idNumber = 1;    }
    static  Id() { instance = null; }

    private        int idNumber;
    private static Id  instance;
}

public class TestIdSingleton {
    public static void Main() {
        Id id1 = Id.GetInstance();
        Id id2 = Id.GetInstance();
        Id id3 = Id.GetInstance();

        System.Console.WriteLine( id1.GetIdNumber() );
        System.Console.WriteLine( id2.GetIdNumber() );
        System.Console.WriteLine( id3.GetIdNumber() );
    }
}
```

The following output is generated:

```
1
2
3
```

In the preceding example, programmers that are familiar with the side effects of C-like operators will notice that the body of the GetIdNumber method can be replaced by a single statement { return idNumber++; }, which returns the idNumber value and then (post-)increments the idNumber field. A full description of all C# operators is provided in Chapter 5.

Although the initialization of data fields can be done at declaration, for example,

```
    private int idNumber = 1;
```

Tip   it is not a good programming practice. Instead, every instance field should be initialized in the same place, grouped either in a method or directly in the constructor. That being said, all instance fields that are initialized when declared are automatically inserted in any case at the beginning of the constructor body. Therefore, the following code:

```
class Id {
    public Id () { }
    private int number = 1;
}
```

is converted by the C# compiler to:

```
class Id {
    public Id () { number = 1; }
    private int number;
}
```

A Digression on Formatting

Similar to the print functions of C, the .NET string formatting methods, including Console.WriteLine, take a formatting string as its first argument followed by zero or more arguments. Each of the arguments is formatted according to its corresponding specifier in the formatting string. Therefore, the formatting string contains one specifier for each argument. Each specifier is defined as:

EBNF

```
"{" n ("," "-"? w)? (":" f)? "}"
```

where n is the zero-based index of the argument(s) following the format string, where minus (-) specifies left justification, where w is the field width, and where f is the type of format. Both left justification and type of format are optional. The sharp (#) and 0 are digit and zero placeholders, respectively. For example, the simple formatting string with four parameters given here:

```
Console.WriteLine("{0}, {1}, {2}, and {3}!", 1, 2, 3, "go");
```

outputs the following string:

1, 2, 3, go!

Table 3.1 summarizes the types of numeric formats, and the following program illustrates their use. The character bar (|) in the formatting strings is used to highlight the resultant string and any possible alignment.

```
using System;

class Format {
    static void Main() {
        Console.WriteLine("|{0:C}|{1:C}|", 1.23, -1.23);
        Console.WriteLine("|{0:D}|{1:D4}|", 123,  -123);
        Console.WriteLine("|{0:F}|{1:F4}|", 1.23, 1.23);
        Console.WriteLine("|{0:E}|{1:G}|", 1.23, 1.23);
```

```
        Console.WriteLine("|{0:P}|{1:N}|",  1.23, 1.23);
        Console.WriteLine("|{0:X}|{1:X5}|{2,5:X}|{3,-5:X}|", 255, 255, 255, 255);
        Console.WriteLine("|{0:#.00}|{1:0.00}|{2,5:0.00}|{3,-5:0.00}|",
                          .23, .23, .23, .23);
    }
}
```

Output:

```
|$1.23|($1.23)|
|123|-0123|
|1.23|1.2300|
|1.230000E+000|1.23|
|123.00 %|1.23|
|FF|000FF|   FF|FF   |
|.23|0.23| 0.23|0.23 |
```

3.1.4 Declaring Destructors

The garbage collector in C# is an automatic memory management scheme that scans for objects that are no longer referenced and are therefore eligible for destruction. Hence, memory allocated to an object is recouped automatically by a garbage collector when the object is no longer accessible (or reachable). Although the garbage collector may be invoked directly using the GC.Collect method, this practice sidesteps the heuristics and complex algorithms that are used to optimize system performance. Unless there are compelling reasons to do otherwise, garbage collection is best left to the system rather than the programmer. It is safer, easier, and more efficient.

However, an object may acquire resources that are unknown to the garbage collector, such as peripheral devices and database connections. These resources are the responsibility of the object itself and, therefore, the logic to release these resources must be

Type of Format	Meaning
c or C	Currency
d or D	Decimal
e or E	Scientific with "e" or "E" (6 digits)
f or F	Fixed-point (12 digits)
g or G	General (the most compact between E and F)
n or N	Number
p or P	Percent
x or X	Hexadecimal

Table 3.1: Numeric format types.

implemented in a special method called a **destructor**. Although an object may be instantiated in any number of ways, at most one destructor is declared per class. A destructor, as shown here for the class Id, where Id is preceded by a tilde (˜), cannot be inherited, overloaded, or explicitly invoked.

```
public class Id {
    ˜Id () { /* release of resources */ }
}
```

Instead, each destructor is invoked automatically but non-deterministically at the end of a program or by the garbage collector itself. To ensure that a destructor is invoked immediately once an object is no longer referenced, the IDisposable .NET design pattern should be used as described in Section 9.1. Such a destructor is also called a **finalizer** in the .NET context.

Tip

3.2 Parameter Passing

As described earlier in the chapter, each method in C# has an optional sequence of formal parameters. Each formal parameter, in turn, represents a special kind of local variable that specifies the type of argument that must be passed to the given method. Like other local variables, formal parameters are allocated on the stack when a method is invoked and are deallocated when the method completes its execution. Therefore, the lifetime of a parameter and the lifetime of its method are synonymous. Finally, arguments are passed to formal parameters in one of two ways: **by value** or **by reference**. These ways are explored in greater detail in the following two sections.

3.2.1 Passing Arguments by Value

When an argument is passed by value, the formal parameter is initialized to a copy of the actual argument. Therefore, the actual argument itself cannot be modified by the invoked method. In the following example, an integer variable p is passed by value to a formal parameter of the same name. Although the formal parameter may change its local copy of p, the value of p in the main program retains its original value after the invocation of ParambyValue.

```
using System;

class ParambyValue {
    static void Fct(int p) {
        Console.WriteLine("In Fct: p = {0}", ++p);
    }
    static void Main() {
        int p = 1;
        Console.WriteLine("Before: p = {0}", p);
        Fct(p);
```

```
        Console.WriteLine("After:   p = {0}", p);
    }
}
```

Output:

```
Before: p = 1
In Fct: p = 2
After:  p = 1
```

3.2.2   Passing Arguments by Reference

When an argument is passed by reference, any changes to the formal parameter are reflected by the actual argument. In C#, however, there are two types of reference parameters: ref and out. If the formal parameter is preceded by the modifier ref then the actual argument must be explicitly initialized before invocation and be preceded by the modifier ref as well. In the following example, the variables a and b in the Main method are explicitly initialized to 1 and 2, respectively, *before* the invocation of Swap. Explicit initialization precludes implicit initialization by default and therefore, without the assignment of 1 and 2 to a and b, respectively, the default values of 0 would raise a compilation error.

```
using System;

class ParamByRef {
    static void Swap(ref int a, ref int b) {
        int t = a;
        a = b;
        b = t;
    }
    static void Main() {
        int a = 1;
        int b = 2;
        Console.WriteLine("Before: a = {0}, b = {1}", a, b);
        Swap(ref a, ref b);
        Console.WriteLine("After:   a = {0}, b = {1}", a, b);
    }
}
```

Output:

```
Before: a = 1, b = 2
After:  a = 2, b = 1
```

If the formal parameter and actual argument are preceded by the modifier out then the actual argument does not need to be initialized before invocation. In other words, the return value is independent of the initial value (if any) of the actual argument. The modifier out is used to indicate that the formal parameter will be assigned a value to be returned to its corresponding argument. Since the use of an unassigned variable is not allowed in C#, this modifier can be used to initialize (or reset) local variables to default values as shown:

```
using System;

class ParamByRefWithOut {
    static void SetRange(out int min, out int max) { min = 0; max = 255; }

    static void Main() {
        int min, max;

        SetRange(out min, out max);
        Console.WriteLine("Begin:  min = {0}, max = {1}", min, max);
        min++; max--;
        Console.WriteLine("Change: min = {0}, max = {1}", min, max);
        SetRange(out min, out max);
        Console.WriteLine("End:    min = {0}, max = {1}", min, max);
    }
}
```

Output:

```
Begin:  min = 0, max = 255
Change: min = 1, max = 254
End:    min = 0, max = 255
```

In the preceding examples, all arguments were of the integer type int. Reference types, however, can also be passed by value or by reference. Because a reference-type argument points to an object stored on the heap and does not represent the object itself, modifications to the object can be made using both parameter-passing mechanisms. Passing a reference-type argument by value simply copies the memory address of the object to the formal parameter. Passing a reference-type argument by reference implies that the pointer itself can be modified and reflected by the actual argument. By changing the reference-type parameter, the pointer is modified to reference an entirely different object of the same class. If that is not the intent, then passing a reference-type argument by value ensures that only the object itself and not the reference to the object can be modified. The following example illustrates this behavior.

```
using System;

class Counter {
    public  void Inc()      { count++; }
    public  int  GetCount() { return count; }
    private int  count;
```

```
}
class ParamByValByRefWithObjects {
    static void SayBye(ref string msg) { msg = "Bye!"; }
    static void SayGoodBye(string msg) { msg = "Goodbye!"; }

    static void IncR(ref Counter c) {
        c = new Counter();
        c.Inc();
        Console.Write("cR = {0} ", c.GetCount());
    }
    static void IncV(Counter c) {
        c = new Counter();
        c.Inc();
        Console.Write("cV = {0} ", c.GetCount());
    }
    static void Main() {
        string msg = "Hello!";
        Console.Write("{0} ", msg);
                                                        // (1)
        SayGoodBye(msg);
        Console.Write("{0} ", msg);
                                                        // (2)
        SayBye(ref msg);
        Console.WriteLine("{0} ", msg);
                                                        // (3)
        Counter cm = new Counter();
        Console.WriteLine("cm = {0}", cm.GetCount());
                                                        // (4)
        IncV(cm);
        Console.WriteLine("cm = {0}", cm.GetCount());
                                                        // (5)
        IncR(ref cm);
        Console.WriteLine("cm = {0}", cm.GetCount());
    }                                                   // (6)
}
```

Output:

```
Hello! Hello! Bye!
cm = 0
cV = 1 cm = 0
cR = 1 cm = 1
```

In Figure 3.1, steps 1 to 6 correspond to the comments in the listing above. At (1), the reference variable msg points to the literal string object "Hello!". Between (1) and (2),

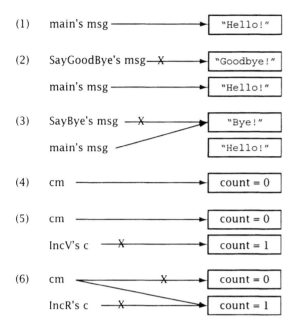

Figure 3.1: Parameter passing by value and by reference with objects.

the formal parameter msg of SayGoodBye is assigned a copy of the actual argument msg in Main. The parameter msg is then assigned a reference to the literal string "Goodbye!". Once the method completes its execution, the reference to "Goodbye!" is lost as indicated by the X, and there is no impact on msg in Main. Between (2) and (3), the actual argument msg of Main is passed by reference to msg of SayBye. The parameter msg is then assigned a reference to the literal "Bye!", which is also reflected by msg in Main. The literal string object "Hello!", then, is no longer reachable and is marked for garbage collection.

At (4), the object cm is created and initialized to zero by default. Between (4) and (5), the argument cm of Main is passed by value to c of IncV. Hence, c is a copy of the reference cm. The parameter c is then assigned a reference to a new object of Counter. The count field of c is incremented by 1 and displayed. However, once the IncV method completes its execution, the reference to c is lost, and there is no impact on cm in Main. On the other hand, when cm is passed by reference, the creation of a new Counter in the IncR method is assigned directly to cm in Main. Therefore, the reference cm to the original object is lost and replaced by a reference to the object created within IncR. Output at (6) confirms that c and cm refer to the same object.

3.2.3 Passing a Variable Number of Arguments

In C/C++, trying to pass a variable number of arguments via the varargs structure compromises the type-checking capabilities of the compiler. To enforce type safety, the C# language is equipped with a third parameter modifier called params. The modifier params is followed by an open array of a specific type. Because the array is expecting values of a given type, type checking is enforced at compile time. In the following example, the method Fct is expecting to receive zero or more integer arguments, each of which is stored consecutively in the open array called args. Because the number of arguments is variable, the params modifier can only be applied to the last parameter.

```
using System;

class ParamByRefWithParms {
    static void Fct(params int[] args) {
        Console.Write    ("{0} argument(s): ", args.Length);
        for (int n = 0; n < args.Length; n++)
            Console.Write("{0} ", args[n]);
        Console.WriteLine();
    }
    static void Main() {
        Console.WriteLine("      args[n]: 0 1 2 3");
        Fct();
        Fct(1);
        Fct(1, 2);
        Fct(1, 2, 3);
        Fct(new int[] {1, 2, 3, 4});
    }
}
```
Output:
```
     args[n]: 0 1 2 3
0 argument(s):
1 argument(s): 1
2 argument(s): 1 2
3 argument(s): 1 2 3
4 argument(s): 1 2 3 4
```

The last invocation of Fct in the main program passes an anonymous array.

3.2.4 Using the this Reference

The keyword this is an argument that is implicitly passed to each instance method and serves as a self-reference to the current object. Using the this reference, one can differentiate between a method argument and a data field that share the same name, as shown:

```
public class Counter {
    public  Counter(int count) { this.count = count; }

    private int count;
}
```

Overuse of the this reference, however, may impair readability. Alternatively, a common style convention used in C++, Java, and C# adds an underscore as a prefix or suffix to the local data member: Tip

```
public class Counter {
    public Counter(int count) { _count = count; }

    private int _count;
}
```

A current method may also be accessed via the this reference. For instance, suppose that the Counter class included an additional method called Init to set or reset count to a specific value. In the following example, the method Init is called from the Counter constructor:

```
public class Counter {
    public  Counter(int count)   {
        this.Init(count);            // Same as Init(count)
    }
    public   void Init(int count) {
        this.count = count;
    }

    private int count;
}
```

Because the this prefix is implicitly understood, it is generally not included in the invocation of a current method.

   Finally, the this reference can be used as part of a **callback**. A callback is a way for one object, A for example, to retain a reference to another object B so that A may "call back" a method in B at any time. The purpose of a callback is to anonymously invoke a method by referencing only the object, in our case A, that retains the other reference to B. Hence, the reference to B is hidden within A. In the next example, an amount of money is calculated both with and without a discount. An instance of the Amount class is first created on line 26 and its reference is passed to two static methods on lines 31 and 35, respectively. The first method called TotalWithNoDiscount gives no discount and simply retrieves the value of a using its Get method. The second method called TotalWithDiscount calculates a 20% discount. This method first creates an instance of Discount via the CreateDiscount method of Amount. In CreateDiscount on line 6, the constructor of Discount is invoked and the current reference of Amount is passed and assigned to amount within the newly created instance of Discount on line 11. Once the instance of Discount is created and retains the reference to Amount, its Apply method is invoked on line 20. Within Apply, the amount reference is used to call back the Get method of Amount, retrieve its value, and return the discounted value (line 13).

```
1        using System;
2
3        public class Amount {
4            public  Amount(double buy)        { this.buy = buy;                }
5            public  double   Get()            { return buy;                    }
6            public  Discount CreateDiscount() { return new Discount(this); }
7            private double   buy;
8        }
9
10       public class Discount {
11           public  Discount(Amount amount) { this.amount = amount; }
12           public  double Apply() {
13               return amount.Get() * 0.80; // Callback amount to apply
14           }                               // 20% discount.
15           private Amount amount;
16       }
17
18       public class TestCallback {
19           public static double TotalWithDiscount(Amount a) {
20               return a.CreateDiscount().Apply(); // Create a discount
21           }                                      // then apply.
22           public static double TotalWithNoDiscount(Amount a) {
23               return a.Get();
24           }
25           public static void Main() {
26               Amount a = new Amount(60.00);
27
28               // Use amount without applying a discount (no call back).
29
30               Console.WriteLine("Please pay {0:C} (no  discount)",
31                               TotalWithNoDiscount(a));
32               // Use amount and apply a discount (call back).
33
34               Console.WriteLine("Please pay {0:C} (20% discount)",
35                               TotalWithDiscount(a));
36           }
37       }
```

Output:

```
Please pay $60.00 (no  discount)
Please pay $48.00 (20% discount)
```

3.2.5 Overloading Methods

Overloading a method means to declare several methods of the same name. But in order to distinguish among methods, each one must have a distinct parameter list, bearing in mind that the return type and the parameter modifier params are not part of a method signature.

```
1    class MethodOverloading {
2        void Fct(int i)            { ... }
3        int  Fct(int i)            { ... } // error: same signature as line 2
4        void Fct(char c)           { ... }
5        void Fct(int[] args)       { ... }
6        void Fct(params int[] args) { ... } // error: same signature as line 5
7    }
```

3.3 Class Reuse

One of the principal benefits of object-oriented technology is the ability to reuse and extend classes. The growing libraries of reusable code in Java and C# reflect the importance and economy of building code from existing components. Reusing code that has weathered extensive testing gives rise to software products that are more robust, maintainable, and reliable. In this section, we examine two fundamental ways, **inheritance** and **aggregation**, that create classes from ones that already exist. To draw a comparison between the two ways, a simple class called Counter is first defined.

```
public class Counter {
    public        Counter()           { SetCount(0); }
    public        Counter(int count)  { SetCount(count); }
    public   int  GetCount()          { return count; }
    public   void SetCount(int count) { this.count = count; }

    private int  count;
}
```

The class Counter has two constructors, a parameterless constructor that initializes count to 0 and an overloaded constructor that initializes count to its single parameter. Both constructors invoke SetCount. The class also includes the method GetCount that returns the current value of count.

We will now extend the Counter class, first via aggregation and second via inheritance, to create another class called BoundedCounter. Objects of the BoundedCounter class behave essentially the same as those objects of Counter, but with one key difference: The private data member count is only valid between two user-defined values, min and max. Although the class BoundedCounter places the onus on the client to check that count falls between min and max, provisions are made to return these bounds for testing.

3.3.1 Using Aggregation

Aggregation, otherwise known as a "**has-a**" or "part-of" relationship, gathers one or more objects from various classes and places them inside another class. Aggregation, therefore, reuses classes by assembling objects of existing classes to define, at least in part, the data members and methods of a new class. In order to define the class BoundedCounter, a single object of the Counter class is placed inside BoundedCounter along with two additional data members, min and max. Also included are methods to return the minimum and maximum values, GetMax and GetMin, as well as a method InitRange to set the bounds. By default, the count for an object of BoundedCounter is initialized to min upon creation.

```
public class BoundedCounter {
    public  BoundedCounter (int min, int max) {
        this.c = new Counter(min);                 // Creates a private Counter c
        InitRange(min, max);
    }
    private  void InitRange(int min, int max) {
        this.min = min;
        this.max = max;
    }
    public  int  GetCount()          { return c.GetCount(); }// Reuses object c
    public  void SetCount(int count) { c.SetCount(count); }  // Reuses object c
    public  int  GetMin()            { return min; }
    public  int  GetMax()            { return max; }

    private Counter c;                 // Reuses object Counter c by aggregation
    private int     min;
    private int     max;
}
```

Although aggregation does work to define BoundedCounter, it is not a particularly elegant solution. The methods GetCount and SetCount of BoundedCounter are reimplemented using the existing methods of Counter. In this case, where behavior is common, inheritance provides a better mechanism than aggregation for class reuse. In Section 3.3.3, the opposite is demonstrated.

3.3.2 Using Inheritance

Inheritance, otherwise known as an "**is-a**" or "kind-of" relationship, allows a class of objects to reuse, redefine, and possibly extend the functionality of an existing class. Therefore, one class, called the derived or subclass, "inherits" all data members and methods of its base or superclass with the exception of instance constructors. Also, it should be noted with respect to the encapsulation principle that private data members of the base class are not directly accessible from their derived classes except through protected or public methods.

Rather than being inherited, instance constructors of the superclass are called either implicitly or explicitly upon creation of an object from the derived class. This exception is best motivated by noting that an object from an inherited class is a "specialized" instance of the base class. Without first creating an instance of the base class, it is simply not possible to create an instance of the derived class. If the base class has no constructor and a default constructor is generated automatically by the compiler, then the compiler can also generate a default constructor for the derived class. Otherwise, the derived class must have at least one constructor.

Like Java, C# only supports single inheritance; that is, a class can only inherit from one other class at a time. Although multiple inheritance is more flexible, reuse is also more difficult. However, as will be seen in Chapter 7, C# does offer a sound software engineering alternative by allowing the implementation of multiple interfaces rather than classes.

Syntactically, one class inherits from another by placing a colon (:) between the name of the derived class and the name of the base class. In our next example, class BoundedCounter : Counter could be read as "class BoundedCounter inherits from class Counter". In this case, BoundedCounter is the derived class and Counter is the base class.

```
1    public class BoundedCounter : Counter {
2        public BoundedCounter() : base() {
3            InitRange(0, Int32.MaxValue);
4        }
5        public BoundedCounter(int min, int max) : base(min) {
6            InitRange(min, max);
7        }
8        private  void InitRange(int min, int max) {
9            this.min = min;
10           this.max = max;
11       }
12       public  int  GetMin()    { return min; }
13       public  int  GetMax()    { return max; }
14
15       private int min;
16       private int max;
17   }
```

The Keyword base

The base keyword is used to access members of the base class from within a derived class. In the previous example, several BoundedCounter constructors can be implemented by reusing the Counter class constructors. Each of the two BoundedCounter constructors explicitly creates an instance of Counter by calling the appropriate constructor of Counter using the keyword base and the proper number of parameters (lines 2–7). In the context of a constructor, the keyword base may only be used within the initialization list that precedes the body of the constructor (lines 2 and 5). Only once an instance of Counter has been created are the data fields min and max initialized to complete the creation of an object from BoundedCounter. Since constructors cannot be inherited, the keyword base is indispensable. Another use of the keyword base within derived classes is presented in the next section.

The Keyword new

In C#, a warning message is generated by the compiler when a method is hidden by inheritance in an unintentional manner. For example, the method M in the derived class D hides the one defined in the base class B:

```
class B    { public void M() {} }
class D : B { public void M() {} } // Warning: M() in class D hides M()
                                   // in class B.
```

In order to express this intention explicitly, the new modifier must be used. This modifier, when placed before a member of the derived class, explicitly hides the inherited member with the same signature. Hence, the following code removes the warning:

```
class B    {     public void M() {} }
class D : B { new public void M() {} } // No warning.
                                       // Hiding is now explicit.
```

Using both keywords, new and base, a method can be reused when behavior of a base class is invoked by the corresponding method of the derived class. In the following short example, the class ExtendedCounter inherits from the class Counter. The derived method Tick reuses the same method (and implementation) of its base class by invoking the Tick method of its parent. It is worth noting again that the keyword new is required to remove the warning and to state clearly that the derived Tick method hides the one in the base class. To avoid a recursive call, however, the invocation of Tick is prefixed by the keyword base. The return type of the derived class must match or be a subclass of the return type of the base method as well.

```
class Counter {
    public bool Tick() { ... }
    ...
}

class ExtendedCounter : Counter {
    public new bool Tick() {
        ...              // Optional computation before
        base.Tick();     // Reuse the Tick method from Counter
        ...              // Optional computation after
    }
    ...
}
```

The Extension of Functionality

The class BoundedCounter extends the functionality of Counter with the methods GetMin, GetMax, and InitRange. Unlike aggregation, the methods GetCount and SetCount are inherited and not reimplemented. Even the Counter data field c disappears. In Chapter 7, we show how behavior can be overridden or redefined using abstract classes. But for now, the common behavior of Counter and its subclass BoundedCounter is exactly the same.

To create an instance of BoundedCounter with minimum and maximum boundaries of 0 and 9 respectively, we are able to invoke all public (and protected) methods available from Counter even if these methods are not visible by looking at the class definition of BoundedCounter alone.

```
BoundedCounter bc = new BoundedCounter(0,9);

int countValue = bc.GetCount();   // From Counter
int minValue   = bc.GetMin();     // From BoundedCounter
int maxValue   = bc.GetMax();     // From BoundedCounter
```

If bc is an instance of BoundedCounter which is derived from Counter, then bc can also be assigned to a Counter object c as shown below. The extra functionality of bc, that is, GetMin, GetMax, and InitRange, is simply not available to c.

```
Counter c = bc;

int countValue = c.GetCount();   // OK.
int minValue   = c.GetMin();     // Error: No GetMin method in the
                                 // Counter class.
      countValue = c.count;      // Error: No access to private members.
```

An inherited class like BoundedCounter has access to all public and protected data fields and methods of its base class. Private members are the only exceptions. Also by inheritance, a hierarchy of classes is established. In the preceding example, BoundedCounter is a subclass of Counter, and Counter is a superclass of BoundedCounter. By default, all classes are derived from the root class object and therefore, all methods defined in object can be called by any C# object. Consequently, every class other than object has a superclass. If the superclass is not specified then the superclass defaults to the object class.

A Digression on Constructor/Destructor Chaining

Objects are built from the top down. A constructor of a derived class calls a constructor of its base class, which in turn calls a constructor of its superclass, and so on, until the constructor of the object class is invoked at the root of the class hierarchy. The body of the object constructor then runs first, followed by the body of its subclass and so on down the class hierarchy. This action is called **constructor chaining**. However, if the first statement in a constructor is not an explicit call to a constructor of the superclass using the keyword base then an implicit call to base() with no arguments is generated. Of course, if the superclass does not have a parameterless constructor then a compilation error is generated. It is however possible that a constructor calls another constructor within the same class using the keyword this:

```
public class Counter {
    public       Counter() : this(0) { }
    public       Counter(int count)  { this.count = count; }
    ...
}
```

The first constructor calls the second with zero as its parameter. At this point, the second constructor implicitly calls the parameterless constructor of its superclass with base() *before* assigning 0 to its local data member count.

Whereas objects are created from the top down, objects are destroyed in the reverse fashion from the bottom up. For example, when an object of BoundedCounter is created, the constructor of Counter is executed before the constructor of BoundedCounter as expected. However, when an object of BoundedCounter is destroyed upon completion of the method Main, the destructor of BoundedCounter is completed before the destructor of Counter.

```
class Counter {
    public  Counter () { System.Console.WriteLine(" Counter"); }
            ˜Counter () { System.Console.WriteLine("˜Counter"); }
}

class BoundedCounter : Counter {
    public  BoundedCounter () { System.Console.WriteLine(" BoundedCounter"); }
            ˜BoundedCounter () { System.Console.WriteLine("˜BoundedCounter"); }
}

class TestDestructor {
    public static void Main() {
        BoundedCounter bc = new BoundedCounter();
    }
}
```

Output:

```
 Counter
 BoundedCounter
˜BoundedCounter
˜Counter
```

3.3.3 Comparing Aggregation and Inheritance

Although the BoundedCounter class was best implemented using inheritance, aggregation proves equally adept in other situations. For example, consider the following class Stream, which offers a behavior consisting of two methods, Read and Write:

```
class Stream {
    public int  Read()       { ... }
    public void Write(int i) { ... }
    ...
}
```

If a new class called StreamReader is interested only in the Read behavior of the Stream class then inheritance is not a good choice. With inheritance, the entire behavior of the Stream class, including its Write method, is exposed and is accessible.

```
class StreamReader : Stream {
    // By inheritance, both Read and Write methods are available
}
...
StreamReader  s = new StreamReader();
s.Write(0);        // Write is called by mistake
```

Aggregation proves to be a more appropriate choice in this case. Exact behavior is realized by selecting only those methods of Stream that define the behavior of StreamReader, no more and no less. Unwanted behavior, such as Write, is not exposed. Consider now the following C# code using aggregation:

```
class StreamReader {
    public  int Read() { // Read is now the only method available.
        return s.Read();
    }
    private Stream s;
}
...
StreamReader  s = new StreamReader();
s.Write(0);        // Compilation error
```

In this case, only the Read method is reimplemented. Any attempt to access the Write method of Stream results in a compilation error, an excellent reminder of the added restriction. However, if one class does include and extend the *entire* behavior of another class, then inheritance is preferred. Otherwise, if only partial behavior is required or dispersed among several classes then aggregation is more appropriate.

3.3.4 Using Protected Methods

In Chapter 2, the protected modifier was applied to a data field or method to restrict access to its own class and subclasses. To illustrate the use of the protected modifier with respect to methods, suppose that a parameterless constructor is added to the Stream class given previously. This constructor invokes a protected method called Init:

```
class Stream {
    public          Stream()                { Init(0); }
    protected void Init(long position)       { this.position = position; }
    public int      Read()                  { ... }
    public void     Write(int i)            { ... }
    public long     GetLength()             { return length; }

    private long length;    // The length of the stream in bytes.
    private long position;  // The current position within the stream.
}
```

The purpose of the Init method is to localize in a single place the common initialization procedure for a Stream object, albeit in this case for a single data member. Therefore, all constructors of Stream and its derived classes may invoke Init before or after performing any specialized initializations. Furthermore, once a Stream object has been created, the Init method also allows the class and its derived classes to reset the object to its initial configuration. Finally, the protected modifier preserves a private view for the clients of Stream and its derived classes. The following example presents a subclass called MyStream that reuses the base Init method in its own local Init before performing other initializations:

```
class MyStream : Stream {
    public MyStream() : base() {
        Init();
    }
    protected void Init() {
        base.Init(base.GetLength()); // To read stream in reverse order.
        // Other local initializations (mode, size, ...)
    }
    ...
}
```

The full impact of protected access when combined with the virtual and override modifiers is described in Chapter 4.

Exercises

Exercise 3-1. Write two methods that receive an Id object—one by reference MR and the other by value MV. Each of them changes the first name of an Id object and prints the change. Add print statements before and after the invocation of each method to see the results.

Exercise 3-2. A person can be defined as an identification having a first name, a last name, and an e-mail address. Use inheritance to define the class Person by reusing the class Id, and write a Main method that creates a few people.

Exercise 3-3. A contact can be defined as a person that has an e-mail address. Use aggregation to define the class Contact by reusing both Id and Email classes, and write a Main method that creates a few contacts.

chapter 4

Unified Type System

Introduced in 1980, Smalltalk prided itself as a pure object-oriented language. All values, either simple or user-defined, were treated as objects and all classes, either directly or indirectly, were derived from an object root class. The language was simple and conceptually sound. Unfortunately, Smalltalk was also inefficient at that time and therefore, found little support for commercial software development. In an effort to incorporate classes in C and without compromising efficiency, the C++ programming language restricted the type hierarchy to those classes and their subclasses that were user-defined. Simple data types were treated as they were in C.

In the early 1990s, Java reintroduced the notion of the object root class but continued to exclude simple types from the hierarchy. Wrapper classes were used instead to convert simple values into objects. Language design to this point was concerned (as it should be) with efficiency. If the Java virtual machine was to find a receptive audience among software developers, performance would be key.

As processor speeds have continued to rapidly increase, it has become feasible to revisit the elegance of the Smalltalk language and the concepts introduced in the late 1970s. To that end, the C# language completes, in a sense, a full circle where all types are organized (unified) into a hierarchy of classes that derive from the object root class. Unlike C/C++, there are no default types in C# and, therefore, all declared data elements are explicitly associated with a type. Hence, C# is also strongly typed, in keeping with its criteria of reliability and security.

This chapter presents the C# unified type system, including reference and value types, literals, conversions, boxing/unboxing, and the root object class as well as two important predefined classes for arrays and strings.

55

4.1   Reference Types

Whether a class is predefined or user-defined, the term class is synonymous with type. Therefore, a class is a type and a type is a class. In C#, types fall into one of two main categories: **reference** and **value**. A third category called **type parameter** is exclusively used with generics (a type enclosed within angle brackets <Type>) and is covered later in

Section 8.2:

EBNF

    Type = ValueType | ReferenceType | TypeParameter .

Reference types represent hidden pointers to objects that have been created and allocated on the heap. As shown in previous chapters, objects are created and allocated using the new operator. However, whenever the variable of a reference type is used as part of an expression, it is implicitly dereferenced and can therefore be thought of as the object itself. If a reference variable is not associated with a particular object then it is assigned to null by default.

The C# language is equipped with a variety of reference types, as shown in this EBNF definition:

EBNF

    ReferenceType = ClassType | InterfaceType | ArrayType | DelegateType .
    ClassType   = TypeName | "object" | "string" .

Although the definition is complete, each reference type merits a full description in its own right. The ClassType includes user-defined classes as introduced in Chapter 2 as well as two predefined reference types called object and string. Both predefined types correspond to equivalent CLR .NET types as shown in Table 4.1.

The object class represents the root of the type hierarchy in the C# programming language. Therefore, all other types derive from object. Because of its importance, the object root class is described fully in Section 4.6, including a preview of the object-oriented tenet of polymorphism. Arrays and strings are described in the two sections that follow, and the more advanced reference types, namely interfaces and delegates, are presented in Chapter 7.

4.2   Value Types

The value types in C# are most closely related to the basic data types of most programming languages. However, unlike C++ and Java, all value types of C# derive from the object

C# Type	Corresponding CLR .NET Type
string	System.String
object	System.Object

Table 4.1: Reference types and their corresponding .NET types.

class. Hence, instances of these types can be used in much the same fashion as instances of reference types. In the next four subsections, simple (or primitive) value types, nullable types, structures, and enumerations are presented and provide a complete picture of the value types in C#.

4.2.1 Simple Value Types

Simple or primitive value types fall into one of four categories: Integral types, floating-point types, the character type, and the boolean type. Each simple value type, such as char or int, is an alias for a CLR .NET class type as summarized in Table 4.2. For example, bool is represented by the System.Boolean class, which inherits in turn from System.Object.

A variable of boolean type bool is either true or false. Although a boolean value can be represented as only one bit, it is stored as a byte, the minimum storage entity on many processor architectures. On the other hand, two bytes are taken for each element of a boolean array. The character type or char represents a 16-bit unsigned integer (Unicode character set) and behaves like an integral type. Values of type char do not have a sign. If a char with value 0xFFFF is cast to a byte or a short, the result is negative. The eight integer types are either signed or unsigned. Note that the length of each integer type reflects current processor technology. The two floating-point types of C#, float and double, are defined by the IEEE 754 standard. In addition to zero, a float type can represent non-zero values ranging from approximately $\pm 1.5 \times 10^{-45}$ to $\pm 3.4 \times 10^{38}$ with a precision of 7 digits. A double type on the other hand can represent non-zero values ranging from approximately $\pm 5.0 \times 10^{-324}$ to $\pm 1.7 \times 10^{308}$ with a precision of 15-16 digits. Finally, the decimal type can represent non-zero values from $\pm 1.0 \times 10^{-28}$ to approximately $\pm 7.9 \times 10^{28}$ with

C# Type	Corresponding CLR .NET Type
bool	System.Boolean
char	System.Char
sbyte	System.SByte
byte	System.Byte
short	System.Int16
ushort	System.UInt16
int	System.Int32
uint	System.UInt32
long	System.Int64
ulong	System.UInt64
float	System.Single
double	System.Double
decimal	System.Decimal

Table 4.2: Simple value types and their corresponding .NET classes.

Type	Contains	Default	Range
bool	true or false	false	n.a.
char	Unicode character	\u0000	\u0000 .. \uFFFF
sbyte	8-bit signed	0	-128 .. 127
byte	8-bit unsigned	0	0 .. 255
short	16-bit signed	0	-32768 .. 32767
ushort	16-bit unsigned	0	0 .. 65535
int	32-bit signed	0	-2147483648 .. 2147483647
uint	32-bit unsigned	0	0 .. 4294967295
long	64-bit signed	0	-9223372036854775808 .. 9223372036854775807
ulong	64-bit unsigned	0	0 .. 18446744073709551615
float	32-bit floating-point	0.0	see text
double	64-bit floating-point	0.0	see text
decimal	high precision	0.0	see text

Table 4.3: Default and range for value types.

28-29 significant digits. Unlike C/C++, all variables declared as simple types have guaranteed default values. These default values along with ranges for the remaining types (when applicable) are shown in Table 4.3.

4.2.2 Nullable Types

C# 2.0 A **nullable** type is any value type that also includes the null reference value. Not surprisingly, a nullable type is only applicable to value and not reference types. To represent a nullable type, the underlying value type, such as int or float, is suffixed by the question mark (?). For example, a variable b of the nullable boolean type is declared as:

```
bool? b;
```

Like reference and simple types, the nullable ValueType? corresponds to an equivalent CLR .NET type called System.Nullable<ValueType>.

An instance of a nullable type can be created and initialized in one of two ways. In the first way, a nullable boolean instance is created and initialized to null using the new operator:

```
b = new bool? ( );
```

In the second way, a nullable boolean instance is created and initialized to any member of the underlying ValueType as well as null using a simple assignment expression:

```
b = null;
```

Once created in either way, the variable b can take on one of three values (true, false or null). Each instance of a nullable type is defined by two read-only properties:

1. HasValue of type bool, and

2. Value of type ValueType.

Although properties are discussed in greater detail in Chapter 7, they can be thought of in this context as read-only fields that are attached to every instance of a nullable type. If an instance of a nullable type is initialized to null then its HasValue property returns false and its Value property raises an InvalidOperationException whenever an attempt is made to access its value.[1] On the other hand, if an instance of a nullable type is initialized to a particular member of the underlying ValueType then its HasValue property returns true and its Value property returns the member itself. In the following examples, the variables nb and ni are declared as nullable byte and int, respectively:

```
1      class NullableTypes {
2          static void Main(string[] args) {
3              byte? nb = new byte?(); // Initialized to null
4                                      // (parameterless constructor).
5                  nb = null;          // The same.
6                                      // nb.HasValue returns false.
7                                      // nb.Value throws an
8                                      // InvalidOperationException.
9
10                 nb = 3;             // Initialized to 3.
11                                     // nb.HasValue returns true.
12                                     // nb.Value returns 3.
13             byte  b  = 5;
14                   nb = b;           // Convert byte  into byte?
15             int?  ni = (int?)nb;    // Convert byte? into int?
16                   b  = (byte)ni;    // Convert int?  into byte.
17                   b  = (byte)nb;    // Convert byte? into byte.
18                   b  = nb;          // Compilation error:
19                                     // Cannot convert byte? into byte.
20         }
21     }
```

Any variable of a nullable type can be assigned a variable of the underlying ValueType, in this case byte, as shown above on line 14. However, the converse is not valid and requires explicit casting (lines 15–17). Otherwise, a compilation error is generated (line 18).

---

[1]Exceptions are fully discussed in Chapter 6.

4.2.3   Structure Types

The **structure** type (struct) is a value type that encapsulates other members, such as constructors, constants, fields, methods, and operators, as well as properties, indexers, and nested types as described in Chapter 7. For efficiency, structures are generally used for small objects that contain few data members with a fixed size of 16 bytes or less. They are also allocated on the stack without any involvement of the garbage collector. A simplified EBNF declaration for a structure type is given here:

EBNF

```
StructDecl = "struct" Id (":" Interfaces)? "{" Members "}" ";"
```

For each structure, an implicitly defined default (parameterless) constructor is always generated to initialize structure members to their default values. Therefore, unlike classes, explicit default constructors are not allowed. In C#, there is also no inheritance of classes for structures. Structures inherit only from the class System.ValueType, which in turn inherits from the root class object. Therefore, all members of a struct can only be public, internal, or private (by default). Furthermore, structures cannot be used as the base for any other type but can be used to implement interfaces.

   The structure Node encapsulates one reference and one value field, name and age, respectively. Neither name nor age can be initialized outside a constructor using an initializer.

```
struct Node {
    public Node(string name, int age) {
        this.name = name;
        this.age  = age;
    }
    internal string name;
    internal int    age;
}
```

An instance of a structure like Node is created in one of two ways. As with classes, a structure can use the new operator by invoking the appropriate constructor. For example,

```
Node node1 = new Node();
```

creates a structure using the default constructor, which initializes name and age to null and 0, respectively. On the other hand,

```
Node node2 = new Node ( "Michel", 18 );
```

creates a structure using the explicit constructor, which initializes name to Michel and age to 18. A structure may also be created without new by simply assigning one instance of a structure to another upon declaration:

```
Node node3 = node2;
```

However, the name field of node3 refers to the same string object as the name field of node2. In other words, only a shallow copy of each field is made upon assignment of one structure to another. To assign not only the reference but the entire object itself, a deep copy is required, as discussed in Section 4.6.3.

Because a struct is a value rather than a reference type, self-reference is illegal. Therefore, the following definition, which appears to define a linked list, generates a compilation error.

```
struct Node {
    internal string name;
    internal Node   next;
}
```

4.2.4 Enumeration Types

An **enumeration** type (enum) is a value type that defines a list of named constants. Each of the constants in the list corresponds to an underlying integral type: int by default or an explicit base type (byte, sbyte, short, ushort, int, uint, long, or ulong). Because a variable of type enum can be assigned any one of the named constants, it essentially behaves as an integral type. Hence, many of the operators that apply to integral types apply equally to enum types, including the following:

```
==  !=  <  >  <=  >=  +  -  ˆ  &  |  ˜  ++  --  sizeof
```

as described in Chapter 5. A simplified EBNF declaration for an enumeration type is as follows:

EBNF

```
EnumDecl = Modifiers? "enum" Identifier (":" BaseType)? "{" EnumeratorList "}" ";"
```

Unless otherwise indicated, the first constant of the enumerator list is assigned the value 0. The values of successive constants are increased by 1. For example:

```
enum DeliveryAddress { Domestic, International, Home, Work };
```

is equivalent to:

```
const int Domestic = 0;
const int International = 1;
const int Home = 2;
const int Work = 3;
```

It is possible to break the list by forcing one or more constants to a specific value, such as the following:

```
enum DeliveryAddress { Domestic, International=2, Home, Work };
```

In this enumeration, Domestic is 0, International is 2, Home is 3, and Work is 4. In the following example, all constants are specified:

```
enum DeliveryAddress {Domestic=1, International=2, Home=4, Work=8};
```

The underlying integral type can be specified as well. Instead of the default int, the byte type can be used explicitly for the sake of space efficiency:

```
enum DeliveryAddress : byte {Domestic=1, International=2, Home=4, Work=8};
```

Unlike its predecessors in C++ and Java, enumerations in C# inherit from the System.Enum class providing the ability to access names and values as well as to find and convert existing ones. A few of these methods are as follows:

- Accessing the name or value of an enumeration constant:
  ```
  string   GetName  (Type enumType, object value)
  string[] GetNames (Type enumType)
  Array    GetValues(Type enumType)
  ```

- Determining if a value exists in an enumeration:
  ```
  bool IsDefined(Type enumType, object value)
  ```

- Converting a value into an enumeration type (overloaded for every integer type):
  ```
  object ToObject(Type enumType, object value)
  object ToObject(Type enumType, intType value)
  ```

Historically, enumerations have been used as a convenient procedural construct to improve software readability. They simply mapped names to integral values. Consequently, enumerations in C/C++ were not extensible and hence not object oriented. Enumerations in C#, however, are extensible and provide the ability to add new constants without modifying existing enumerations, thereby avoiding massive recompilations of code.

At the highest level, value types are subdivided into three categories: StructType, EnumType, and NullableType, the former including the simple types, such as char and int. The complete EBNF of all value types in C# is summarized below, where TypeName is a user-defined type identifier for structures and enumerations:

EBNF

```
ValueType    = StructType | EnumType | NullableType .
StructType   = TypeName | SimpleType .
SimpleType   = NumericType | "bool" .
NumericType  = IntegralType | RealType | "decimal" | "char" .
IntegralType = "sbyte" | "short" | "int" | "long" | "byte" | "ushort" |
               "uint" | "ulong" .
RealType     = "float" | "double" .
EnumType     = TypeName .
NullableType = ValueType "?" .
```

4.3 Literals

The C# language has six literal types: integer, real, boolean, character, string, and null. Integer literals represent integral-valued numbers. For example:

```
123            (is an integer by default)
0123           (is an octal integer, using the prefix 0)
123U           (is an unsigned integer, using the suffix U)
123L           (is a long integer, using the suffix L)
123UL          (is an unsigned long integer, using the suffix UL)
0xDecaf        (is a hexadecimal integer, using the prefix 0x)
```

Real literals represent floating-point numbers. For example:

```
3.14    .1e12 (are double precision by default)
3.1E12  3E12  (are double precision by default)
3.14F         (is a single precision real, using the suffix F)
3.14D         (is a double precision real, using the suffix D)
3.14M         (is a decimal real, using the suffix M)
```

Suffixes may be lowercase but are generally less readable, especially when making the distinction between the number 1 and the letter l. The two boolean literals in C# are represented by the keywords: `Tip`

```
true   false
```

The character literals are the same as those in C but also include the Unicode characters (\udddd):

```
\ (continuation)   '\n'   '\t'   '\b'   '\r'   '\f'   '\\'   '\''   '\"'
0ddd    or  \ddd
0xdd    or  \xdd
0xdddd  or  \udddd
```

Therefore, the following character literals are all equivalent:

```
'\n'    10    012    0xA    \u000A    \x000A
```

String literals represent a sequence of zero or more characters—for example:

```
"A string"
""              (an empty string)
"\""            (a double quote)
```

Finally, the null literal is a C# keyword that represents a null reference.

4.4 **Conversions**

In developing C# applications, it may be necessary to convert or **cast** an expression of one type into that of another. For example, in order to add a value of type float to a value of type int, the integer value must first be converted to a floating-point number before addition is performed. In C#, there are two kinds of conversion or casting: implicit and explicit. **Implicit conversions** are ruled by the language and applied automatically without user intervention. On the other hand, **explicit conversions** are specified by the developer in order to support runtime operations or decisions that cannot be deduced by the compiler. The following example illustrates these conversions:

```
1                       // 'a' is a 16-bit unsigned integer.
2   int  i = 'a';       // Implicit conversion to 32-bit signed integer.
3   char c = (char)i;   // Explicit conversion to 16-bit unsigned integer.
4
5   Console.WriteLine("i as int  = {0}", i);         // Output 97
6   Console.WriteLine("i as char = {0}", (char)i);   // Output a
```

The compiler is allowed to perform an implicit conversion on line 2 because no information is lost. This process is also called a widening conversion, in this case from 16-bit to 32-bit. The compiler, however, is not allowed to perform a narrowing conversion from 32-bit to 16-bit on line 3. Attempting to do char c = i; will result in a compilation error, which states that it cannot implicitly convert type int to type char. If the integer i must be printed as a character, an explicit cast is needed (line 6). Otherwise, integer i is printed as an integer (line 5). In this case, we are not losing data but printing it as a character, a user decision that cannot be second-guessed by the compiler. The full list of implicit conversions supported by C# is given in Table 4.4.

From	To Wider Type
byte	decimal, double, float, long, int, short, ulong, uint, ushort
sbyte	decimal, double, float, long, int, short
char	decimal, double, float, long, int, ulong, uint, ushort
ushort	decimal, double, float, long, int, ulong, uint
short	decimal, double, float, long, int
uint	decimal, double, float, long, ulong
int	decimal, double, float, long
ulong	decimal, double, float
long	decimal, double, float
float	double

Table 4.4: Implicit conversions supported by C#.

Conversions from int, uint, long, or ulong to float and from long or ulong to double may cause a loss of precision but will never cause a loss of magnitude. All other implicit numeric conversions never lose any information.

In order to prevent improper mapping from ushort to the Unicode character set, the former cannot be implicitly converted into a char, although both types are unsigned 16-bit integers. Also, because boolean values are not integers, the bool type cannot be implicitly or explicitly converted into any other type, or vice versa. Finally, even though the decimal type has more precision (it holds 28 digits), neither float nor double can be implicitly converted to decimal because the range of decimal values is smaller (see Table 4.3).

To store enumeration constants in a variable, it is important to declare the variable as the type of the enum. Otherwise, explicit casting is required to convert an enumerated value to an integral value, and vice versa. In either case, implicit casting is not done and generates a compilation error. Although explicit casting is valid, it is not a good programming practice and should be avoided.

| Tip |

```
DeliveryAddress  da1;
            int  da2;

da1 = DeliveryAddress.Home;   // OK.
da2 = da1;                    // Compilation error.
da2 = (int)da1;              // OK, but not a good practice.
da1 = da2;                    // Compilation error.
da1 = (DeliveryAddress)da2;   // OK, but not a good practice.
```

Implicit or explicit conversions can be applied to reference types as well. In C#, where classes are organized in a hierarchy, these conversions can be made either up or down the hierarchy, and are known as **upcasts** or **downcasts**, respectively. Upcasts are clearly implicit because of the type compatibility that comes with any derived class within the same hierarchy. Implicit downcasts, on the other hand, generate a compilation error since any class with more generalized behavior cannot be cast to one that is more specific and includes additional methods. However, an explicit downcast can be applied to any reference but is logically correct only if the attempted type conversion corresponds to the actual object type in the reference. The following example illustrates both upcasts and downcasts:

```
1   public class TestCast {
2       public static void Main() {
3           object o;
4           string s = "Michel";
5           double d;
6
7           o = s;            // Implicit upcast.
8           o = (object)s;    // Explicit upcast (not necessary).
9           s = (string)o;    // Explicit downcast (necessary).
10          d = (double)o;    // Explicit downcast (syntactically correct) but ...
```

```
11          d *= 2.0;        // ...throws an InvalidCastException at runtime.
12      }
13  }
```

An object reference o is first assigned a string reference s using either an implicit or an explicit upcast, as shown on lines 7 and 8. An explicit downcast on line 9 is logically correct since o contains a reference to a string. Hence, s may safely invoke any method of the string class. Although syntactically correct, the explicit downcast on line 10 leads to an InvalidCastException on the following line. At that point, the floating-point value d, which actually contains a reference to a string, attempts to invoke the multiplication method and thereby raises the exception.

4.5 Boxing and Unboxing

Since value types and reference types are subclasses of the object class, they are also compatible with object. This means that a value-type variable or literal can (1) invoke an object method and (2) be passed as an object argument without explicit casting.

```
int    i = 2;
i.ToString();    // (1) equivalent to 2.ToString();
                 // which is 2.System.Int32::ToString()

i.Equals(2);     // (2) where Equals has an object type argument
                 // avoiding an explicit cast such as i.Equals( (object)2 );
```

Boxing is the process of implicitly casting a value-type variable or literal into a reference type. In other words, it allows value types to be treated as objects. This is done by creating an optimized temporary reference type that refers to the value type. Boxing a value via explicit casting is legal but unnecessary.

```
int    i = 2;
object o = i;           // Implicit casting (or boxing).
object p = (object)i;   // Explicit casting (unnecessary).
```

On the other hand, it is not possible to unbox a reference type into a value type without an explicit cast. The intent must be clear from the compiler's point of view.

```
object o;
...
short  s = (short)o;
```

The ability to treat value types as objects bridges the gap that exists in most programming languages. For example, a Stack class can provide push and pop methods that take and return value and reference objects:

```
class Stack {
    public object pop()          { ... }
    public void   push(object o) { ... }
}
```

4.6 The Object Root Class

Before tackling the object root class, we introduce two additional method modifiers: virtual and override. Although these method modifiers are defined in detail in Chapter 7, they are omnipresent in every class that uses the .NET Framework. Therefore, a few introductory words are in order.

A method is **polymorphic** when declared with the keyword virtual. Polymorphism allows a developer to invoke the same method that behaves and is implemented differently on various classes within the same hierarchy. Such a method is very useful when we wish to provide common services within a hierarchy of classes. Therefore, polymorphism is directly tied to the concept of inheritance and is one of the three hallmarks of object-oriented technology.

4.6.1 Calling Virtual Methods

Any decision in calling a virtual method is done at runtime. In other words, during a virtual method invocation, it is the runtime system that examines the object's reference. An object's reference is not simply a physical memory pointer as in C, but rather a virtual logical pointer containing the information of its own object type. Based on this information, the runtime system determines which actual method implementation to call. Such a runtime decision, also known as a polymorphic call, dynamically binds an invocation with the appropriate method via a virtual table that is generated for each object.

When classes already contain declared virtual methods, a derived class may wish to refine or reimplement the behavior of a virtual method to suit its particular specifications. To do so, the signature must be identical to the virtual method except that it is preceded by the modifier override in the derived class. In the following example, class D overrides method V, which is inherited from class B. When an object of class D is assigned to the parameter b at line 13, the runtime system dynamically binds the overridden method of class D to b.

```
1   class B {
2       public virtual  void V() { System.Console.WriteLine("B.V()"); }
3   }
4   class D : B {
5       public override void V() { System.Console.WriteLine("D.V()"); }
6   }
```

```
7   class TestVirtualOverride {
8       public static void Bind(B b) {
9           b.V();
10      }
11      public static void Main() {
12          Bind( new B() );
13          Bind( new D() );
14
15          new D().V();
16      }
17  }
```

Output:

```
B.V()
D.V()
D.V()
```

With this brief overview of the virtual and override modifiers, let us now take a comprehensive look at the object root class.

The System.Object class is the root of all other classes in the .NET Framework. Defining a class like Id (page 30) means that it inherits implicitly from System.Object. The following declarations are therefore equivalent:

```
class Id { ... }
class Id : object { ... }
class Id : System.Object { ... }
```

As we have seen earlier, the object keyword is an alias for System.Object.

The System.Object class, shown below, offers a few common basic services to all derived classes, either value or reference. Of course, any virtual methods of System.Object can be redefined (overridden) to suit the needs of a derived class. In the sections that follow, the methods of System.Object are grouped and explained by category: parameterless constructor, instance methods, and static methods.

```
namespace System {
    public Object {
        // Parameterless Constructor
        public Object();

        // Instance Methods
        public    virtual string ToString();
        public            Type   GetType();
        public    virtual bool    Equals(Object o);
        public    virtual int     GetHashCode();
        protected virtual void    Finalize();
```

```
        protected          object MemberwiseClone();

        // Static Methods
        public static bool Equals(Object a, Object b);
        public static bool ReferenceEquals(Object a, Object b);
    }
}
```

4.6.2 Invoking the Object Constructor

The Object() constructor is both public and parameterless and is invoked by default by all derived classes either implicitly or explicitly. The following two equivalent declarations illustrate both invocations of the base constructor from System.Object:

```
class Id {
    Id() { ... }            // Invoking Object() implicitly.
    ...
}

class Id {
    Id() : base() { ... }  // Invoking Object() explicitly.
    ...
}
```

4.6.3 Using Object Instance Methods

Often used for debugging purposes, the ToString virtual method returns a string that provides information about an object. It allows the client to determine where and how information is displayed—for example, on a standard output stream, in a GUI, through a serial link, and so on. If this method is not overridden, the default string returns the fully qualified type name (namespace.className) of the current object.

The GetType method returns the object description (also called the metadata) of a Type object. The Type class is also well known as a meta-class in other object-oriented languages, such as Smalltalk and Java. This feature is covered in detail in Chapter 10.

The following example presents a class Counter that inherits the ToString method from the System.Object class, and a class NamedCounter that overrides it (line 11). The Main method in the test class instantiates three objects (lines 19–21) and prints the results of their ToString invocations (lines 23–25). In the case of the object o (line 23), System.Object corresponds to its Object class within the System namespace. For the objects c and nc (lines 24 and 25), Counter and NamedCounter correspond, respectively, to their classes within the default namespace. The last three statements (lines 27–29) print the names representing the meta-class Type of each object.

```
1    using System;
2
3    public class Counter {
4        public void Inc() { count++; }
5        private int count;
6    }
7    public class NamedCounter {
8        public NamedCounter(string aName) {
9            name = aName; count = 0;
10       }
11       public override string ToString() {
12           return "Counter '"+name+"' = "+count;
13       }
14       private string name;
15       private int    count;
16   }
17   public class TestToStringGetType {
18       public static void Main() {
19           Object        o = new Object();
20           Counter       c = new Counter();
21           NamedCounter  nc = new NamedCounter("nc");
22
23           Console.WriteLine(" o.ToString() = {0}",  o.ToString());
24           Console.WriteLine(" c.ToString() = {0}",  c.ToString());
25           Console.WriteLine("nc.ToString() = {0}", nc.ToString());
26
27           Console.WriteLine("Type of o    = {0}",  o.GetType());
28           Console.WriteLine("Type of c    = {0}",  c.GetType());
29           Console.WriteLine("Type of nc   = {0}", nc.GetType());
30       }
31   }
```

Output:

```
 o.ToString() = System.Object
 c.ToString() = Counter
nc.ToString() = Counter 'nc' = 0
Type of o    = System.Object
Type of c    = Counter
Type of nc   = NamedCounter
```

The virtual implementation of Object.Equals simply checks for identity-based equality between the parameter object o and the object itself. To provide value-based equality for derived classes, the Equals method must be overridden to check that the two objects are instantiated from the same class and are identical member by member. A good ip implementation tests to see first if the parameter o is null, second if it is an alias (this), and third if it is not of the same type using the operator is. In C#, this method is not equivalent to the operation == unless the operator is overloaded.

The GetHashCode virtual method computes and returns a first-estimate integer hash code for each object that is used as a key in the many hash tables available in System.Collections. The hash code, however, is only a necessary condition for equality and therefore obeys the following properties:

1. If two objects are equal then both objects must have the same hash code.

2. If the hash code of two objects is equal then both objects are not necessarily equal.

A simple and efficient algorithm for generating the hash code for an object applies the exclusive OR operation to its numeric member variables. To ensure that identical hash codes are generated for objects of equal value, the GetHashCode method must be overridden for derived classes.

The following example presents a class Counter that inherits the Equals and GetHashCode methods from the System.Object class, and a class NamedCounter that over-rides them (lines 14 and 25). The Main method in the test class instantiates six objects (lines 33–38) and prints their hash codes (lines 40–45). Notice that all hash codes are unique except for the two identical objects nc1 and nc3. All the other lines (47–56) compare objects with themselves, null, and an instance of the class Object.

```
1    using System;
2
3    public class Counter {
4        public  void Inc() { count++; }
5        private int  count;
6    }
7    public class NamedCounter {
8        public NamedCounter(string aName) { name = aName; }
9        public void Inc()                 { count++; }
10       public int  GetCount()            { return count; }
11       public override string ToString() {
12           return "Counter '"+name+"' = "+count;
13       }
14       public override bool Equals(object o) {
15           if (o == null) return false;
16           if (GetHashCode() != o.GetHashCode()) return false;
17                                    // Is same hash code?
18           if (o == this) return true;
19                                    // Compare with itself?
20           if (!(o is NamedCounter)) return false;
21                                    // Is same type as itself?
22           NamedCounter nc = (NamedCounter)o;
23           return name.Equals(nc.name)  &&  count == nc.count;
```

```
24      }
25      public override int GetHashCode() {
26          return name.GetHashCode() ^ count;                      // Exclusive or.
27      }
28      private string name;
29      private int    count;
30  }
31  public class TestHashCodeEquals {
32      public static void Main() {
33          Object          o = new Object();
34          NamedCounter nc1 = new NamedCounter("nc1");
35          NamedCounter nc2 = new NamedCounter("nc2");
36          NamedCounter nc3 = new NamedCounter("nc1");
37          Counter      c1 = new Counter();
38          Counter      c2 = new Counter();
39
40          Console.WriteLine("HashCode    o = {0}",    o.GetHashCode());
41          Console.WriteLine("HashCode nc1 = {0}", nc1.GetHashCode());
42          Console.WriteLine("HashCode nc2 = {0}", nc2.GetHashCode());
43          Console.WriteLine("HashCode nc3 = {0}", nc3.GetHashCode());
44          Console.WriteLine("HashCode  c1 = {0}",  c1.GetHashCode());
45          Console.WriteLine("HashCode  c2 = {0}",  c2.GetHashCode());
46
47          Console.WriteLine("nc1 == null? {0}", nc1.Equals(null)?"yes":"no");
48          Console.WriteLine("nc1 == nc1?  {0}", nc1.Equals(nc1) ?"yes":"no");
49          Console.WriteLine("nc1 == o?    {0}", nc1.Equals(o)   ?"yes":"no");
50          Console.WriteLine("nc1 == nc2?  {0}", nc1.Equals(nc2) ?"yes":"no");
51          Console.WriteLine("nc1 == nc3?  {0}", nc1.Equals(nc3) ?"yes":"no");
52
53          Console.WriteLine(" c1 == null? {0}", c1.Equals(null) ?"yes":"no");
54          Console.WriteLine(" c1 == c1?   {0}", c1.Equals(c1)   ?"yes":"no");
55          Console.WriteLine(" c1 == o?    {0}", c1.Equals(o)    ?"yes":"no");
56          Console.WriteLine(" c1 == c2?   {0}", c1.Equals(c2)   ?"yes":"no");
57      }
58  }
```

Output:

```
HashCode    o = 54267293
HashCode nc1 = 1511508983
HashCode nc2 = -54574958
HashCode nc3 = 1511508983
HashCode  c1 = 18643596
HashCode  c2 = 33574638
nc1 == null? no
```

```
nc1 == nc1?   yes
nc1 == o?     no
nc1 == nc2?   no
nc1 == nc3?   yes
 c1 == null?  no
 c1 == c1?    yes
 c1 == o?     no
 c1 == c2?    no
```

The last two methods of the Object class are protected to be securely available only to derived classes. The Finalize method when overridden is used by the garbage collector to free any allocated resources before destroying the object. Section 9.1 illustrates how the C# compiler generates a Finalize method to replace an explicit destructor.

The MemberwiseClone method returns a member-by-member copy of the current object. Although values and references are duplicated, subobjects are not. This type of cloning is called a **shallow copy**. To achieve a shallow (or bitwise) copy, the method Object.MemberwiseClone is simply invoked for the current object. In this way, all the non-static value and reference fields are copied. Although a shallow copy of a value field is non-problematic, the shallow copy of a reference-type field does not create a duplicate of the object to which it refers. Hence, several objects may refer to the same subobjects. The latter situation is often undesirable and therefore, a **deep copy** is performed instead. To achieve a deep copy, the method Object.Memberwiseclone is invoked for the current object *and* its subobject(s).

The following example shows three classes that clearly express the impact of each kind of cloning. The Value class contains a value-type field called v. After creating an object v1 and incrementing its value (lines 31–32), v2 is initialized as a clone of v1 and then incremented (lines 33–34). The first two lines of output show that the v2 object is independent of v1, though v2 had the same value as v1 at the time of the cloning. In this case, a shallow copy is sufficient.

The ShallowCopy class contains a reference-type field called r (line 17) that is cloned in the same way as the Value class (compare lines 7 and 15). The object sc1 is then created on line 39 with a reference to the object v2. In cloning sc1 into sc2 (line 40), both objects are now pointing to the same object v2. Increasing the value of v2 and printing objects sc1 and sc2 clearly shows that the subobject v2 is not duplicated using a shallow copy.

Finally, the DeepCopy class also contains a reference-type field r (line 27) but with a different implementation of the method Clone. As before, the object dc1 is created on line 46 with a reference to object v2. In cloning dc1 into dc2 (line 47), a temporary object reference clone of type DeepCopy is first initialized to a shallow copy of the current object dc1 (line 23). On line 24, the subobject v2 is cloned as well. The object clone is then returned from the method Clone and assigned to dc2. Increasing the value of v2 and printing objects dc1 and dc2 shows that the reference field r of each object points to a distinct instance of the Value class. On one hand, the object dc1 refers to v2, and on the other hand, the object dc2 refers to a distinct instance of Value, which was created as an identical copy of v2. The output illustrates the impact of creating two distinct subobjects owned by two different objects dc1 and dc2.

```
1    using System;
2
3    public class Value {
4        public void Inc() { v++; }
5        public override string ToString() { return "Value("+v+")"; }
6        public object Clone() { // Shallow copy of v
7            return this.MemberwiseClone();
8        }
9        private int v;
10   }
11   public class ShallowCopy {
12       public ShallowCopy(Value v) { r = v; }
13       public override string ToString() { return r.ToString(); }
14       public object Clone() { // Shallow copy of r
15           return this.MemberwiseClone();
16       }
17       private Value r;
18   }
19   public class DeepCopy {
20       public DeepCopy(Value v) { r = v; }
21       public override string ToString() { return r.ToString(); }
22       public object Clone() { // Deep copy of r
23           DeepCopy clone = (DeepCopy)this.MemberwiseClone();
24           clone.r = (Value)r.Clone();
25           return clone;
26       }
27       private Value r;
28   }
29   public class TestClone {
30       public static void Main() {
31           Value v1 = new Value();
32           v1.Inc();
33           Value v2 = (Value)v1.Clone();
34           v2.Inc();
35
36           Console.WriteLine("v1.ToString = {0}", v1.ToString());
37           Console.WriteLine("v2.ToString = {0}", v2.ToString());
38
39           ShallowCopy sc1 = new ShallowCopy(v2);
40           ShallowCopy sc2 = (ShallowCopy)sc1.Clone();
41           v2.Inc();
```

```
42
43            Console.WriteLine("sc1.ToString = {0}", sc1.ToString());
44            Console.WriteLine("sc2.ToString = {0}", sc2.ToString());
45
46            DeepCopy dc1 = new DeepCopy(v2);
47            DeepCopy dc2 = (DeepCopy)dc1.Clone();
48            v2.Inc();
49
50            Console.WriteLine("dc1.ToString = {0}", dc1.ToString());
51            Console.WriteLine("dc2.ToString = {0}", dc2.ToString());
52        }
53  }
```

Output:

```
v1.ToString = Value(1)
v2.ToString = Value(2)
sc1.ToString = Value(3)
sc2.ToString = Value(3)
dc1.ToString = Value(4)
dc2.ToString = Value(3)
```

Some important best practices can be noted from the preceding examples. It is strongly   Tip
recommended to always override the ToString method. The HashCode and Equals methods
must always be overridden[2] when you wish to compare the objects of that type in your
application. When comparing objects, first invoke the HashCode method to avoid unnecessary comparisons among instance members. If the hash codes are not equal then objects
are not identical. On the other hand, if hash codes are equal then objects may be identical.
In that case, a full comparison using the Equals method is applied. Note that GetType and
MemberwiseClone methods cannot be overridden since they are not virtual.

4.6.4 Using Object Static Methods

The static method Equals tests for a value-based equality between two Object parameters.
On line 11 in the following example, a value-based comparison is made between two int
(or System.Int32) objects. Because the values of x and y are both 1, equality is True. When
making the same value-based comparison between two reference types, such as a and b
on line 13, the hash codes of each object are used instead.

The static method ReferenceEquals on the other hand tests for a reference-based
identity between the two Object parameters. The method returns True if the two objects
are not distinct, that is, if they have the same reference value. Because objects x and y as
well as objects a and b are all distinct, the comparison for reference-based identity returns

---

[2]If you forget to implement HashCode, the compiler will give you a friendly warning.

False on lines 12 and 14. If both methods, Equals and ReferenceEquals, refer to the same object including null then True is returned as shown on lines 17 through 20.

```
1    using System;
2
3    public class TestObjectEquals {
4        public static void Main() {
5            int x = 1;
6            int y = 1;
7            Object a = new Object();
8            Object b = new Object();
9
10           Console.WriteLine("{0} {1} {2} {3}",
11                           Object.Equals(x, y),
12                           Object.ReferenceEquals(x, y),
13                           Object.Equals(a, b),
14                           Object.ReferenceEquals(a, b));
15           a = b;
16           Console.WriteLine("{0} {1} {2} {3}",
17                           Object.Equals(a, b),
18                           Object.ReferenceEquals(a, b),
19                           Object.Equals(null, null),
20                           Object.ReferenceEquals(null, null));
21       }
22   }
```

Output:

```
True False False False
True True True True
```

4.7 Arrays

Arrays in C# are objects and derive from System.Array. They are the simplest collection or data structure in C# and may contain any value or reference type. In fact, an array is the only collection that is part of the System namespace. All other collections that we cover later, such as hash tables, linked lists, and so on are part of System.Collections. In C#, arrays differ from other collections in two respects:

1. They are declared with a specific type. All other collections are of object type.

2. They cannot change their size once declared.

Tip   These differences make arrays more efficient vis-à-vis collections, but such improvements may not be significant in light of today's processor speeds. Nonetheless, it is always recommended to use profilers to carefully verify where a processor spends its time and to isolate those sections of code that need to be optimized.

4.7.1 Creating and Initializing Arrays

Arrays are zero-indexed collections that can be one- or multi-dimensional and are defined in two steps. First, the type of array is declared and a reference variable is created. Second, space is allocated using the new operator for the given number of elements. For example, a one-dimensional array is defined as follows:

```
int[] myArray;          // (1)
myArray = new int[3];  // (2)
```

At step (1), a reference variable called myArray is created for an int array. At step (2), space is allocated to store three int values. The square brackets [] must be placed after the type in both steps (1) and (2). Only at step (2), however, are the actual number of elements placed within the brackets. Here, array size is specified by any well-defined integral expression. Hence,

```
myArray = new int[a + b];
```

defines an array of size a+b as long as the result of the expression is integral. As in Java but contrary to C/C++, C# is not allowed to define a fixed-size array without the use of the new operator. Therefore, attempting to specify the size within the square brackets at step (1) generates a compilation error.

```
int[3] myArray;         // Compilation error.
```

Finally, like C/C++ and Java, the previous two steps may be coalesced into one line of code:

```
int[] myArray = new int[3];
```

So far, the myArray array has been declared, but each array element has not been explicitly initialized. Therefore, each array element is initialized implicitly to its default value, in this case, 0. It is important to note that if the array type was our Id class instead of int—in other words, a reference type instead of a value type—then myArray would be an array of references initialized by default to null.

Elements in the array, however, can be initialized explicitly in a number of ways. The use of an initializer, as in C/C++ and Java, is often preferred to declare and initialize an array at the same time:

```
int[] myArray = { 1, 3, 5 };
```

In this case, the compiler determines the number of integers within the initializer and implicitly creates an array of size 3. In fact, the preceding example is equivalent to this more explicit one:

```
int[] myArray = new int[3] { 1, 3, 5 };
```

For an array of objects, each element is a reference type and, therefore, each object is either instantiated during the array declaration as shown here:

```
Id[] ids = {
    new Id("Michel", "de Champlain"),
    new Id("Brian", "Patrick")
};
```

or instantiated after the array declaration:

```
Id[] ids = new Id[2];

ids[0] = new Id("Michel", "de Champlain");
ids[1] = new Id("Brian", "Patrick");
```

4.7.2   Accessing Arrays

Elements of an array are accessed by following the array name with an index in square brackets. Bearing in mind that indices begin at 0, myArray[2] accesses the third element of myArray. In the following example, the first and last elements of myArray are initialized to 1, and the second element is initialized to 3.

```
myArray[0] = 1;
myArray[1] = 3;
myArray[2] = myArray[0];
```

When attempting to access an array outside of its declared bounds, that is, outside 0..n-1 for an array of size n, the runtime system of C# throws an IndexOutOfRangeException. Therefore, unlike C/C++, C# provides a greater level of security and reliability.

4.7.3   Using Rectangular and Jagged Arrays

C# supports two kinds of multi-dimensional arrays: rectangular and jagged. **Rectangular arrays** like matrices have more than one index and have a fixed size for each dimension. The comma (,) separates each dimension in the array declaration as illustrated here:

```
int[,]  matrix = new int[2,3];     // 2x3 matrix (6 elements).
int[,,] cube   = new int[2,3,4];   // 2x3x4 cube (24 elements).
```

Accessing the element at the first row and second column of the matrix is done as follows:

```
matrix[0,1];  // matrix [ <row> , <column> ]
```

Jagged arrays are "arrays of arrays" where each element is a reference pointing to another array. Unlike rectangular arrays, jagged arrays may have a different size for each dimension. In the following example, `jaggedMatrix` allocates space for eight integer elements, three in the first row and five in the second:

```
int[][] jaggedMatrix = new int[2][]; // An array with 2 arrays (rows).
jaggedMatrix[0] = new int[3];        // A row of 3 integers.
jaggedMatrix[1] = new int[5];        // A row of 5 integers.
```

Accessing the element at the first row and second column of the `jaggedMatrix` is done as follows:

```
jaggedMatrix[0][1];  // jaggedMatrix [ <row> ] [ <column> ]
```

Of course, attempting to access `jaggedMatrix[0][3]` throws an `IndexOutOfRangeException`.

Although access to rectangular arrays is more efficient than access to jagged arrays, the latter is more flexible for cases such as sparse matrices. Nonetheless, dimensions for both rectangular and jagged arrays are fixed. When dimensions must grow or when fixed sizes cannot be determined by the application requirements, collections, which are discussed in Chapter 8, are a far more flexible alternative to multi-dimensional arrays.

4.8 Strings

Strings in C# are objects and derive from `System.String`, alias `string`. Each string is an immutable sequence of zero or more characters. Any attempt, therefore, to change a string via one of its methods creates an entirely new string object. A string is often initialized to a **string literal**, a sequence of zero or more characters enclosed in double quotes, such as `"Csharp"`. A string is also zero-based. Hence, the first character of a string is designated at index 0. Table 4.5 defines the prototypes for a subset of string methods.

Method Name	Formal Parameter	Return Type	Description
ToUpper	none	string	Converts all of the characters to uppercase.
ToLower	none	string	Converts all of the characters to lowercase.
IndexOf	int *c*	int	Returns index of the 1st occurrence of the character *c*.
IndexOf	string *s*	int	Returns index of the 1st occurrence of the substring *s*.
Concat	string *s*	string	Concatenates the string *s* to the end.
Substring	int *index*	string	Returns new string as the substring starting at *index*.

Table 4.5: String method prototypes.

4.8.1   Invoking String Methods

Both "Csharp" as a string literal and cs as defined here are instances of the string class:

```
string cs = "Csharp";
```

Therefore, both the literal and the reference variable are able to invoke instance string methods to yield equivalent results:

```
"Csharp".IndexOf('C') // Returns 0 (the first letter's index of "Csharp").
cs.IndexOf('C')       // The same.

"Csharp".ToUpper      // Returns "CSHARP".
cs.ToUpper            // The same.
```

4.8.2   Concat, IndexOf, and Substring Methods

The Concat method is an overloaded static method that returns a new string object made up of the concatenation of its one or more string parameters. For example,

```
string a, b, c;

a = "C";
b = "sharp";
c = String.Concat(a, b);
```

As a result of the last statement, c refers to "Csharp". The same result can be accomplished in a single line in one of two ways:

```
string c = String.Concat("C", "sharp");
```

or:

```
string c = "C" + "sharp";
```

In the latter case, the operator + is overloaded.

The IndexOf method is also overloaded and returns the integer position of the first occurrence of a character or string parameter in a particular instance of a string. If the occurrence is not found then −1 is returned. The IndexOf method is illustrated using name:

```
string name = "Michel de Champlain";
           // 01234567...

System.Console.WriteLine(name.IndexOf('M'));    // Returns 0
System.Console.WriteLine(name.IndexOf('d'));    // Returns 7
System.Console.WriteLine(name.IndexOf("de"));   // Returns 7
System.Console.WriteLine(name.IndexOf('B'));    // Returns -1
```

The Substring method creates a new string object that is made up of the receiver string object starting at the given index. For example,

```
string lastName = "Michel de Champlain".Substring(7);
```

As a result, lastName refers to "de Champlain".

4.8.3 The StringBuilder Class

Each manipulation of an immutable string created by System.String results in a new string object being allocated on the heap. Many of these immutable strings will be unreachable and eventually garbage collected. For example:

```
1    string myName = "Michel";
2
3    myName = String.Concat(myName, " de");
4    myName = String.Concat(myName, " Champlain");
```

The above concatenation has instantiated five strings: three for the literal strings ("Michel", " de", and " Champlain"), one as the result of the concatenation on line 3 ("Michel de"), and another as the last concatenation on line 4 ("Michel de Champlain"). Repeating concatenations or making intensive manipulations on immutable strings within loops may be very inefficient. To improve performance, the StringBuilder class in the namespace System.Text is a better choice. It represents instead mutable strings that are allocated only once on the heap.

| Tip |

An object of the StringBuilder class allows a string of up to 16 characters by default and grows dynamically as more characters are added. Its maximum size may be unbounded or increased to a configurable maximum. This example shows the equivalent concatenation of strings using the Append method:

```
StringBuilder myName = new StringBuilder("Michel");

myName.Append(" de");
myName.Append(" Champlain");
```

The three literal strings are still allocated, but only one StringBuilder object assigned to myName is allocated and reused.

In addition to methods such as Insert, Remove, and Replace, the StringBuilder class is equipped with a number of overloaded constructors:

```
public StringBuilder()
public StringBuilder(int capacity)
public StringBuilder(int capacity, int maxCapacity)
public StringBuilder(string value, int capacity)
public StringBuilder(string value, int index, int length, int capacity)
```

The first parameterless constructor creates an empty string with an initial capacity of 16 characters. The second constructor creates an empty string with a specified initial capacity. The third adds a maximum capacity. The fourth constructor specifies the initial string and its capacity. And finally, the last constructor specifies the initial (sub)string, where to start (index), its length, and its initial capacity.

The System.Text namespace also contains classes that represent ASCII, Unicode, UTF-7, and UTF-8 character encoding schemes. These classes are very useful when developing applications that interact with a user through byte I/O streams.

Exercises

Exercise 4-1. Improve the class Id by adding GetHashCode() and Equals() methods in order to efficiently compare Id objects. Test these methods with a separate test program.

Exercise 4-2. Write a class StringTokenizer that extracts tokens from a string delimited by separators, as follows:

```
public class StringTokenizer {
    public StringTokenizer(string line)                     { ... }
    public StringTokenizer(string line, string separators) { ... }
    public string[] GetTokens()                            { ... }
}
```

Noting that separators are blanks and tabs by default, use the following two instance methods for support:

```
public string[] Split(params char[] separators)
public char[]   ToCharArray()
```

The Split() method divides a string into an array of strings based on the given separators, and the ToCharArray() method copies the characters within a string into a character array.

chapter **5**

Operators, Assignments, and Expressions

Operators, assignments, and expressions are the rudimentary building blocks of those programming languages whose design is driven in large part by the underlying architecture of the von Neumann machine. And C# is no exception.

An expression in its most basic form is simply a literal or a variable. Larger expressions are formed by applying an operator to one or more operands (or expressions). Of all operators, the most fundamental is the assignment operator that stores the result of an expression in a variable. Because variables are expressions themselves, they can be used as operands in other expressions and hence, propel a computation forward.

In this chapter, we present all variations of the arithmetic, conditional, relational, and assignment operators in C#. We discuss which simple types and objects are valid for each operator and what types and values are generated for each expression. Because most operators in C# are derived from the lexicon of C/C++, explanations are relatively short but always augmented with simple examples. To disambiguate the order of expression evaluation, the rules of precedence and associativity are also presented along with the powerful notion of operator overloading that was first introduced in Chapter 3.

5.1 Operator Precedence and Associativity

An **expression** in C# is a combination of operands and operators and is much like expressions in C. An **operand** is a literal or a variable, and an **operator** acts upon the operands to return to a single value. Table 5.1 lists all the operators in order of precedence from highest (Primary) to lowest (Assignment). Operators with the same precedence appear on the same line of the table. However, before presenting the operators starting from those

Category	Operators	Associativity
Primary (*Highest*)	x.y f(x) a[x] x++ x-- (x) new	→
	typeof sizeof checked unchecked	
Unary	+ - ˜ ! ++x --x (Type)x	←
Multiplicative	* / %	→
Additive	+ -	→
Shift	<< >>	→
Relational/Type Testing	< <= > >= is as	→
Equality	== !=	→
Logical AND	&	→
Logical XOR	^	→
Logical OR			→
Conditional Logical AND	&&	→
Conditional Logical OR	||	→
Null Coalescing	??	←
Conditional	?:	→
Assignment	= += -= *= /= %= |= ^= &= >>= <<=	←

Table 5.1: Precedence and associativity rules for all operators in C#.

with the lowest precedence, we pause to explain the rules for "deterministic" evaluation, namely the rules of precedence and associativity.

Precedence rules determine which operator should be applied first. For operators with different precedence, the one with the highest precedence is always applied first. For example, a+b*c is evaluated as a+(b*c). **Associativity rules**, on the other hand, determine which operator should be applied first among operators with the same precedence. There are two kinds of associativity:

- **Left associativity** groups operators from left to right (→). For example, a + b - c is evaluated as ((a+b)-c).

- **Right associativity** groups operators from right to left (←). For example, a = b = c is evaluated as (a=(b=c)).

Later in this chapter we will cover why the order of evaluation is important if expressions have side effects and short circuits.

5.2 Assignment Operators

5.2.1 Simple Assignment

EBNF

The **assignment operator** with the following syntax assigns the result of the expression on the right-hand side to the variable on the left-hand side:

```
Variable "=" Expression .
```

The destination Variable and the source Expression must be type compatible. The Variable can store either a simple data value or an object reference.

Assignments of Simple Values

Examples:

```
int a, b, c;

a = 1;       // OK.
b = a;       // OK.
a = c;       // Error: Variable must be initialized before used.
1 = a;       // Error: Destination must be a variable.
c = (a + b); // OK.
(a + b) = c; // Error: Destination must be a variable.
```

The assignment operator has the lowest precedence, allowing the expression on the right-hand side to be evaluated before any assignment:

```
int a;

a = 1;
System.Console.WriteLine(a);

a = a - 1;                      // - has higher precedence than =
System.Console.WriteLine(a);

a = 2 + a * 3;                  // (2 + (0 * 3))
System.Console.WriteLine(a);
```

Output:

```
1
0
2
```

Assignments of References

Examples:

```
Id id1 = new Id("Frank", 1);
Id id2 = new Id("Emma", 2);

id2 = id1;
```

Copying references by assignment does not copy the content of the source object, only its reference. Now id2 refers to the same Id object as id1, and the previous object Id("Emma", 2) is eligible for garbage collection.

5.2.2 Multiple Assignments

An assignment always returns the value of the expression on the right-hand side as a result. Therefore, initializing several variables to a common value or reference using multiple assignment statements:

```
int a, b, c;

a = 1; b = 1; c = 1;
```

can be reduced to a single statement using **multiple assignments** as shown:

```
a = b = c = 1;   // a = (b = (c = 1));
```

The preceding example illustrates the importance of right associativity for the assignment operator.

5.3 Conditional Operator

The **conditional operator** evaluates a boolean expression, and, depending on its resultant value (either true or false), executes one of two expressions as defined here:

EBNF

```
ConditionalOperator = Condition "?" ExprIfConditionTrue ":" ExprIfConditionFalse.
```

The conditional operator, therefore, is equivalent to a simple if-else statement:

```
if ( Condition )
    ExprIfConditionTrue
else
    ExprIfConditionFalse
```

For example:

```
minimum = a < b ? a : b;
```

is equivalent to:

```
if (a < b)
    minimum = a;
else
    minimum = b;
```

Another example:

```
absolute = a < 0 ? -a : a;
```

is equivalent to:

```
if (a < 0)
    absolute = -a;
else
    absolute = a;
```

This operator can be nested but becomes rapidly unreadable:

```
a?b?c:d:e  // Evaluates as (a?(b?c:d):e)
```

5.4 Null Coalescing Operator

Given that a represents an operand of a nullable or reference type, the **null coalescing operator** is defined as in Table 5.2.

Name	Notation	Meaning
Null Coalescing	a ?? b	Returns a if a is non-null, otherwise returns b.

Table 5.2: Null coalescing operator.

Example:

```
using System;

public class CoalescingNull {
    public static void Main(string[] args) {
        bool?  a = true;
        bool?  b = false;
        object o = null;

        Console.WriteLine("|{0,4}|{1,4}|{2,4}|{3,4}|",
                        a??b, a??o, o??b, o??o );
    }
}
```

Output:

```
|True|True|False|    |
```

5.5 Conditional Logical Operators

Given that a and b represent boolean expressions, the **conditional logical operators** are defined as in Table 5.3.

Name	Notation	Meaning
Conditional Logical AND	a && b	true if both operands are true, otherwise false
Conditional Logical OR	a || b	true if either or both operands are true, otherwise false
Conditional Logical NOT	!a	true if the operand is false, otherwise false

Table 5.3: Conditional logical operators.

These operators are much like logical (bitwise) operators except that their evaluation is short-circuited. The short-circuit eliminates unnecessary evaluations. If the value of a is false then the expression a && b also evaluates to false without the need to evaluate b. Similarly, if the value of a is true then the expression a || b also evaluates to true without the need to evaluate b. Table 5.4 summarizes all combinations of boolean values.

a	b	a && b	a || b
true	true	true	true
true	false	false	true
false	true	false	true
false	false	false	false

Table 5.4: Values for conditional logical operators.

Example:

```
using System;

public class ConditionalLogical {
    public static void Main(string[] args) {
        bool t, b, f = false;
        t = b = true;

        Console.WriteLine( (t && t) +" "+ (t && f) +" "+ (f && t) +" "+
                           (f && f) );
        Console.WriteLine( (t || t) +" "+ (t || f) +" "+ (f || t) +" "+
                           (f || f) );
```

```
            // t&&b       where f not evaluated (short-circuited)
            Console.Write("{0} ",    t&&b || f );

            // f || b   where t not evaluated (short-circuited)
            Console.Write("{0} ",    f&&t || b );

            // f || f   where b not evaluated (short-circuited)
            Console.Write("{0} ",    f || f&&b );

            // t&&b       where f not evaluated (short-circuited)
            Console.WriteLine("{0}", f || t&&b );
        }
    }
```

Output:

```
True False False False
True True True False
True True False True
```

5.6 Logical Operators

Given that a and b are corresponding bit values in the left-hand and right-hand operands, respectively, the **logical (bitwise) operators** are defined as in Table 5.5.

Name	Notation	Meaning
Logical NOT	˜a	Invert the bit value (Complement)
Logical AND	a & b	1 if both bits are 1, otherwise 0
Logical OR	a | b	1 if either or both bits are 1, otherwise 0
Logical XOR	a ˆ b	1 if and only if one of the bits is 1, otherwise 0

Table 5.5: Logical operators.

a	b	˜a	a & b	a | b	a ˆ b
1	1	0	1	1	0
1	0	0	0	1	1
0	1	1	0	1	1
0	0	1	0	0	0

Table 5.6: Values for logical operators.

Valid types for logical operators are integers and boolean.

Example:

```
public class LogicalBitwise {
    public static void Main(string[] args) {
        ushort a = 0x005A; // in binary = 0000 0000 0101 1010
        ushort b = 0x3C5A; // in binary = 0011 1100 0101 1010

        System.Console.WriteLine( "{0:x}",  a & b );
        System.Console.WriteLine( "{0:x}",  a | b );
        System.Console.WriteLine( "{0:x}",  a ^ b );
        System.Console.WriteLine( "{0:x}", ~a     );
        System.Console.WriteLine( "{0:x}", ~b     );
    }
}
```

Output:

```
5a
3c5a
3c00
ffffffa5
ffffc3a5
```

5.6.1   Logical Operators as Conditional Logical Operators

The logical bitwise operators may also be used as conditional logical operators since they can be applied to boolean operands and return a bool value. Given that a and b represent boolean expressions, the logical operators are defined as in Table 5.7.

Name	Notation	Meaning
Logical NOT	!a	Returns the complement of the truth value of a (negation)
Logical AND	a & b	true if both operands are true, otherwise false
Logical OR	a | b	true if either or both operands are true, otherwise false
Logical XOR	a ^ b	true if and only if one operand is true, otherwise false

Table 5.7: Logical operators as conditional logical operators.

Note that the logical operators & and | have the same truth values as their corresponding conditional operators, && and || (Table 5.8).

a	b	!a	a & b	a | b	a ^ b
true	true	false	true	true	false
true	false	false	false	true	true
false	true	true	false	true	true
false	false	true	false	false	false

Table 5.8: Values for logical operators.

5.6.2 Compound Logical Assignment Operators

Given that a and b represent integral expressions, the compound logical assignment operators are defined as in Table 5.9.

Name	Notation	Meaning
Compound Logical AND	b &= a	b = (Type) (b & (a))
Compound Logical OR	b |= a	b = (Type) (b | (a))
Compound Logical XOR	b ^= a	b = (Type) (b ^ (a))

Table 5.9: Compound logical assignment operators.

Based on the preceding table, a and b are first promoted to int and the result is implicitly narrowed to the destination (Type) of b upon assignment:

```
byte b  = 0x62; // 0x62
     b &= 0x0F; // 0x62 & 0x0F => 0x00000002 (now an int)
             // 0x02            (cast back to a byte)
```

Example:

```
using System;

public class CompoundLogical {
    public static void Main(string[] args) {
        bool t, b, f = false;
        t = b = true;

        Console.WriteLine( (t & t) +" "+ (t & f) +" "+ (f & t) +" "+
                           (f & f) );
        Console.WriteLine( (t | t) +" "+ (t | f) +" "+ (f | t) +" "+
                           (f | f) );
```

```
            // t&b      where f not evaluated (short-circuited)
            Console.Write("{0} ", t&b | f);

            // f   | b   where t not evaluated (short-circuited)
            Console.Write("{0} ", f&t | b);

            // f | f     where b not evaluated (short-circuited)
            Console.Write("{0} ", f | f&b);

            //      t&b   where f not evaluated (short-circuited)
            Console.Write("{0} ", f | t&b);
            Console.Write("{0} ", f &= t | t);       // (1) f=(f&(t|t))
            Console.WriteLine("{0}", f = f & t | t); // (2) f=((f&t)|t)
        }
    }
```

Output:

```
True False False False
True True True False
True True False True False True
```

Note that assignments (1) and (2) give different results for the same value of the operands.

5.7 Equality Operators

5.7.1 Simple Value Type Equality

Given that a and b represent operands of simple value types, the simple-type **equality operators** are defined as in Table 5.10.

Name	Notation	Meaning
Equal	a == b	true if a and b have the same simple value, otherwise false
Not Equal	a != b	true if a and b have different simple values, otherwise false

Table 5.10: Simple value type equality operators.

Example:

```
public class Equality {
    public static void Main(string[] args) {
        System.Console.WriteLine( 9  == 9  );
        System.Console.WriteLine( 0  != 1  );
```

```
        System.Console.WriteLine( '9' == 9    ); // Operands are promoted
                                               // as ints.
        System.Console.WriteLine( '0' == 0x30 ); // Operands are promoted
                                               // as ints.
    }
}
```

Output:

```
True
True
False
True
```

When comparing floating-point numbers, bear in mind that values are approximated to a finite number of bits.

5.7.2 Object Reference and Value Equality

The predefined reference-type equality operators == and != accept operands of type object. Testing two object references o1 and o2 using Object.ReferenceEquals(o1, o2) is equivalent to:

```
(object)o1 == (object)o2
```

Examples:

```
bool    b;
Name    m1 = new Name("Michel");
Name    m2 = new Name("Michel");
string  m3 = "Michel";

b  = m2 == m3;  // Compile-time error (incompatible type).
b  = m1 == m2;  // False (two different objects).

m1 = m2;        // Alias to the same object m2.
b  = m1 == m2;  // True (same reference).
```

The null reference can be assigned and compared to any object reference. The Object.Equals method also returns true only if the object is compared to itself:

```
class Object {
    ...
    bool Equals(Object o) { return o == this; }
    ...
}
```

However, it is common practice to overload the equality operators and to override the Equals method in derived classes to provide object value rather than object reference equality as shown in Section 4.6. `Tip`

5.8 Relational Operators

Given that a and b represent numeric expressions, the **relational operators** are defined as in Table 5.11.

Name	Notation	Meaning
Less Than	a < b	true if a is less than b, otherwise false
Less Than or Equal	a <= b	true if a is less than or equal to b, otherwise false
Greater Than	a > b	true if a is greater than b, otherwise false
Greater Than or Equal	a >= b	true if a is greater than or equal to b, otherwise false

Table 5.11: Relational operators.

All relational operators are binary operators and all operands are promoted, if necessary, to numeric values. The evaluation results in a boolean value. Relational operators have a lower precedence than arithmetic operators, but a higher precedence than the assignment operators.

Example:

```
public class Relational {
    public static void Main(string[] args) {
        System.Console.WriteLine( 1   <  2   );
        System.Console.WriteLine( 3   <= 4   );
        System.Console.WriteLine( 5   >  6   );
        System.Console.WriteLine( 7   >= 8   );
        System.Console.WriteLine( 5.5 >= 5.0 );
        System.Console.WriteLine( 'A' <  'a' ); // Operands are promoted
                                                // as ints.
    }
}
```

Output:

True
True
False
False
True
True

5.8.1 Type Testing

Two additional operators in C# are used for type testing: is and as. The is operator defined next returns a boolean value and is used to determine at runtime if an object is an instance of Type or any type compatible with (derived from) Type.

EBNF

```
IsOperator = Expression "is" Type .
```

If the result of the is operator is true then Expression can be successfully converted to Type via explicit reference casting or implicit boxing/unboxing. In other words, the is operator verifies if an object is compatible with another instance of any derived class within the same hierarchy of classes. If the Expression is null, then the result is false. The following example illustrates implicit unboxing on line 6 and the need to explicitly cast on line 8 in order to invoke the specific ToUpper method of the string class:

```
1   using System;
2
3   public class TestIs {
4       private static void PrintValue(object o) {
5           if (o is Int32)
6               Console.WriteLine("Integer value in hexadecimal = {0:X}", o);
7           if (o is string)
8               Console.WriteLine("String  value in upper case  = {0}",
9                                 ((string)o).ToUpper());
10      }
11      public static void Main(string[] args) {
12          PrintValue(10);
13          PrintValue("Michel");
14      }
15  }
```

Output:

```
Integer value in hexadecimal = A
String  value in upper case  = MICHEL
```

The as operator defined next is a conditional type conversion. It attempts to perform a downcast on the result of an expression and if unsuccessful, returns a null value. If only an explicit cast is performed on the expression using the () operator, an unsuccessful cast will raise an InvalidCastException. The as operator, therefore, is used to avoid this situation by returning a null value rather than risk a possible termination of the application.

EBNF

```
AsOperator = Expression "as" Type .
```

The preceding definition is equivalent to the following ternary condition:

```
Expression is Type ? (Type) Expression : (Type) null
```

Example:

```
public class TypeTesting {
    public static void Main(string[] args) {
        object o = "Michel";
        char[] c = o as char[];    // c = (char[])null
        string s = o as string;    // s = (string)o

        System.Console.WriteLine( "{0}",  c == null );
        System.Console.WriteLine( "{0}",  s.Equals("Michel") );
    }
}
```

Output:

True
True

The as operator cannot be applied to value types.

5.9 Shift Operators

Given that a contains the value whose bits are to be shifted and n is the number of times to shift, the **shift operators** are defined as in Table 5.12.

Name	Notation	Meaning
Shift left	a << n	Shift all bits to the left n times, filling with 0 from the right.
Shift right	a >> n	Shift all bits to the right n times, filling with sign bit from the left.

Table 5.12: Shift operators.

Note that a is either int, uint, long, or ulong and that n is always an int type. Since char, byte, and short operands are promoted to either int or long, the result of applying these shift operators is always either an int or a long value.

5.9.1 Compound Shift Assignment Operators

Given that a and b represent integral operands, the **compound shift assignment operators** are defined as in Table 5.13.

Name	Notation	Meaning
Compound Shift Assignment Left (sign fill)	b <<= a	b = (Type) (b << (a))
Compound Shift Assignment Right (sign fill)	b >>= a	b = (Type) (b >> (a))

Table 5.13: Compound shift assignment operators.

Example:

```
public class Shift {
    public static void Main(string[] args) {
        byte a = 0x06; // In binary = 0000 0110
        byte b = 0x06; // In binary = 0000 0110

        System.Console.WriteLine("{0:x}",       (a >> 1) | (b << 1) );
        System.Console.WriteLine("{0:x}({1})", (-a >> 2), (-a >> 2) );
        System.Console.WriteLine("{0:x}({1})", (-a << 2), (-a << 2) );
    }
}
```

Output:

```
f
fffffffe(-2)
ffffffe8(-24)
```

5.10 Arithmetic Operators

5.10.1 Multiplicative Operators

Given that a and b represent operands of numeric data types, the **multiplicative operators** are defined as in Table 5.14.

Name	Notation	Meaning
Multiplication	a * b	a multiplied by b
Division	a / b	a divided by b
Modulus	a % b	a mod b

Table 5.14: Binary multiplicative operators.

If either a or b is a floating-point value, then the result of a multiplication or division is a floating-point value as well. If a and b are integral values, then the result of a multiplication or division is also integral (and truncated if necessary). The modulus operator returns the remainder of a division performed on either floating-point or integral operands.

Examples:

```
13 % 5       // 3
11.5 % 2.5   // 1.5
10 / 0       // DivideByZeroException
4.0 / 5      // 0.8
4.0 / 0.0    // Infinity (positive infinity)
-4.0 / 0.0   // -Infinity (negative infinity)
0.0 / 0.0    // NaN (not-a-number)
```

Because C# uses the IEEE 754 formats for floating-point types, dividing a non-zero number by zero generates Infinity or -Infinity as a result. Similarly, dividing zero by zero generates NaN as a result.

5.10.2 Additive Operators

Given that a and b represent operands of numeric data types, the **additive operators** are defined as in Table 5.15.

Name	Notation	Meaning
Addition	a + b	a is added to b
Subtraction	a - b	b is subtracted from a

Table 5.15: Binary additive operators.

If either a or b is a floating-point value, then the result of an addition or subtraction is a floating-point value as well. If a and b are integral values, then the result of an addition or subtraction is also integral.

Examples:

```
13 + 5       // 18
13.0 + 5     // 18.0
13 - 5       // 8
11.5 - 2.5   // 9.0
```

The binary operator + also acts as a string concatenation if one or both of the operands is a string object. If only one of the operands is a string, the other is implicitly converted to its string representation method before the concatenation is performed. For non-string objects, this conversion is performed using the ToString method. The result of the concatenation is always a new string object.

For example:

```
"1 + 1 is not equal to " + 1 + 1
```

is evaluated as:

```
((("1 + 1 is not equal to ") + 1) + 1)
```

and results in the following string:

```
"1 + 1 is not equal to 11"
```

5.10.3 checked/unchecked Operators

The result of an arithmetic expression that falls outside the limits or range of an integral destination variable generates an **overflow error**. In C#, these errors can be checked or disabled at compile-time or runtime, and at the level of expressions, blocks, or the entire source file.

Checking for overflow at compile-time is limited to constant expressions. In the following example, the constant expression MAX+1 exceeds the range of sbyte $(-128 .. +127)$ and is therefore not assignable to i. Hence, a compilation error is generated.

```
class Index {
    private       sbyte i;
    private const sbyte MAX = 127;
    public Index() { i = MAX+1; }  // Compile error: Constant value '128'
                                   // cannot be converted to a 'sbyte'.
}
```

Checking for overflow at runtime is achieved at the level of the entire source file using the compiler option /checked. This option, however, is turned off by default (i.e., /checked-). Therefore, when the following source file called TestChecked.cs is compiled without the /checked option:

```
class Index {
    private       sbyte i;
    private const sbyte MAX = 127;

    public Index()    { i = MAX; }
    public sbyte I()  { return ++i; }

    public static void Main() {
        System.Console.WriteLine("{0}", new Index().I());
    }
}
```

it is equivalent to explicitly turning off all overflow checking:

```
csc /checked- TestChecked.cs
```

Running this program will (incorrectly) output -128. On the other hand, if the source file is recompiled by turning on all overflow checking with the /checked+ option, then the program throws a System.OverflowException.

   Overflow can also be checked at a finer granularity using the operators checked and unchecked. Even though these operators are part of the primary category, it is appropriate to discuss them at this point since they are related to arithmetic operations on integral types. The checked and unchecked operators, applied to either expressions or block statements, have the following syntax:

EBNF

```
CheckedExpr   = "checked" "(" expression ")" .
CheckedStmt   = "checked" "{" statement+ "}" .
UncheckedExpr = "unchecked" "(" expression ")" .
UncheckedStmt = "unchecked" "{" statement+ "}" .
```

Instead of compiling a source file with the checked option on, overflow checking can be limited to particular expressions with the compiler option disabled. Using the preceding example, only the expression ++i may be checked for overflow within the I method:

```
{ return checked(++i); }
```

Although the compiler option checked is turned off, a System.OverflowException is still generated. Likewise, if the source file is compiled with the checked option turned on, then in order to avoid the exception, overflow checking for the expression ++i can be disabled as follows:

```
{ return unchecked(++i); }
```

If several statements within a method are to be checked/unchecked for overflow, then the checked or unchecked operator can be applied to a block of statements as shown here:

```
public sbyte I() {
    unchecked {
        // Other statements...
        return ++i;
    }
}
```

5.10.4 Compound Arithmetic Assignment Operators

EBNF

The **compound arithmetic assignment operator** has the following syntax:

```
Variable Op"=" Expression .
```

and the following meaning:

```
Variable "=" "(" Type ")" "(" Variable Op "(" Expression ")" ")" .
```

Given that v and e represent a variable and expression of a numeric data type, the compound arithmetic assignment operators are defined as in Table 5.16.

Name	Notation	Meaning
Multiplication Assignment	v *= e	v = (T) (v*(e))
Division Assignment	v /= e	v = (T) (v/(e))
Modulus Assignment	v %= e	v = (T) (v%(e))
Addition Assignment	v += e	v = (T) (v+(e))
Subtraction Assignment	v -= e	v = (T) (v-(e))

Table 5.16: Compound arithmetic assignment operators.

An implied type cast (T) in compound assignments is necessary.

Examples:

```
int i = 2;
i *= i + 4;  // i = (int) (i * (i + 4))

byte b = 2;
b += 10;     // b = (byte) ((int)b + 10)
b = b + 10;  // Error: explicit cast required.
```

5.11 Unary Operators

Given that a represents an operand of a numeric data type, the **unary operators** are defined as in Table 5.17.

Name	Notation	Meaning
Unary Plus	+a	a remains unchanged
Unary Minus	-a	a is negated

Table 5.17: Unary arithmetic operators.

The associativity of the unary operators is from right to left:

```
int value = - -10; // (-(-10))
```

Notice that the blank is needed to separate the unary operators. Otherwise, the expression would be interpreted as the decrement operator --.

Both logical unary operators, ! (boolean NOT) and ˜ (bitwise NOT), have already been presented in Sections 5.5 and 5.6, respectively.

5.11.1   Prefix and Postfix Operators

The increment (++) and decrement (--) operators come in two flavors: **prefix** and **postfix**. In the prefix case, the increment or decrement operator is placed before a simple data type variable. For example:

```
++a     // a = a + 1
```

In the postfix case, the increment or decrement operator is placed after a simple data type variable. For example:

```
a--    // a = a - 1
```

These operators have the side effect of changing the value of a simple data type variable by plus one for an increment and minus one for a decrement. The prefix operator increments or decrements the simple data type variable before the expression in which it appears is evaluated. The postfix operator increments or decrements the simple data type variable after the expression in which it appears is evaluated.

Consider the following sequence of instructions and the resultant values for a and b after each instruction is executed:

```
int b = 6;
int a = ++b;
            // a = 7, b = 7
a = b++;
            // a = 7, b = 8
++b;
            // a = 7, b = 9
a = --b;
            // a = 8, b = 8
a = b--;
            // a = 8, b = 7
```

These operators are very useful for updating variables in loops where only the side-effect of the operator is of interest. Even if both are considered unary operators, postfix operators are in the primary category and therefore evaluated before the prefix operators. The following example illustrates the precedence of the ++ postfix operator over its prefix one:

```
class TestPrePost {
    public static void Main() {
```

```
    int a, b;

    a = b = 1;
    System.Console.Write("{0} ",     a++ + ++b); // 1 + 2 = 3
    a = b = 1;
    System.Console.Write("{0} ",     a++ + b++); // 1 + 1 = 2
    a = b = 1;
    System.Console.Write("{0} ",     ++a + b++); // 2 + 1 = 3
    a = b = 1;
    System.Console.Write("{0} ",     ++a + ++b); // 2 + 2 = 4
    a = 1;
    System.Console.Write("{0} ",     a++ + ++a); // 1 + 3 = 4
    a = 1;
    System.Console.WriteLine("{0} ", ++a + a++); // 3 + 1 = 4
  }
}
```

Output:

3 2 3 4 4 4

5.11.2 Explicit Casts

C# is a strongly typed language and therefore checks for type compatibility at compile-time. As seen in Section 5.8.1, some checks are only possible at runtime using the is and as operators. An operator, however, can have incompatible operands, for example, assigning a char to a byte. In that case, a cast must be used to explicitly indicate the type conversion as follows:

EBNF

```
    CastExpr = "(" Type ")" Expression .
```

At runtime, a cast applied to either a simple value or a reference results in a new value of Type and is called an **explicit cast** (or **conversion**). For example:

```
    byte b = 0x34;
    char c = (char)b; // c = 0x0034 or '4'
         b = (byte)c; // b = 0x34;
```

It is worth noting again that if types are not compatible at runtime, then an InvalidCastException is thrown.

5.12 Other Primary Operators

The [ ] notation is used to declare and construct arrays and to access array elements. The x.y, f(x), and (x) notations are used to access members, to invoke methods, and to pass arguments, respectively. All these operators, including the new operator to create objects, have been covered in Chapter 3.

The typeof operator defined next returns the System.Type object for a class. This object contains information about all members of the given class.

EBNF

```
TypeofExpr = "typeof" "(" Type ")" .
```

The same object can also be obtained by calling GetType with any instance of the class. Hence, Type t = typeof(Id); is equivalent to:

```
Id   id = new Id();
Type t  = id.GetType();
```

As a final note, the typeof operator is particularly useful when an instance of the type is not available to invoke GetType.

5.13 Overloadable Operators

Overloading an operator in C# allows us to define an operator in the context of a new type. This feature is very similar to the one in C++. However, not all operators can be over-loaded including member access (x.y), method invocation (f(x)), array indexing (a[x]), or the =, &&, ||, ?:, checked, unchecked, new, typeof, as, and is operators. Overloading an operator, however, should only be done when the meaning is clear from its context. Some excellent candidates for operator overloading are == (equal), != (not equal), + (addition), and - (subtraction).

Tip

In Section 4.6, the Equals method for the Counter class was reimplemented to be used in the following manner:

```
Counter c1  = new Counter();
Counter c2  = new Counter();
bool result = c1.Equals(c2);
```

The operator == can also be overloaded for our Counter class in order to compare two counters more succinctly as:

```
bool result = c1 == c2;
```

The implementation of overloaded operators as shown next for == and != is defined by a method called operator followed by the operator itself. Here, two parameters are passed that correspond to the two operands.

```
class Counter {
    . . .
    public static bool operator ==(Counter left, Counter right) {
        // Check if left and right refer to the same object
        // or are both null.
```

```
        if (Object.ReferenceEquals(left, right))
            return true;

        // Check if one of them is null.
        if (Object.ReferenceEquals(left,  null) ||
            Object.ReferenceEquals(right, null))
            return false;

        return left.Equals(right);
    }

    public static bool operator !=(Counter left, Counter right) {
        return !(left == right);
    }
    ...
}
```

In this case, the Equals method (and the operator ==) are reused.

Table 5.18 illustrates the relationship between operator and method notations for unary and binary operators. In this table, op denotes any overloadable operator. A unary operator has only a single operand, and a binary operator has both left and right operands. An operator cannot be redefined if it has the same signature as a predefined operator in C#.

Overloadable Operator	Notation	Method Notation
Unary operator	op operand	operator op (operand)
Unary postfix (++ and --)	operand op	operator op (operand)
Binary operator	left op right	operator op (left, right)

Table 5.18: Method notations for overloadable operators.

Exercises

Exercise 5-1. Improve class Id by adding the overloaded operators == and !=.

Exercise 5-2. Write similar TypeTesting classes that create Person and Id objects and pass them as parameters to a static method Print(Id id) in order to identify objects at runtime using type-testing operators.

chapter **6**

Statements and Exceptions

In C#, statements fall into one of three categories: labeled, declaration, and embedded. This is shown by the following EBNF definition: EBNF

```
Stmt = LabeledStmt | DeclStmt | EmbeddedStmt .
```

Embedded statements include the full gamut of conditional, iterative, and transfer statements that one would expect in any high-level language. Additional constructs for mutual exclusion and the use of resources are also provided.

In this chapter, we first present one type of embedded statement called the block statement. Declaration statements and all other embedded statements are then discussed with particular emphasis on the exception-handling mechanism of C#. Because of their limited use and appeal, labeled statements are only described in the narrow context of the goto and switch statements.

6.1 Block Statement

A **block** is an embedded statement that encloses zero or more statements within a pair of opening and closing braces: EBNF

```
Block = "{" Stmts? "}" .
```

Each statement in a block is executed in sequence, but the block itself returns no value. Although a block is not required for only one statement, it is a useful practice to enclose Tip
a single statement within braces, as would become required if additional statements were added. For example, if a debugging Write is added to this statement:

```
if ( x > 0 )
    x = temp;
```

107

then braces are required to enclose the two statements as a single block:

```
if ( x > 0 ) {
    x = temp;
    Console.Write("Value of x is {0}.", x);
}
```

Finally, if code is not reachable within a block, then a compilation error is generated.

6.2 Declaration Statements

A **declaration statement** declares and initializes one or more local variables or constants of a given type. In the case of a constant, the type must be preceded by the keyword const and the initialization must be explicit. Variables need not be explicitly initialized upon declaration since number, character, and reference-type variables are initialized by default to 0, '\0', and null, respectively. The complete EBNF definition for declaration statements is given here:

EBNF

```
DeclStmt                = ( LocalVariableDecl | LocalConstantDecl ) ";" .
LocalVariableDecl       = Type LocalVariableDecltorList .
LocalVariableDecltor    = Identifier ( "=" LocalVariableInitializer )? .
LocalVariableInitializer = Expr | ArrayInitializer .
LocalConstantDecl       = "const" Type ConstantDecltorList .
ConstantDecltor         = Identifier "=" ConstantExpr .
```

For example:

```
float number;
const String name = "Michel";
int n = 2, m;
int len[] = { 1, n, 3 };
```

A variable declaration can appear anywhere in a block, and not just at the beginning as in C. The scope of the variable, however, ranges from its point of declaration to the end of the innermost block in which it is declared. For example:

```
{
    ...
    for (int n = 0; n < 8; n++) {
        // n is in the scope of the for
        ...
    }
    ...
    char c;   // Declaration closer to its related code
    ...
}
```

Finally, any variable that is used *before* declaration or is accessed outside its scope generates a compilation error.

6.3 Embedded Statements

Embedded statements in C# include many of the well-known constructs in C/C++ and Java, such as block statements (described previously), expression statements, empty statements, selection statements, and iteration statements. A summary of these statements and others in C# are listed in the following EBNF definition and described in the sections that follow.

EBNF

```
EmbeddedStmt = ExprStmt | EmptyStmt | Block | SelectionStmt
             | IterationStmt | JumpStmt | TryStmt | CheckedStmt
             | UncheckedStmt | LockStmt | UsingStmt | YieldStmt .
```

6.3.1 Expression and Empty Statements

An **expression statement** is simply an expression with a semicolon at the end. However, only the following types of expressions can become statements:

- Method invocations,
- Object creation expressions (with new),
- Assignment expressions containing = or op= operators, and
- Expressions with ++ and -- operators (prefix or postfix).

The complete EBNF definition of an expression statement is given here:

EBNF

```
ExprStmt = StmtExpr ";" .
StmtExpr = InvocationExpr | ObjectCreationExpr | Assignment |
           PostIncExpr   | PostDecExpr    | PreIncExpr | PreDecExpr .
```

An **empty statement**, on the other hand, is simply represented by a semicolon.

EBNF

```
EmptyStmt = ";" .
```

An empty statement is often used in conjunction with the for statement as illustrated here:

```
for (i = 0; i < n  && A[i]!=x; i++)
    ;   // Empty statement
```

In this case, all the necessary comparisons and assignments that search for value x in array A of size n are encapsulated as part of the control mechanism of the for statement itself.

6.3.2 Selection Statements

Selection statements allow a program to choose one of a number of possible actions for execution. These selection statements include the if and switch statements.

if *Statement*

EBNF   The syntax of the if statement is:

```
IfStmt = "if" "(" BooleanExpr ")" EmbeddedStmt1 ( "else" EmbeddedStmt2 )? .
```

where the else part of the if statement is optional. If the condition specified by BooleanExpr evaluates to true then the action specified by EmbeddedStmt1 is performed. Otherwise, EmbeddedStmt2 is executed whenever present. Two variations of the if statement, with and without the else part, are illustrated in the following single example:

```
bool directionUp;
...

if (directionUp)       { // If statement with an else part
    if (++count > max) { // Nested if statement without an else part
        count = min;
        return true;
    }
} else {
    if (--count < min) { // Nested if statement without an else part
        count = max;
        return true;
    }
}
return false;
```

Another variation of the if statement uses the else if clause to select one of many alternatives. In the following example, this variation selects one of four alternatives based on the value of an operator character. A similar example using the switch statement is presented in the next subsection.

```
char operator;
...

if (operator == '+') {
    ...
} else if (operator == '-') {
    ...
} else if (operator == '*') {
    ...
```

```
} else {  // Default case
    ...
}
```

switch *Statement*

The switch statement is used to choose one of many alternative actions based on the value of an expression Expr as shown here:

EBNF

```
SwitchStmt    = "switch" "(" Expr ")"  SwitchBlock .
SwitchBlock   = "{" SwitchSections? "}" .
SwitchSection = SwitchLabels StmtList .
SwitchLabel   = ( "case" ConstantExpr ":" ) | ( "default"  ":" ) .
```

A switch statement is executed as follows:

- The switch expression is evaluated. Only expressions that evaluate to an integral, character, enumerated, or string type are permitted.

- If one of the case label constants is equal to the expression, control is transferred to the list of statement(s) following the case label that is matched. After execution of the associated statement(s), a break statement must be used to reach the end of the switch statement. Unlike C/C++ and Java, control does *not* fall through to the next case section unless a goto statement is used. In fact, the traditional fall-through strategy results in a compilation error in C#.

- If no case label is equal to the value of the expression, the default label (if any) is executed.

Example:

```
char  op;
long  int1, int2;
...

switch (op) {
    case '+': Console.WriteLine(" = {0}", int1 + int2); break;
    case '-': Console.WriteLine(" = {0}", int1 - int2); break;
    case 'x': goto case '*';  // To obtain a fall through
    case '*': Console.WriteLine(" = {0}", int1 * int2); break;
    case '/': if ( int2 != 0 )
                    Console.WriteLine(" = {0}", int1 / int2);
              else
                    Console.WriteLine("Divide by zero");
              break;
    default:  Console.WriteLine("Invalid operator: must be + - * x /");
              break;
}
```

6.3.3 Iteration Statements

Iteration statements, or loops, allow a single statement or block to be executed repeatedly. The loop condition is a boolean expression that determines when to terminate the loop. C# provides four kinds of loops: while, do-while, for, and foreach statements.

while *Statement*

EBNF The syntax of the while loop is:

```
WhileStmt = "while" "(" BooleanExpr ")" EmbeddedStmt .
```

EmbeddedStmt is executed zero or more times until the BooleanExpr evaluates to false.

Example:

```
Console.Write("Countdown: ");
int sec = 9;
while ( sec >= 0 )
    Console.Write("{0} ", sec--);

Console.WriteLine("... Go!");
```

Output:

```
Countdown: 9 8 7 6 5 4 3 2 1 0 ... Go!
```

do-while *Statement*

EBNF The syntax of the do-while loop is:

```
DoStmt = "do" EmbeddedStmt "while" "(" BooleanExpr ")" ";" .
```

EmbeddedStmt is executed one or more times until the BooleanExpr evaluates to false.

Example (giving the same output):

```
Console.Write("Countdown: ");
int sec = 9;
do
    Console.Write("{0} ", sec--);
while ( sec >= 0 );

Console.WriteLine("... Go!");
```

for *Statement*

The syntax of the for loop is:

EBNF

```
ForStmt = "for" "(" ForInitializer? ";" ForCondition? ";" ForIterator? ")"
        EmbeddedStmt .
```

and is equivalent to the following statements:

```
ForInitializer
"while" "(" ForCondition ")" "{"
    EmbeddedStmt
    ForIterator
"}"
```

where:

EBNF

```
ForInitializer = LocalVarDecl | StmtExprList .
ForCondition   = BooleanExpr .
ForIterator    = StmtExprList .
```

Example (giving the same output):

```
Console.Write("Countdown: ");
for (int sec = 9; sec >= 0; --sec)
    Console.Write("{0} ", sec);

Console.WriteLine("... Go!");
```

An infinite for loop that prints dots:

```
for (;;)
    Console.Write(".");
```

is equivalent to the following while statement:

```
while (true)
    Console.Write(".");
```

foreach *Statement*

The syntax of the foreach loop is:

EBNF

```
ForeachStmt = "foreach" "(" Type Identifier "in" Expr ")" EmbeddedStmt .
```

The foreach statement enumerates the elements of a given collection and executes the embedded statement for each one. The Type and Identifier declare a read-only iteration variable to be used locally within the scope of the embedded statement. During the loop execution, this iteration variable represents a collection element. A compilation error occurs if the variable is (1) modified via assignment or the ++ and -- operators or (2) passed as a ref or out parameter.

Example:

```
int[] evenNumbers = { 2, 4, 6, 8 };

foreach (int n in evenNumbers)
    Console.Write("{0} ", n);

Console.WriteLine();
```

Output:

```
2 4 6 8
```

6.3.4 Jump Statements

C# offers five kinds of **jump statements** that unconditionally transfer control in an application: goto, continue, break, return, and exception handling (throw and try) statements. Because of its importance, exception handling is discussed separately in the next section.

goto *and Labeled Statements*

A **labeled statement** allows a statement to be preceded by an Identifier label. Labels are permitted within blocks only, and their scope includes any nested blocks.

EBNF

```
LabeledStmt = Identifier ":" EmbeddedStmt .
```

In C#, the name of an identifier label never conflicts with any other identifier for local variables, fields, and so on. Outside the normal sequence of execution, a labeled statement is reached by using a goto statement within the same scope (or block). In general, the goto statement transfers control to any statement that is marked by a label including a case label as defined here:

EBNF

```
GotoStmt = "goto" ( Identifier | ("case" ConstantExpr) | "default" ) ";" .
```

The goto statement must be within the scope of the label. Otherwise, a compilation error is generated.

continue *Statement*

The continue statement starts a new iteration of the innermost enclosing while, do-while, for, or foreach by prematurely ending the current iteration and proceeding with the next iteration, if possible.

EBNF

```
ContinueStmt = "continue" ";" .
```

Example:

```
for (int i = 0; i < 10; ++i) {
    if (i % 2 == 0) continue;
    Console.Write(i + " ");
}
Console.WriteLine();
```

Output:

```
1 3 5 7 9
```

The continue and goto statements are not recommended unless absolutely necessary   Tip
for improving the readability or optimizing the performance of a method. Justification,
therefore, should be a well-thought-out compromise between clarity and efficiency.

break *Statement*

The break statement is used in labeled blocks, loops (while, do-while, for, or foreach),
and switch statements in order to transfer control out of the current context, that is, the
innermost enclosing block.   EBNF

```
BreakStmt = "break" ";" .
```

Example (giving the same output as the for):

```
Console.Write("Countdown: ");
for (int sec = 9;;) {
    if (sec < 0) break;
    Console.Write("{0} ", sec--);
}
Console.WriteLine("... Go!");
```

return *Statement*

The return statement returns control to the caller of the current method and has one of
two forms: void (using return;) and non-void (using return Expr;) as shown here: EBNF

```
ReturnStmt = "return" Expr? ";" .
```

Example:

```
using System;

class Factorial {
    // non-void method must return a value
    static int Process(int i) {
        if (i > 0)                    // termination test
            return i * Process(i-1); // recursion invocation
```

```
        else
            return 1;
    }

    public static void Main(string[] args) {
        if (args.Length == 0) {
            Console.WriteLine("Usage: Factorial <n>");
            return; // main is a void method that can use return.
        }
        int n = Int32.Parse(args[0]);
        Console.WriteLine(n + "! = " + Process(n));
    }
}
```

In the case of the non-void return, the type of the Expr value must be compatible with the return type specified by the method. For example, if 1.0 is returned instead of 1 in the previous example, then a compilation error is generated. Therefore, the static method Int32.Parse is used to convert the string args[0] to its integer equivalent.

6.3.5   checked/unchecked Statements

The checked and unchecked statements control the context of overflow checking for integral-type arithmetic operations and conversions. These statements were covered in Chapter 5.

6.3.6   lock and using Statements

| EBNF |

The lock statement delimits an embedded statement as a mutually exclusive, critical section for an object represented by the expression Expr.

```
LockStmt = "lock" "(" Expr ")" EmbeddedStmt .
```

Because no implicit boxing is performed on Expr, the expression must be a reference type. Otherwise, a compile-time error is generated. The lock mechanism itself is implemented with a monitor synchronization primitive (generated by the C# compiler) that ensures that only one thread (at a time) is exclusively active in a critical section.

The using statement in C# acquires one or more resources, executes a statement, and

| EBNF |

then disposes of the resource(s).

```
UsingStmt           = "using" "(" ResourceAcquisition ")" EmbeddedStmt .
ResourceAcquisition = LocalVarDecl | Expr .
```

Both the lock and using statements are covered in greater detail in Chapter 9 in the context of threads and input/output, respectively.

6.4 Exceptions and Exception Handling

Software developers have long realized that moving from a procedural to an object-oriented approach requires a completely different mindset. Similarly, using exceptions, as opposed to the traditional approach of returning flags, provides a completely different and far more reliable method of tackling errors. In this section, we present the C# exception-handling mechanism as a modern approach to robust error management. In doing so, we will show how exceptions:

- Separate error-handling code from normal code and
- Make applications more readable and maintainable.

6.4.1 What Is an Exception?

An **exception** is an unexpected error condition. It is not a simple event, such as reaching the end of an input stream. For example, when the scanner of a compiler reads the next character from a file, you expect that it will eventually "reach the end." This is expected behavior, as shown here:

```
while ( (c = inputStream.Read()) != EOF )
    assembleToken(c);

inputStream.Close();
```

It is therefore important to note that an exception *really* means an exceptional condition that cannot be predicted. The following are some examples:

- Hardware failures,
- Floppy disk ejected while reading,
- Serial connection disconnected while transmitting, and
- Resource exhaustion.

Checking the above situations requires extensive manual polling and testing to ensure robust behavior. In fact, there are situations where testing and polling are simply inadequate. For example, reading a stream of binary values of different sizes, it is still possible and unexpected to read past the end-of-file.

```
while ( !inputStream.Eof() )
    process( inputStream.GetStructure() );

inputStream.Close();
```

Unexpected situations are not easy to determine. However, it is important not to (ab)use exceptions as a way to report situations with simple and predictable behavior.

6.4.2 Raising and Handling Exceptions

Without exception handling, dealing with errors increases the length of the resultant code often at the expense of its clarity. **Exception handling**, on the other hand, is a mechanism for dealing more systematically with exceptional error conditions. It works by transferring execution to a handler when an error occurs. By separating the code that may generate errors from the code that handles them, this mechanism allows the detection of errors without adding special conditions to test return values or flags.

An exception is said to be raised (or thrown) when an unexpected error condition is encountered and it is said to be handled (or caught) at the point to which control is transferred. Appropriate action is then taken by the exception handler including rethrowing the exception to another handler, if necessary. Because an exception unconditionally transfers control to an exception handler, the code within the block and beyond the point where the exception is raised is not reached.

The System namespace contains the class Exception as the root of the exception-handling hierarchy in the .NET Framework. The Exception class is composed of two immediate subclasses, SystemException and ApplicationException. The SystemException class is defined as the base class for all predefined (.NET) system exceptions that are thrown by the runtime system. The ApplicationException class was originally intended to be used as the base class for all application (user-defined) exceptions declared outside the .NET Framework. Because the code to handle user-defined exceptions is typically specific to an application, it is very unlikely that an instance of ApplicationException will ever be

Tip

needed. Although logically sound, in practice, ApplicationException adds an extraneous layer to the exception hierarchy. As a consequence, Microsoft strongly suggests that user-defined exceptions inherit directly from Exception rather than ApplicationException. A partial list of the most common system exceptions and where to define user-defined exceptions is given here:

```
Exception (root)
    SystemException
        ArithmeticException
            DivideByZeroException
            OverflowException
        FormatException
        IndexOutOfRangeException
        InvalidCastException
        IOException
        NullReferenceException
        TypeLoadException
            DllNotFoundException
            EntryPointNotFoundException
        ...
```

```
<UserDefinedExceptions>

ApplicationException    // Not recommended as a root for
                        // user-defined exceptions.
```

6.4.3 Using the throw Statement

Every exception in C# is an instance of the class System.Exception or one of its subclasses. Therefore, the following throw statement raises an exception associated with the object evaluated by the expression Expr.

EBNF

```
ThrowStmt = "throw" Expr? ";" .
```

If the evaluation of Expr returns null, a System.NullReferenceException is thrown instead. Since exceptions are objects, they must be created before being thrown and can be used to carry information from the point at which an exception occurs to the handler that catches it. In the following example, an IOException is raised by creating an instance of the IOException class.

```
void OpenFile(File f) {
    ...

    if ( !f.Exists() )
        throw new IOException("File doesn't exist");
    ...
}
```

As mentioned previously, the class System.Exception serves as the root class for all user-defined exceptions. It is strongly recommended that the name for each new user-defined exception reflect its cause and end with the suffix Exception. The following application presents the definition and use of a new exception class called DeviceException. As recommended, the exception is equipped with three constructors. The first (line 4) is the basic parameterless constructor, the second (line 5) is the one that is primarily used to create exceptions to be thrown, and the third (line 6) wraps (inner) exceptions with more information to be thrown if needed.

Tip

```
1   using System;
2
3   public class DeviceException : Exception {
4       public DeviceException() { }
5       public DeviceException(string msg) : base(msg) { }
6       public DeviceException(string msg, Exception inner) : base(msg, inner) {}
7   }
8
9   public class Device {
```

```
10      // Where an exception is thrown.
11      public byte Read() {
12          byte b = 0;
13
14          if (!status)
15              throw new DeviceException("Cannot read.");
16          //...
17          return b;
18      }
19
20      // Where an exception is thrown (by the runtime system).
21      public void Process()   {
22          int num = 2;
23          int den = 0;
24          // ...
25
26          // The next statement will generate
27          // an arithmetic exception: DivideByZeroException.
28
29          System.Console.WriteLine( num/den );
30          System.Console.WriteLine( "done." );
31      }
32      private bool status = false;
33  }
34
35  class TestException1 {
36      public static void Main() {
37          new Device().Process();
38      }
39  }
```

The class Device is defined with two methods, Read and Process. When method Process is invoked on line 37 and because den is initialized to 0, the predefined DivideByZeroException is implicitly raised. This exception is thrown by the runtime system and generates the following message:

```
Unhandled Exception: System.DivideByZeroException: Attempted to divide by zero.
    at TestException1.Main()
```

Suppose now that the method Process is replaced by Read on line 37. When method Read is invoked and because status is initialized to false, the user-defined DeviceException is explicitly raised on line 15 and the following message is generated:

```
Unhandled Exception: DeviceException: Cannot Read.
    at Device.Read()
    at TestException1.Main()
```

6.4.4 Using the `try-catch` Statement

When the exceptions DivideByZeroException and DeviceException were raised in methods Process and Read, respectively, neither exception was caught and handled. To associate a block of code within which an exception may occur with the appropriate exception handlers, a try-catch statement is used. This statement clearly separates the code that raises an exception from the code that handles it.

```
try {
    // A block of code where one or more exceptions may be raised.
} catch ( ExceptionType1 e1 ) {
    // An exception handler for ExceptionType1.
} catch ( ExceptionType2 e2 ) {
    // An exception handler for ExceptionType2.
} finally {
    // A block of code that is unconditionally executed upon exit
    // from the try block.
}
```

In the previous example, the try block defined a checked region of code where an exception might be raised. Once an exception is raised using the throw statement, execution is transferred to the appropriate exception handler. Hence, if an exception of type ExceptionType2 is raised within the try block, then control is transferred to the second exception handler. The parameter e2 is optional and depends on whether or not information contained within the object is required when the exception is handled. To match an exception with its handler, the catch clauses are examined in order. A match is made when the exception raised belongs to, or can be implicitly converted to, the class specified in the parameter of the exception handler. Hence, to handle multiple exceptions as done above, the most specific catch block must precede a more generic one as shown next. Otherwise, a compiler error is generated. Clearly, the Exception root class catches all types of exceptions and therefore must follow all other handlers. Furthermore, only one catch block is executed for each exception that is raised.

```
try {
    ...
} catch (SpecificException e) {      //  From specific.
    // Handle a specific exception    //
} catch (GenericException e) {       //  To more generic.
    // Handle a more generic exception  //
} catch (Exception e ) {             //  To most generic.
    // Handles all exceptions
}
```

In general, it is a best practice for an application to only catch those exceptions that it can handle. An OutOfMemoryException is a typical exception that an application should not catch because it is unable to recover from it.   Tip

Because try-catch statements may be nested, if no match is found in the current try-catch statement then the search proceeds outward to the catch clause(s) associated with the innermost enclosing try statement (if any). If no match is found within a method, the search continues with the catch clauses associated with the try statement that encloses the point of invocation. This process of matching an exception with its handler is called **propagating** (or "bubbling up") an exception. Once an exception is caught, however, the exception may be rethrown within its handler and the propagation process is reignited from that point. The reraising of an exception is done using the throw statement with or without an expression. If the throw is used without an expression, any interim assignment to the exception variable (if present) does *not* alter the original exception.

```
try {
    ...
} catch (ExceptionType2 e2) {
    e2 = new ExceptionType2(...);
    throw;                         // Original exception is used.
}
```

On the other hand, if the throw is used with an expression that redefines the exception, then the updated exception is used.

```
try {
    ...
} catch (ExceptionType2 e2) {
    throw new ExceptionType2 (...);  // New exception is used.
}
```

It is also possible that the exception handler can throw an entirely different exception (in this case, ExceptionType1) as shown here:

```
try {
    ...
} catch (ExceptionType2 e2) {
    throw new ExceptionType1 (...);
}
```

Once an exception handler is found and the appropriate code is executed, execution resumes at the point following the try-catch statement that contains the final handler. If no exception handler is found, a default exception handler is invoked and prints useful information about where the exception was thrown. This information is also known as the **stack trace**, an example of which is found at the end of the previous section. In any case, the program terminates if no exception handler is explicitly found.

Whether or not an exception is raised within a try block, the finally clause is *always* executed before control is transferred elsewhere. Even a return, goto, or throw statement within the try or catch clauses does not preclude its execution. The finally clause is optional and must immediately follow the last catch block as shown here. If the finally clause is present, the catch blocks are also optional. Therefore, the try statement must be associated with one or more catch clauses and/or a finally clause.

```
try {
    ...
} catch (SpecificException e) {       //  From specific.
    // Handle a specific exception.
} catch (GenericException e) {        //  To more generic.
    // Handle a more generic exception.
} finally {
    // Always executed
}
```

The finally clause provides a graceful mechanism for exiting a try block whether or not an exception is thrown. It is also useful when some clean-up or release of resources is required. It is good practice to keep the finally block as simple as possible. For example, the following code ensures that a device is released even if an exception occurs. | Tip |

```
Device d = null;
try {
    //  d.open();
} catch (DeviceException  e) {
    // Recovery code.
} finally {
    if (d != null) d.close();
}
```

It is not good practice to catch and immediately rethrow the same exception. If only | Tip | resources need to be cleaned up or released then a try/finally block works fine since an exception is propagated automatically without an explicit rethrow. Of course, a handler may throw a different exception whenever required. The following example clarifies the three ways and implications of (re)throwing an exception:

```
try {...} catch (Exception e) { if (...) throw; }
try {...} catch (Exception e) { if (...) throw e; }
try {...} catch (Exception e) { if (...) throw
                            new DeviceException("Message", e); }
```

The first way (throw;) rethrows the same exception and preserves the original stack trace. Because no additional information is added to the exception and no additional computation such as error logging is performed, it is better to omit the catch block altogether and allow the exception to propagate automatically to the next level. The second way (throw e;) rethrows the same exception but generates a new stack trace by overwriting the stack trace of the original exception. Rethrowing an exception in this way is not recommended | Tip | since information is lost. Finally, the third way preserves the original information of the exception and, hence, the cause of the error by passing its reference to a new exception. In this case, an instance of DeviceException is created using its third constructor (line 6 on page 119) by passing "Message" and e to msg and inner, respectively.

EBNF

The complete EBNF definition of the try-catch statement is given here.

```
TryStmt = "try" Block ( CatchClauses | FinallyClause )? |
                      ( CatchClauses   FinallyClause )? .

CatchClauses = ( SpecificCatchClauses  GeneralCatchClause? ) |
               ( SpecificCatchClauses? GeneralCatchClause  ) .

SpecificCatchClause = "catch" "(" ExceptionType Identifier? ")" Block .
GeneralCatchClause  = "catch" Block .
FinallyClause       = "finally" Block .
```

6.4.5 An Extended Example

Using an object dev of the Device class presented in the previous section, the Init method of LowLevelDeviceDriver given here invokes methods Read and Process. Although dev can throw one of two exceptions, LowLevelDeviceDriver does not handle the exceptions and, instead, propagates these exceptions to DeviceManager1.

```
public class LowLevelDeviceDriver {
    public LowLevelDeviceDriver() { dev = new Device(); }

    // When the exception is not handled and propagated up to the caller.
    public void Init() {
        dev.Read();     // May throw a DeviceException.
        dev.Process();  // May throw a DivideByZeroException.
    }
    private Device dev;
}
```

In the class DeviceManager1, given here, a call to the Init method of LowLevelDeviceDriver appears within a try statement. This is where the exceptions are handled and a message is printed.

```
public class DeviceManager1 {
    public DeviceManager1() { dd = new LowLevelDeviceDriver(); }

    public void Init() {  // When the exception is handled.
        try {
            dd.Init();
        } catch(DeviceException e) {
            Console.WriteLine("Handled in DeviceManager1 [{0}]", e);
```

```
            } catch(DivideByZeroException e) {
                Console.WriteLine("Handled in DeviceManager1 [{0}]", e);
            }
        }
        private LowLevelDeviceDriver dd;
    }
```

Because DeviceManager1 handles the DeviceException and does not throw any further exceptions, the class DeviceSecureManager as shown next, and any other class that invokes the Init method of DeviceManager1, is relieved of any further error handling.

```
    public class DeviceSecureManager {
        public DeviceSecureManager() { dm = new DeviceManager1(); }

        // When the exception is handled by a subobject DeviceManager.
        public void Init() {
            dm.Init();
        }
        private DeviceManager1 dm;
    }
```

Now consider a HighLevelDeviceDriver that uses a LowLevelDeviceDriver object called lldd.

```
    public class HighLevelDeviceDriver {
        public HighLevelDeviceDriver() { lldd = new LowLevelDeviceDriver(); }

        // When the exception is partially handled by HighLevelDeviceDriver
        // and is rethrown (or relayed) to DeviceManager2.
        public void Init() {
            try {
                lldd.Init();
            } catch(DeviceException e) {
                Console.WriteLine("Handled in HighLevelDD and rethrown[{0}]", e);
                // Some additional handling here...
                throw new DeviceException(e.Message, e);
            }
        }
        private LowLevelDeviceDriver lldd;
    }
```

In this case, the HighLevelDeviceDriver not only prints a message but also rethrows or relays the DeviceException to DeviceManager2 as shown here.

```
    public class DeviceManager2 {
        public DeviceManager2() { dd = new HighLevelDeviceDriver(); }
```

```
        // When the exception is handled by several catchers that rethrow.
        public void Init() {
            try {
                dd.Init();
            } catch(DeviceException e) {
                Console.WriteLine("Handled in DeviceManager2 [{0}]", e);
            }
        }
        private HighLevelDeviceDriver dd;
    }
```

Exercises

Exercise 6-1. Use a foreach statement to enumerate an array of Id objects in order to print their first and last names.

Exercise 6-2. Complete the GetName method in the EmailFormat class presented here. This method returns a formatted string representing an Id object in a specified string format as described in Section 1.3.

```
    public class EmailFormat {
        private static readonly string[] formats = {
                "F.L", "L.F", "F.Last", "Last.F", "First.Last", "Last.First",
                "F+L", "L+F", "F+Last", "Last+F", "First+Last", "Last+First",
                "F_L", "L_F", "F_Last", "Last_F", "First_Last", "Last_First",
                "Other."
        };
        public static string[] GetFormats() { return formats; }
        public static string  GetDefault() { return "First.Last"; }
        public static string  GetName(string format, Id id) { ... }
    }
```

Exercise 6-3. Write a word count wc utility similar to the one available on a Unix-like platform. This utility counts lines, words, and characters from the standard input (or input redirected from a file). A word is a string of characters delimited by spaces, tabs, and newlines. The optional arguments specify counts (l for lines, w for words, and c for characters) as shown here:

```
    WcCommandLine = "wc" Options? .
    Option        = "-l" | "-w" | "-c" .
```

Exercise 6-4. The System.UInt32.Parse method converts the string representation of a number to its 32-bit unsigned, integer equivalent. This static method may generate three possible exceptions: `ArgumentNullException`, `FormatException`, and `OverflowException`. One limitation of this parse method is its inability to verify specific minimum and maximum values within its range (`MinValue..MaxValue`).

Write a class `Input` that has a static method `GetUint` that reads an unsigned decimal number from standard input between a minimum and a maximum unsigned value and returns the corresponding `uint` (using `UInt32.Parse`). A user-defined `InputOverflowException` is needed:

```
public class InputOverflowException : Exception {
    public InputOverflowException(uint min, uint max) {
        this.min = min; this.max = max;
    }
    public override string ToString() {
        return "Integer value must be within ["+min+".."+max+"].";
    }
    private uint min, max;
}
public class Input {
    public static uint GetUInt(string msg, uint min, uint max) { ... }

    public static void Main() {
        bool validNumber = false;
        while (!validNumber) {
            try {
                uint n = GetUInt("Enter a number: ", 0, 9);
                System.Console.WriteLine("The number entered is: {0}", n);
                validNumber = true;
            }
            catch (InputOverflowException e) {
                System.Console.WriteLine("InputOverflow: " + e.ToString());
            }
            catch (OverflowException e) {
                System.Console.WriteLine("Overflow: " + e.Message);
            }
            catch (FormatException e) {
                System.Console.WriteLine("Format: " + e.Message);
            }
        }
    }
}
```

as well as a main program that exercises the methods as follows:

```
Enter a number: +
Format: Input string was not in a correct format.
```

```
Enter a number: -1
Overflow: Value was either too large or too small for a UInt32.
Enter a number: 712635412735427345127364452743651274
Overflow: Value was either too large or too small for a UInt32.
Enter a number: 10
InputOverflow: Integer value must be within [0..9].
Enter a number: 3
The number entered is: 3
```

chapter **7**

Advanced Types, Polymorphism, and Accessors

In Chapter 4, the basic notion of a reference type was presented. In this chapter, the more advanced, and certainly more important, reference types of C# are presented. These include delegates, events, abstract classes, and interfaces. Delegates are "object-oriented function pointers" that are not attached to any particular type, but rather to any method that shares its signature. Hence, delegates are used extensively to support callbacks, events, and anonymous methods. Abstract classes and interfaces, on the other hand, are used to extract common behavior and to offer generic (non-dedicated) connection points or references to any client of a derived class. Although they both support the notion of decoupling in object-oriented software development, interfaces in particular are used to "atomize" behavior. Hence, a class may selectively derive and implement behavior from one or more interfaces.

The notion of polymorphism, first mentioned in Chapter 4 with respect to the `object` class, is one of the three pillars of object-oriented programming, along with classes and inheritance. But it is polymorphism that acts as the hinge that gives classes and inheritance their potency and flexibility. By dynamically binding method calls (messages) with their methods, polymorphism enables applications to make decisions at runtime and move away from the rigidity of compile-time logic. As we shall see, it is a notion that has redefined programming methods, both literally and conceptually.

The chapter also includes a discussion on properties and indexers, the two accessor types that are provided with the C# language. Properties are an elegant solution for the traditional getters and setters of data members. Indexers are a flexible implementation of the [ ] operator and are used whenever a class is better seen as a virtual container of data. Finally, the chapter offers a few words on nested types, showing an equivalent implementation using internal types within a namespace.

129

7.1 Delegates and Events

A **delegate** is a reference type to an instance or static method that shares the same signature as the delegate itself. Therefore, any instance of a delegate can refer to a method that shares its signature and thereby "delegate" functionality to the method to which it is assigned. In order to encapsulate an instance or static method, the delegate is instantiated with the method as its parameter. Of course, if the method does not share the same signature as the delegate, then a compiler error is generated. Hence, delegates are type-safe and are declared according to the following EBNF definition:

EBNF

```
DelegateDecl = DelegateModifiers? "delegate"
               Type Identifier "(" FormalParameters? ")" ";" .
```

Delegates are derived from a common base class System.Delegate and are an important feature of the C# language. They are used to implement callbacks, support events, and enable anonymous methods, each of which is described in greater detail in the following three subsections.

7.1.1 Using Delegates for Callbacks

Generally, using delegates involves three steps: declaration, instantiation, and invocation. Each of these steps is illustrated with the following example, where two classes, Message and Discount, use delegates MessageFormat and DiscountRule. The two delegates encapsulate message formats and discount rules, respectively.

```
1   delegate double DiscountRule();                    // Declaration
2   delegate string MessageFormat();                   // Declaration
3
4   class Message {
5       public        string Instance() { return "You save {0:C}"; }
6       public static string Class()    { return "You are buying for {0:C}"; }
7       public        void   Out(MessageFormat format, double d) {
8           System.Console.WriteLine(format(), d);
9       }
10  }
11  class Discount {
12      public static double Apply(DiscountRule rule, double amount) {
13          return rule()*amount;        // Callback
14      }
15      public static double Maximum() { return 0.50; }
16      public static double Average() { return 0.20; }
17      public static double Minimum() { return 0.10; }
18      public static double None()    { return 0.00; }
19  }
20  class TestDelegate1 {
21      public static void Main() {
```

```
22          DiscountRule[] rules = {                    // Instantiations
23              new DiscountRule(Discount.None),
24              new DiscountRule(Discount.Minimum),
25              new DiscountRule(Discount.Average),
26              new DiscountRule(Discount.Maximum),
27          };
28          // Instantiation with a static method
29          MessageFormat format = new MessageFormat(Message.Class);
30
31          double buy = 100.00;
32          Message msg = new Message();
33
34          msg.Out(format, buy);                       // Invocation
35
36          // Instantiation with an instance method
37          format = new MessageFormat(msg.Instance);
38
39          foreach (DiscountRule r in rules) {
40              double saving = Discount.Apply(r, buy); // Invocation
41              msg.Out(format, saving);                // Invocation
42          }
43      }
44  }
```

On lines 1 and 2, the delegates, DiscountRule and MessageFormat, are first declared. Since an instance of a delegate may only refer to a method that shares its signature, instances of both delegates in this case may only refer to methods without parameters. It is worth noting that unlike a method, the return type is part of a delegate's signature. On lines 22–27, 29, and 37, six delegates are instantiated. Delegates for the four discount rules are stored in an array called rules of type DiscountRule. Delegates for message formats are assigned on two occasions to a reference variable called format of type MessageFormat. In the first assignment on line 29, format refers to the static method Class. On the second assignment on line 37, format refers to the instance method Instance. It is important to remember that the method passed as a parameter can only be prefixed by the class name (Message) for a static method and by an object name (msg) for an instance method. All methods of rules are static and, therefore, prefixed by their class name Discount.

Once the delegates have been instantiated, the methods to which they refer are invoked or "called back." On line 34, the first instance of format is passed to the method Out along with the parameter buy. Within Out, the method Class is invoked. The string that Class returns is then used as part of the buy message. For each execution of the foreach loop from lines 39 to 42, a different discount method is passed to the static method Apply. Within Apply on line 13, the appropriate discount rule is invoked and the saving is returned. On line 41, the second instance of format is passed to the method Out along with the parameter saving. This time, the method Instance is "called back"

within Out and returns a string that is used as part of the saving message. The output of
TestDelegate1 is given here:

```
You are buying for $100.00
You save $0.00
You save $10.00
You save $20.00
You save $50.00
```

In C#, more than one delegate can be subscribed in reaction to a single callback. But in
order to do so, each delegate object must have a void return value. The following example
illustrates how to display different integer formats (views).

```
1   delegate void IntView(int c);
2
3   class View {
4       public static void AsChar(int c) {
5           System.Console.Write("'{0}' ", (char)c);
6       }
7       public static void AsHexa(int c) {
8           System.Console.Write("0x{0:X} ", c);
9       }
10      public static void AsInt(int c) {
11          System.Console.Write("{0} ", c);
12      }
13  }
14  class TestDelegate2 {
15      public static void Main() {
16          IntView i, x, c, ic, all;
17
18          i = new IntView(View.AsInt);
19          x = new IntView(View.AsHexa);
20          c = new IntView(View.AsChar);
21
22          System.Console.Write("\ni:   ");  i(32);
23          System.Console.Write("\nx:   ");  x(32);
24          System.Console.Write("\nc:   ");  c(32);
25
26          all = i + x + c;  // callbacks in that order
27          System.Console.Write("\nall: ");  all(32);
28
29          ic  = all - x;
30          System.Console.Write("\nic:  ");  ic(32);
31      }
32  }
```

The delegate IntView is first declared on line 1. Hence, any instance of IntView may only refer to a void method that has a single int parameter. The class View from lines 3 to 13 groups together three methods that output a different view of an integer parameter. Three delegates of IntView are instantiated on lines 18–20 and are assigned to each of the three static methods in View. The methods are invoked separately on lines 22–24 with the integer parameter 32. A fourth (composite) delegate called all combines the other three delegates into one using the + operator. When all is invoked on line 27, each method in the combination is invoked in turn. Finally, a delegate can be removed from a combination using the – operator as shown on line 29. The output of TestDelegate2 is shown here:

```
i:    32
x:    0x20
c:    ' '
all: 32 0x20 ' '
ic:  32 ' '
```

7.1.2 Using Delegates for Events

An **event**, another reference type, is simply an occurrence within a program environment that triggers an event handler to perform some action in response. It is analogous in many ways to an exception that is raised and dealt with by an exception handler. However, the handling of an event is achieved using a callback. Event programming is common in graphical user interfaces where input from the user, such as a button click, notifies one or more event handlers to react to its activation.

In C#, one class called the source or subject class fires an event that is handled by one or more other classes called listener or observer classes. Events themselves are declared by placing the keyword event before the declaration of a delegate in the source class. Handlers are associated with an event by combining delegates from observer classes. In the following example, the Subject class defines an event called Changed on line 7.

```
1    delegate void UpdateEventHandler();
2
3    class Subject {
4        private int  data;
5        public  int  GetData()        { return data; }
6        public  void SetData(int value) { data = value; Changed(); }
7        public event UpdateEventHandler Changed;
8    }
9    class Observer {
10       public Observer(Subject s)  { subject = s;  }
11       public Subject GetSubject() { return subject; }
12       private Subject subject;
13   }
```

```
14  class HexObserver : Observer {
15      public HexObserver(Subject s) : base(s) {
16          s.Changed += new UpdateEventHandler(this.Update);
17      }
18      public void Update() {
19          System.Console.Write("0x{0:X} ", GetSubject().GetData());
20      }
21  }
22  class DecObserver : Observer {
23      public DecObserver(Subject s) : base(s) {
24          s.Changed += new UpdateEventHandler(this.Update);
25      }
26      public void Update() {
27          System.Console.Write("{0} ", GetSubject().GetData());
28      }
29  }
30  class TestEvent {
31      public static void Main() {
32          Subject s = new Subject();
33          HexObserver  ho = new HexObserver(s);
34          DecObserver  co = new DecObserver(s);
35
36          for (int c;;) {
37              System.Console.Write("\nEnter a character"+
38                                   "(followed by a return, ctrl-C to exit): ");
39              c = System.Console.Read();
40              s.SetData( c );
41              System.Console.Read(); // Two reads to get rid of the \r\n on PC.
42              System.Console.Read();
43          }
44      }
45  }
```

On line 32, an instance of Subject is created and assigned to s. Its data field is initialized by default to 0 and its Changed event is initialized by default to null (keep in mind that a delegate is a reference type). In order to attach handlers to the event Changed of instance s, the constructors of the two observer classes, in this case HexObserver and DecObserver, are invoked with the parameter s on lines 33 and 34. Each constructor then assigns their respective Update methods (handlers) to the delegate Changed of instance s on lines 16 and 24. It is important to note that the Update methods in both cases must have the same signature as UpdateEventHandler. Otherwise, a compilation error is generated. After a character c is input from the user on line 39, the SetData method of s is invoked on line 40. In addition to updating the data field of s, the event Changed "calls back" each of its associated handlers.

7.1.3 Using Delegates for Anonymous Methods

In the previous sections, a callback or event handler was implemented as a method, and when delegates were later instantiated, the method was passed as a parameter. For example, the Update method on lines 18–20 in the previous HexObserver class was later passed as a parameter on line 16 upon the instantiation of the UpdateEventHandler delegate. An **anonymous method**, on the other hand, allows the body of a callback method or event handler to be declared inline, where the delegate is instantiated as shown here:

```
class HexObserver : Observer {
    public HexObserver(Subject s) : base(s) {
        s.Changed += delegate { System.Console.Write("0x{0:X} ",
                              GetSubject().GetData()); };
    }
}
```

An anonymous method is declared with the keyword delegate followed by a parameter list. `C# 2.0` The inline code is surrounded by braces { }. In the previous case, there was no parameter list because the UpdateEventHandler delegate had no parameters. For the delegate IntView with a single int parameter, the class View can be eliminated altogether using anonymous methods as shown here:

```
delegate void IntView(int v);

class TestDelegate2 {
    public static void Main() {
        IntView i, x, c, ic, all;

        i = delegate(int v) { System.Console.Write("'{0}' ", (char)v); };
        x = delegate(int v) { System.Console.Write("0x{0:X} ", v); };
        c = delegate(int v) { System.Console.Write("{0} ", v); };

        System.Console.Write("\ni:   ");  i(32);
        System.Console.Write("\nx:   ");  x(32);
        System.Console.Write("\nc:   ");  c(32);

        all = i + x + c;  // callbacks in that order
        System.Console.Write("\nall: ");  all(32);

        ic  = all - x;
        System.Console.Write("\nic:  ");  ic(32);
    }
}
```

Anonymous methods are particularly useful in event programming or callback intensive applications used to declare methods (usually delegates) inline with the declaration of the event.

7.1.4 Using Delegate Inferences

A delegate variable may be initialized by passing a method name to the instantiation of its delegate constructor. On line 5 of this example, the variable d is assigned as a delegate for the method Act:

```
1    class C {
2        delegate void D();
3        public void Act() { }
4        public void DoAction() {
5            D d = new D(Act);
6            // ...
7            d();
8        }
9    }
```

C# 2.0 A delegate inference, on the other hand, directly assigns a method name to a delegate variable. Based on the previous example, line 5 can be replaced by:

```
D d = Act;
```

In fact, the C# compiler deduces the specific delegate type and creates the equivalent delegate object underneath.

7.2 Abstract Classes

An **abstract class** is a class that defines at least one member without providing its implementation. These specific members are called abstract and are implicitly virtual. Members can be methods, events, properties, and indexers. The latter two are presented later in this chapter. Because at least one method is not implemented, no instance of an abstract class can be instantiated since its behavior is not fully defined. Furthermore, a subclass of an abstract class can only be instantiated if it overrides and provides an implementation for each abstract method of its superclass. If a subclass of an abstract class does not implement all abstract methods that it inherits, then the subclass is also abstract.

7.2.1 Declaring Abstract Classes

EBNF The declaration of an abstract class is similar to that of a class:

```
AbstractClassDecl      = AbstractClassModifiers? "abstract" "class"
                         Identifier ClassBase? ClassBody ";"? .
AbstractClassModifier = "public" | "protected" | "internal" | "private" .
```

However, it is very important to point out that the access modifiers of an abstract class and those of structures, enumerations, delegates, and interfaces (discussed in the next section) are context dependent. Within a namespace, these type declarations are limited to public or internal. In this context, if the access modifier is not specified then internal is assumed by default. Additional modifiers such as new, protected, and private may be applied to each type of declaration when the declaration is nested within a class. For this case, all applicable modifiers for each type declaration are given in Appendix A. As a final note, neither data nor static methods can be abstract.

7.2.2 Implementing Abstract Classes

An abstract class is most appropriate if it implements some default behavior common to many subclasses and delegates, and the rest of its behavior as specialized implementations. In fact, if all methods are abstract, then it is better to define an interface, as described in the next section, instead of an abstract class. Consider now an abstract class called Counter as defined here.

```
1   using System;
2
3   namespace SubclassConstructors {
4       abstract class Counter {
5           public Counter(int c) { count = c; }
6           public    abstract void    Tick();
7
8           public    int     GetCount()  { return count; }
9           protected void    Inc()       { ++count; }
10          protected void    Dec()       { --count; }
11
12          private   int     count;
13      }
14
15      class DownCounter : Counter {
16          public DownCounter(int count) : base(count) { }
17          public override void Tick() { Dec(); }
18      }
19
20      class UpCounter : Counter {
21          public UpCounter(int count) : base(count) { }
22          public override void Tick() { Inc(); }
23      }
24
25      public class TestAbstractCounter {
26          public static void Main() {
27              Counter[] counters = { new UpCounter(0), new DownCounter(9) };
28
29              for (int c = 0; c < counters.Length ; c++) {
```

```
30              Console.WriteLine("Counter starting at: "
31                              +counters[c].GetCount());
32              for (int n = 0; n < 5; n++) {
33                  Console.Write(counters[c].GetCount());
34                  counters[c].Tick();
35              }
36              Console.WriteLine();
37          }
38      }
39    }
40  }
```

The methods GetCount, Inc, and Dec are fully implemented and, hence, represent common behavior for all subclasses that may derive from Counter. The Tick method, on the other hand, is abstract, requiring subclasses to implement Tick according to their own needs. The two subclasses, DownCounter and UpCounter, inherit from Counter. When Tick is implemented by either subclass, it must be preceded by the modifier override as shown in lines 17 and 22. Hence, implementations are specialized for DownCounter and UpCounter. In this case, the subclass DownCounter decrements count in its implementation of Tick, and the subclass UpCounter increments count in its implementation of Tick. If no modifier precedes an inherited method, a warning and an error is generated indicating that the inherited method in the subclass hides the corresponding method of its parent. But if that is the intent, then the method Tick must be preceded, instead, by the modifier new.

7.2.3 Using Abstract Classes

In the previous class, TestAbstractCounter, the Main method declares an array of Counter called counters. The array is initialized to one instance each of DownCounter and UpCounter (line 27) and, hence, has a length of two. The instance of DownCounter has an initial value of 9, and the instance of UpCounter has an initial value of 0. For each instance, the method Tick is invoked five times (lines 32–35). Depending on whether or not it is an instance of DownCounter or UpCounter, the count is either decremented or incremented as shown by the following output:

```
Counter starting at: 0
01234
Counter starting at: 9
98765
```

7.3 Interfaces

An **interface** is a special type of abstract class. It provides the signature, but no implementation of all its members. Therefore, an interface cannot define data fields, constructors, static methods, and constants. Only instance methods, events, properties, and indexers are permitted, and of course, must be abstract. Like an abstract class, an interface cannot be instantiated and cannot inherit from multiple abstract classes. However, unlike an abstract class, any subclass that inherits an interface *must* implement all members of the interface. If all interface members are not implemented by the concrete subclass, then a compilation error is generated. On the other hand, a compilation error is not generated if an abstract class is not fully implemented by its subclass. For example, a subclass inheriting from an abstract class may only implement two of four abstract methods. The other two methods and the subclass itself remain abstract. Hence, abstract classes give subclasses the freedom to implement or delegate abstract members. Because a subclass may delegate implementation of an abstract member down the class hierarchy, there is no guarantee that a subclass is fully implemented. This freedom, though, is not always useful, especially if the client seeks assurance that a given subclass can be instantiated. For these reasons, we typically say that a subclass "inherits from" an abstract class but "implements" an interface.

In C#, a class can inherit from only one base class but can implement any number of interfaces. This feature is called "single inheritance of classes with multiple inheritance of interfaces." Like subclasses, an interface can also tailor a specific behavior by inheriting from multiple interfaces. But unlike subclasses, an interface does not, and cannot by definition, implement the abstract members of its parent interface. That remains the responsibility of the subclass.

In the .NET Framework, interfaces are often limited to a single method, which reduces ⎡Tip⎤ the likelihood that undesired behavior is inherited. This approach supports the golden rule of inheritance: Always be completely satisfied with inherited behavior. Dealing with interfaces that contain only one method also allows one to pick and choose (by inheritance) those methods that will constitute a new "assembled" behavior. The result is exactly the right combination of methods, no more and no less. For many years, the design-pattern community has promoted the adage: Program to an interface, not to an implementation.

7.3.1 Declaring Interfaces

The declarations of an interface and an abstract class are very similar. Other than their semantic differences concerning inheritance, the interface ICountable given here:

```
interface ICountable {
    bool Tick();
}
```

is equivalent to the abstract class ACountable:

```
abstract class ACountable {
    public abstract bool Tick();
}
```

The ICountable interface prescribes common behavior for all subclasses that inherit from it. Once implemented in a subclass, for example, the method Tick may "bump a count" and return true once a maximum or minimum value has been reached. Syntactically, interface members, such as Tick, are implicitly public and abstract. In fact, no modifier for interface members can be used other than new, which permits an interface member to hide its inherited member. It is also good programming practice to begin an interface name with a capital "I" to distinguish it from a class. The full syntax of an interface declaration is given here:

Tip

EBNF

```
InterfaceDecl = InterfaceModifiers? "interface" Identifier (":" Interfaces)? "{"
                    InterfaceMembers
                "}" ";"? .

InterfaceModifier = "new" | "public" | "protected" | "internal" | "private" .
InterfaceMember   = MethodDecl | PropertyDecl | EventDecl | IndexerDecl .
```

Now consider two common interface declarations. The ICloneable interface declared here is used to create copies of an existing object:

```
public interface ICloneable {
    object Clone();
}
```

Because the return type of Clone is an object reference of the root class, the method Clone is able to return any instance of any class. Another useful interface is IComparable whose method CompareTo compares two objects of the same type.

```
public interface IComparable {
    int CompareTo(object o);
}
```

Once implemented in a subclass, for example, the method CompareTo may return a negative integer if the current object is "less than" its object parameter, zero if it is equal, and a positive integer if it is "greater than." In any case, any class that implements ICountable, ICloneable, or IComparable must implement their respective methods in some way. The implementation, however, does not place semantic constraints on the programmer. The method CompareTo in this case, and the previous methods Tick and Clone, may be implemented in any way as along as the signature of the behavior is satisfied. Common behavior, therefore, means common use of abstract members. Nonetheless, actual behavior as defined by implementation should be predictable and disciplined as shown in the following section.

7.3.2   Implementing Interfaces

As previously pointed out, the members of an interface must be implemented by the class that inherits it. In the following example, the Counter class inherits part of its behavior from the interface ICountable, namely the Tick method. Other methods include ToString that is overridden from the Object class as well as GetCount and SetCount that return and initialize count, respectively.

```
class Counter : ICountable {
    public Counter(int c)      { count = c; }
    public Counter() : this(0) { }

    public override string ToString() { return ""+count; }
                                       // same as count.ToString()
    public    int   GetCount()      { return count; }
    protected void  SetCount(int c) { count = c; }
    public    bool  Tick() { return ++count == System.Int32.MaxValue; }

    private int count;
}
```

The implementation of Tick increments count by one and returns true once the maximum integer value Int32.MaxValue is reached.

If it is recognized that all counters, in addition to those defined by Counter, exhibit a common behavior described by GetCount, then that behavior is best encapsulated and explicitly defined as an interface:

```
public interface IRetrievable {
    int GetCount();
}
```

Furthermore, to make copies of Counter objects, the Counter class may also implement ICloneable. The final changes to the class Counter are highlighted here:

```
class Counter : ICountable, IRetrievable, ICloneable {
    ...
    public object Clone() { return this.MemberwiseClone(); }
    ...
}
```

The class Counter now inherits and implements three interfaces, and each one includes only a single method. Because the signature of the GetCount method in Counter is the same as the corresponding method in IRetrievable, its definition is unaffected. The description for MemberwiseClone is found in Chapter 4; it is implicitly inherited from the root class Object.

7.3.3 Using Interface Methods

Because an interface is typically small and defines a limited behavior, several classes are likely to implement the same interface. Therefore, instances of classes like the following, Counter and BoundedCounter, share a common behavior:

```
public class Counter        : ICloneable, IRetrievable {...}
public class BoundedCounter : IRetrievable              {...}
```

Both classes inherit from the interface IRetrievable and therefore implement its GetCount method. However, only Counter inherits behavior from ICloneable and has access to the Clone method.

If a reference is guaranteed to contain an object of an interface type, then it can be safely cast and seen as an object of that type. In the following example, the method InvokeService retrieves and outputs the count of each object in the counters array. The array parameter, however, may contain instances of both Counter and BoundedCounter, both of which have implemented the IRetrievable interface.

```
void InvokeService(IRetrievable[] counters) {
    for (int n = 0; n < counters.Length; n++)
        System.Console.WriteLine("Counter #{0}: {1}", n,
                                counters[n].GetCount() );
}
```

Since instances of both Counter and BoundedCounter contain GetCount, they can safely invoke it through instances of IRetrievable without explicit casting. However, if an object does not have access to the method of an interface, in this case GetCount, then an InvalidCastException is raised and the program terminates. Casting therefore runs a risk.

Suppose now that the array counters is of type IRetrievable and, hence, is able to contain a mix of instances from Counter and BoundedCounter. Suppose also that only those instances of Counter are to be cloned and returned in a list. Since the Counter class inherits additional behavior called Clone from the ICloneable interface and since this behavior is not available from either the Object class or the IRetrievable interface, explicit casting is insufficient and raises an exception if objects of type BoundedCounter are cloned. In this case, it is far safer to test for compatibility using the is operator, shown here:

```
ArrayList InvokeService(IRetrievable[] counters) {
    ArrayList list = new ArrayList();

    for (int n = 0; n < counters.Length; n++) {
        System.Console.WriteLine("Counter #{0}: {1}", n,
                                counters[n].GetCount() );

        if (counters[n] is ICloneable)
            list.Add( ((ICloneable)counters[n]).Clone() );
    }
    return list;
}
```

In the previous example, there is no reference to any concrete class type, such as Counter and BoundedCounter. There is simply no need to know which objects of what class make up the array counters. Hence, it is easy to add new concrete classes that derive from these interfaces without changing the code of InvokeService.

Delegates and interfaces are two important features of the C# language that can isolate a single method from large classes with many public services. An interface, on one hand, offers only a few public services (typically one) that must be implemented as a contract by the subclass that derives from it. A delegate, however, offers a single public service[1] that is not necessarily related to a particular object or interface. From a caller's point of view, it is only necessary to match the signature of a method with that of the delegate.

7.4 Polymorphism and Virtual Methods

Unlike inheritance, which is a compile-time mechanism, **polymorphism** is the runtime ability of a reference to vary its behavior depending on the type of object that is currently assigned to it. This dynamic routing (or binding) of messages to methods is one of the three hallmarks of object-oriented programming in addition to classes and inheritance. Although making decisions (tests, branching, and so on) at compile-time is very efficient, any change may require considerable recompilation. On the other hand, with polymorphism, decisions can be changed at runtime and routed to the correct behavior.

Dynamic binding does come with some computational overhead. However, faster processors, larger memories, and better compilers have reduced this cost considerably. Nonetheless, tools such as profilers are very helpful in pinpointing those sections of code that can afford the luxury of polymorphism. In any case, it is always worthwhile to investigate the possibility since polymorphism leads to software that is more flexible, extendable, and easier to maintain in the long run.

When a class is designed, it is advantageous to make methods polymorphic or virtual. Therefore, if a method is inherited and does not satisfy the specific requirements of the derived class, it can be redefined and reimplemented. Such a method is said to be **overridden**. In Chapter 4, methods for the BoundedCounter class were inherited "as is" from their base class Counter. In this section, we examine how methods are overridden using the modifier override to redefine the behavior of virtual (polymorphic) methods. Using a suite of counters, we also show how dynamic binding takes place for polymorphic objects.

Tip

7.4.1 Using the Modifiers override and virtual

If an inherited method is to be completely redefined, the corresponding method of the base class must be preceded by the modifier virtual as shown here:

```
class Counter {
    public virtual bool Tick() { ... }
    ...
}
```

---

[1] It could be argued that more than one public service is offered using a combination of delegates but the restrictions are quite severe.

To demonstrate the process of redefining Tick, the class BoundedCounter is reintroduced. A bounded counter is a counter that begins with an initial value and then counts up or down within a range delimited by minimum and maximum values. If the count exceeds the maximum value when counting up, then it is reset to the minimum value. If the count falls below the minimum value when counting down, then it is reset to the maximum value. The default bounded counter starts at 0, has 0 and Int32.MaxValue for its min and max values respectively, and has an directionUp of true. The default increment is 1 unless otherwise established by the method SetIncrement. The full implementation of the BoundedCounter is shown here:

```
class BoundedCounter : Counter {
    public BoundedCounter(int count, int min, int max,
                        bool directionUp) : base (count) {
        this.min = min;
        this.max = max;
        this.directionUp = directionUp;
        this.increment = 1;
    }
    public BoundedCounter() : this(0, 0, Int32.MaxValue, true) { }

    public override string ToString() {
        return GetCount()+"["+GetMin()+".."+GetMax()+"] "
                +(directionUp?"UP":"DOWN");
    }

    // Bumps the count depending of counter's direction and increment.
    public override bool Tick() {
        if (directionUp) {
            if (GetCount() + GetIncrement()  >  GetMax()) {
                SetCount(min);
                return true;
            } else {
                SetCount(GetCount() + GetIncrement());
            }
        } else {
            if (GetCount() - GetIncrement()  <  GetMin()) {
                SetCount(max);
                return true;
            } else {
                SetCount(GetCount() - GetIncrement());
            }
        }
        return false;
    }
```

```
// Gets the minimum count value.
public virtual int GetMin() { return min; }

// Gets the maximum count value.
public virtual int GetMax() { return max; }

// Gets the count's increment.
public virtual int GetIncrement() { return increment; }

// Sets the count's increment.
public virtual void SetIncrement(int n) { increment = n; }

// Gets the count's direction.
public virtual bool getDirection() { return directionUp; }

// Sets the count's direction.
public virtual void setDirection(bool value) {
    if (value != directionUp) directionUp = value;
}
private   int    increment;
private   int    min, max;
private   bool   directionUp;
}
```

The class BoundedCounter inherits from the class Counter. Since Tick is virtual in Counter, it is redefined in BoundedCounter by preceding its implementation of Tick with the modifier override. Overriding a polymorphic method only happens when the name and parameter list of both the parent and derived class are the same. Also note that BoundedCounter introduces several virtual methods (such as GetMin, GetMax, GetIncrement, and so on), which can also be redefined by any class that derives from BoundedCounter.

7.4.2 Adding and Removing Polymorphism

When deciding whether or not to add or remove polymorphism, it is best to look "under the hood" and see how static, instance, and virtual methods are invoked. For optimization purposes, a call to a static (class) method is equivalent to a call in a procedural language. Without dynamic binding, the invocation directly calls the function code entry point. Instance methods are invoked through a this pointer that is implicitly passed as the first parameter and generated automatically by the compiler. Finally, virtual methods are invoked via the runtime system, which interprets a (virtual) object reference. This reference contains two parts: the type of the object invoking the method, and the offset of that method in a method table (also known as a virtual table). The method table is an array of pointers to functions that enables an invocation to be indirectly and dynamically routed to the correct function code entry point.

Clearly, polymorphism comes with a computational overhead. Adding polymorphism via virtual methods involves weighing flexibility against performance. Although database and network accesses tend to be the bottlenecks of today's applications, the use of profilers can still pinpoint where and when optimization is really required.

In the following example, class D inherits from class B and redefines the method signatures of IM, SM, and VM using the new keyword. For the method VM, the polymorphic chain is broken. For methods IM and SM, on the other hand, a new polymorphic chain is started.

```
class B {
    public          void IM() {}      // Instance method.
    public static  void SM() {}      // Static   method.
    public virtual void VM() {}      // Virtual  method.
}

class D : B {
    new public virtual void IM() {} // Redefine instance as virtual method.
    new public virtual void SM() {} // Redefine static as virtual method.
    new public static  void VM() {} // Redefine virtual as static method.
}
```

Further explanation of the new modifier is provided in Section 7.8.

7.4.3 Using Dynamic Binding

Now that the BoundedCounter class is available, four additional counters are presented, including the two subclasses UpCounter and DownCounter, given here:

```
class DownCounter : BoundedCounter {
    public DownCounter(int count) : base(count, 0, 9, false) { }
}

class UpCounter : BoundedCounter {
    public UpCounter(int count) : base(count, 0, 59, true) { }
}
```

These subclasses inherit from BoundedCounter and reuse its constructor with the base keyword. As the names imply, UpCounter increases its count at every Tick, and DownCounter decreases its count at every Tick.

The next refinement is the definition of a cascaded counter. A cascaded counter is a counter that, when it reaches its maximum value, increments a second counter (if attached). In the following CascadedCounter class, this second counter is passed as a parameter and assigned to the private data member upper of type ICountable. If no counter is attached, then null is passed and assigned to upper. Again, the Tick method of CascadedCounter is overridden to implement the dependence of one counter on the other.

Once count, which is inherited from the class Counter, reaches its maximum value, two things occur: count is reset to its minimum value and upper is incremented by one.

```
class CascadedCounter : BoundedCounter {
    public CascadedCounter(int max, ICountable upper) :
        base(0, 0, max, true) {
        this.upper = upper;
    }
    public override bool Tick() {
        bool overflow = false;

        if ( base.Tick() ) {
            SetCount(GetMin());
            if (upper != null) upper.Tick();
            overflow = true;
        }
        return overflow;
    }
    private ICountable  upper;
}
```

Like UpCounter and DownCounter, CascadedCounter is derived from BoundedCounter and invokes the constructor of its parent class using the keyword base.

Finally, an HourMinute class is defined to simulate a simple watch display formatted as hh:mm. In the constructor of this class, which is defined next, two objects of the class CascadedCounter are instantiated and assigned to data members hour and minute of type Counter. Note that Counter type is compatible with any derived objects, such as those from CascadedCounter.

```
class HourMinute : ICountable {
    public HourMinute() {
        hour   = new CascadedCounter(59, null);
        minute = new CascadedCounter(59, hour);
    }
    public bool Tick() { return minute.Tick(); }

    public override string ToString() {
        return String.Format("{0:D2}:{1:D2}", hour.GetCount(),
                             minute.GetCount());
    }
    private Counter hour;
    private Counter minute;
}
```

The hour object, as expected, represents the hour part of the display. It is instantiated with a null reference as a second parameter since there is no link to any upper counter. The minute object is instantiated and receives as its second parameter the hour reference as its upper counter. This is used to trigger an overflow when the maximum number of minutes is reached. Like BoundedCounter, the Tick method of HourMinute is also overridden. Although the minute object is defined as type Counter, its behavior is dynamically routed to the Tick method of CascadedCounter since an object of the latter class is assigned to minute in the constructor method. Hence, when the count of minute reaches 60, the Tick method of CascadedCounter resets the count of minute to 0 and increments the count of hour by one.

    To further demonstrate polymorphic behavior and to test all counters previously mentioned, a test program called TestInterface is shown here:

```
public class TestInterface {
    public static void Main() {
        Counter up = new BoundedCounter(0, 0, 5, true);
        System.Console.WriteLine("UpCounter [0..5] starting at 0: ");
        for (int n = 0; n < 14; n++) {
            System.Console.Write("{0} ", up.GetCount());
            up.Tick();
        }

        Counter down = new BoundedCounter(5, 0, 5, false);
        System.Console.WriteLine("\n\nDownCounter [5..0] starting at 5: ");
        for (int n = 0; n < 14; n++) {
            System.Console.Write("{0} ", down.GetCount());
            down.Tick();
        }

        Counter ch = new UpCounter(5);
        System.Console.WriteLine("\n\nUpCounter [0..59] starting at 5: ");
        for (int n = 0; n < 61; n++) {
            System.Console.Write("{0} ", ch.GetCount());
            ch.Tick();
        }

        Counter cd = new DownCounter(5);
        System.Console.WriteLine("\n\nDownCounter [9..0] starting at 5: ");
        for (int n = 0; n < 14; n++) {
            System.Console.Write("{0} ", cd.GetCount());
            cd.Tick();
        }

        Counter ch2 = new UpCounter(5);
        System.Console.WriteLine("\n\nUpCounter [0..59] starting at 5 by 2: ");
        ((BoundedCounter)ch2).SetIncrement(2);
```

```
for (int n = 0; n < 61; n++) {
    System.Console.Write("{0} ", ch2.GetCount());
    ch2.Tick();
}

Counter cd2 = new DownCounter(5);
System.Console.WriteLine("\n\nDownCounter [9..0] starting at 5 by 2: ");
((BoundedCounter)cd2).SetIncrement(2);
for (int n = 0; n < 14; n++) {
    System.Console.Write("{0} ", cd2.GetCount());
    cd2.Tick();
}

System.Console.WriteLine("\n\nHourMinute:");
HourMinute hhmm = new HourMinute();
for (int n = 0; n < 64; n++) {
    System.Console.Write("{0} ", hhmm.ToString());
    hhmm.Tick();
}
}
```

Variables of type Counter are assigned instances of BoundedCounter, UpCounter, and DownCounter. In all cases, the appropriate Tick method is invoked depending on what type of object is currently assigned to the variable. For example, when variable cd2 of type Counter is assigned an instance of DownCounter then the inherited Tick method of DownCounter would be invoked. Since the Tick method of DownCounter did not redefine the Tick method of BoundedCounter, the behavior of the two is equivalent. Notice the explicit cast that must be applied to the Counter objects, ch2 and cd2, in order to invoke the SetIncrement method of the BoundedCounter class. The sample output of the test program follows:

```
UpCounter [0..5] starting at 0:
0 1 2 3 4 5 0 1 2 3 4 5 0 1

DownCounter [5..0] starting at 5:
5 4 3 2 1 0 5 4 3 2 1 0 5 4

UpCounter [0..59] starting at 5:
5 6 7 8 9 10 11 12 13 14 15 16 17 18 19 20 21 22 23 24 25 26 27 28 29 30 31
32 33 34 35 36 37 38 39 40 41 42 43 44 45 46 47 48 49 50 51 52 53 54 55 56
57 58 59 0 1 2 3 4 5

DownCounter [9..0] starting at 5:
5 4 3 2 1 0 9 8 7 6 5 4 3 2
```

```
UpCounter [0..59] starting at 5 by 2:
5 7 9 11 13 15 17 19 21 23 25 27 29 31 33 35 37 39 41 43 45 47 49 51 53 55
57 59 0 2 4 6 8 10 12 14 16 18 20 22 24 26 28 30 32 34 36 38 40 42 44 46 48
50 52 54 56 58 0 2 4

DownCounter [9..0] starting at 5 by 2:
5 3 1 9 7 5 3 1 9 7 5 3 1 9

HourMinute:
00:00 00:01 00:02 00:03 00:04 00:05 00:06 00:07 00:08 00:09 00:10 00:11 00:12
00:13 00:14 00:15 00:16 00:17 00:18 00:19 00:20 00:21 00:22 00:23 00:24 00:25
00:26 00:27 00:28 00:29 00:30 00:31 00:32 00:33 00:34 00:35 00:36 00:37 00:38
00:39 00:40 00:41 00:42 00:43 00:44 00:45 00:46 00:47 00:48 00:49 00:50 00:51
00:52 00:53 00:54 00:55 00:56 00:57 00:58 00:59 01:00 01:01 01:02 01:03
```

7.5 Properties

A **property** is an accessor that provides and encapsulates access to a data field. In the past, object-oriented languages such as Smalltalk, C++, and Java have simply used conventions to access the data fields of objects and classes. These conventions have centered on the implementation of getter and setter methods to retrieve and update information. In C#, properties are incorporated as field extensions with a syntax that appears to access the data fields directly. Even if properties give this impression, they are nonetheless implemented as methods as described in the following subsections.

7.5.1 Declaring get and set Accessors

In Java, access to a data field is typically implemented with two methods. The two methods, prefixed with get and set, respectively, retrieve and assign values from a data field as follows:

```
class Id {
    public  String  getName()               { return name;  }
    public  void     setName(String value) { name = value; }

    private String  name;
}
```

Using a more intuitive syntax, properties in C# encapsulate two accessor methods called get and set within the same block of code as shown here:

```
class Id {
    public string Name {        // Declaration of the Name property.
        get { return name;  }
```

```
        set { name = value; }
    }
    private string name;        // Declaration of the name field.
}
```

Every set method has exactly one implicit parameter called value with the same type as the field with which the property is associated. Because set accessors have write-only properties, they also have a tendency to throw exceptions when receiving invalid parameters. Therefore, validation may be required before assigning the value parameter to a field member. A get accessor, on the other hand, should not change a data field but merely return its value. It is therefore good practice to avoid throwing exceptions from get accessors since they are primarily used as read-only access to objects.

Tip

To illustrate the invocation of both the get and set accessors, consider the following example:

```
Id id      = new Id();
id.Name    = "Michel";
id.Name    = id.Name + " de Champlain";
```

In this example, an object id is created and its field name is first set to "Michel" through the property Name. On the following line, the get accessor is invoked to retrieve the field name before it is concatenated with " de Champlain". The field name is then set to the resultant string.

Both get and set accessors specify read and write properties that should always return and receive a copy of an object's private data (value or reference type). Although this seems safe enough for value types, care must be exercised for reference types. Returning or receiving a reference to the private data of an object results in sharing what is supposed to be protected and well encapsulated.

7.5.2 Declaring Virtual and Abstract Properties

A property, unlike a field, can be overridden. Therefore, it is good programming practice to declare virtual or abstract properties, especially when behavior needs to be redefined. For example, the Counter class (lines 1–13 of the next example) supports counters within a byte range from 0 to MaxValue (255). Its Max property is used only in the ToString method (line 10). The set accessor (line 6) associated with the count field does not use the Max property for validation. On the other hand, if a BoundedCounter class (lines 15–28) wishes to restrict its range to a specific maximum value at creation time (line 16), then it is important to override the get accessor (line 19) of the Max property and the set accessor (lines 22–25) of the Count property. With this extension, the class Counter does not need to be modified since its ToString method is routed dynamically to the Max property based on the instance of its caller's type.

Tip

```
1  class Counter {
2      public  virtual byte Max {
```

```
3                get { return System.Byte.MaxValue; }
4            }
5        public  virtual byte Count {
6            set { count = value; }
7            get { return count;  }
8        }
9        public override string ToString() {
10           return ""+Count+"[0.."+Max+"]";
11       }
12       private byte count;
13   }
14
15   class BoundedCounter : Counter {
16       public BoundedCounter(byte max) { this.max = max; }
17
18       public  override byte Max    {
19           get { return max; }
20       }
21       public  override byte Count {
22           set {
23               if (value > Max) base.Count = Max;
24               else base.Count = value;
25           }
26       }
27       private byte max;
28   }
29
30   class TestCounter {
31       public static void Main(string[]  args) {
32           Counter c = new Counter();
33           System.Console.WriteLine(c.ToString());
34           c.Count = 4;
35           System.Console.WriteLine(c.ToString());
36
37           c = new BoundedCounter(5);
38           System.Console.WriteLine(c.ToString());
39           c.Count = 6;
40           System.Console.WriteLine(c.ToString());
41       }
42   }
```

Output:

```
0[0..255]
4[0..255]
```

```
0[0..5]
5[0..5]
```

Properties support read-only, write-only, or both read/write access to fields. However, overridden properties are only possible for the accessors that are declared. In other words, a write-only property (using a set) cannot be extended to a read/write property.

As shown next, the use of an interface (lines 1–3) and an abstract class (lines 5–11) is sometimes ideal for specifying the desired accessors of virtual properties. The following example illustrates this combination for the declaration of our previous Counter class:

```
1    interface ICounter {
2        byte Count { set; get; }
3    }
4
5    abstract class Counter : ICounter {
6        public  virtual byte Count {        // Default implementation.
7            set { count = value; }
8            get { return count;  }
9        }
10       private byte count;
11   }
12
13   class Counter2 : Counter {
14       public  virtual byte Max {
15           get { return System.Byte.MaxValue; }
16       }
17       public override string ToString() {
18           return ""+Count+"[0.."+Max+"]";
19       }
20   }
```

The Counter abstract class implements a default behavior for the Count property, and the Counter2 concrete class implements the Max property and ToString method. Note that the interface ICounter, like all interfaces, does not specify an access modifier for its members. They are always implicitly public. Therefore, the property Count in ICounter has public access.

7.5.3 Declaring Static Properties

A static (or class) property behaves like static data and is accessed via its class name. The following Id class increments a static counter number corresponding to the number of Id objects created.

```
1    public class Id {
2        public Id() { ++number; }
```

```
3              static      Id()   { number = 0; }
4      public  static int Number { get { return number; } }
5      private static int number;
6  }
7
8  public class TestCounter {
9      public static void Main(string[]  args) {
10         new Id();
11         System.Console.WriteLine(Id.Number);
12         new Id();
13         System.Console.WriteLine(Id.Number);
14     }
15 }
```

Output:

```
1
2
```

Static properties cannot be referenced through an instance variable and, hence, the following access will generate a compilation error:

```
new Id().Number
```

7.5.4   Declaring Properties with Accessor Modifiers

A typical component is designed with public accessibility for both get and set accessors. But applications may also need accessors with different accessibilities. For example, a public get accessor may need to be combined with a protected or internal set accessor that restricts access to derived classes or classes within the same assembly. In order to achieve this flexibility, accessors too may have access modifiers. These modifiers, however, are not applicable to accessors within an interface.

C# 2.0

If a property has no override modifier then an accessor modifier is allowed only if both get and set accessors are defined. In addition, only one of the two accessors may have a modifier other than public as shown here:

```
public class Counter {
    public virtual byte Count {
        protected set { count = value; } // Accessible to derived classes.
                    get { return count;  } // Accessible to all clients.
    }
    private byte count;
}
```

If an accessor needs to be overridden in the case of a virtual property then the accessors of the override property must match the signatures of the accessors in the virtual property.

For example, if Counter2 inherits from Counter then the virtual property of Counter is overridden as follows:

```
public class Counter2 : Counter {
    public override byte Count {
        protected set { ... }
                   get { ... }
    }
}
```

As a final note, the accessibility of an accessor must be at least as restrictive as that of its encapsulating property, as summarized in Table 7.1.

The complete EBNF definition for a property declaration is given here:

EBNF

```
PropertyDecl      = Attributes? PropertyModifiers? Type MemberName
                    "{" AccessorDecls "}" .
PropertyModifier  = "new" | "public" | "protected" | "internal" | "private"
                    | "static" | "virtual" | "sealed" | "override"
                    | "abstract" | "extern" .
AccessorDecls     = ( GetAccessorDecl SetAccessorDecl? )
                    | ( SetAccessorDecl GetAccessorDecl? ) .
GetAccessorDecl   = Attributes? AccessorModifier? "get" AccessorBody .
SetAccessorDecl   = Attributes? AccessorModifier? "set" AccessorBody .
AccessorModifier  = "protected | "internal" | "private"
                    | ("protected" "internal") | ("internal" "protected") .
AccessorBody      = Block | ";" .
```

Property Modifier	Applicable Accessor Modifiers
public	Any
protected internal	internal, protected, or private
internal or protected	private
private	None

Table 7.1: Restrictive accessibility for accessors.

7.6 Indexers

An **indexer** is an accessor that enables an object to be treated in the same way as an array, where any number and type of parameters can be used as indices. Therefore, defining an indexer in C# is equivalent to redefining the operator [ ]. An indexer is considered when a class is better represented as a virtual container of data that can be retrieved or set using indices. Since an indexer is nameless, its signature is specified by the keyword this followed by its indexing parameters within square brackets. Like methods, indexers can also be overloaded. The following example of an indexer illustrates its use to access an int as an array of bits:

```
1    using System;
2    using System.Text;
3
4    namespace BitIndexer {
5        public class IntBits {
6            public bool this [int index] {
7                get {
8                    if (index < 0 || index >= BitsPerInt)
9                        throw new ArgumentOutOfRangeException();
10
11                   return (bits & (1 << index)) != 0;
12               }
13               set {
14                   if (index < 0 || index >= BitsPerInt)
15                       throw new ArgumentOutOfRangeException();
16
17                   if (value)
18                       bits |= (1 << index);
19                   else
20                       bits &= ~(1 << index);
21               }
22           }
23           public override string ToString() {
24               StringBuilder s = new StringBuilder("[ ");
25               for (int n = 0; n < BitsPerInt; n++)
26                   s.Append(this[n] ? "1 ": "0 ");
27               s.Append("]");
28               return s.ToString();
29           }
30           private      int bits;
31           private const int BitsPerInt = 32;
32       }
33
34       public class TestBitIndexer {
35           public static void Main() {
36               IntBits  ibits = new IntBits();
37
38               ibits[6] = true;             // set
39               bool peek = ibits[2];        // get
40               ibits[6] = ibits[2] || peek; // get and set
```

```
41
42                  Console.WriteLine( ibits.ToString() );
43              }
44          }
45  }
```

An int in C# has 32 bits (line 31). Therefore, validation must be made upon entry to the get (lines 8–9) and set (lines 14–15) accessors to ensure that the index is within the integer bit range 0..31. Otherwise, a ArgumentOutOfRangeException is thrown. Access to an object of IntBits is shown on lines 38–40. Notice that internal use of the get accessor is also made within the ToString method on line 26 in order to peek at an indexed value and to use its corresponding boolean value to append the string "1 " or "0 ".

In terms of modifiers, there are three key differences between an indexer and a property. First, a property is identified by its name whereas an indexer is identified by its signature. Second, a property can be a static member, but an indexer is always an instance member. Third, an indexer must have at least one parameter. In a similar vein, however, the restrictions on accessor modifiers for properties also apply to indexers. The complete EBNF definition for an indexer declaration is given here:

EBNF

```
IndexerDecl     = Attributes? IndexerModifiers? IndexerDecltor
                  "{" AccessorDecls "}" .
IndexerModifier = "new" | "public" | "protected" | "internal" | "private"
                  | "static" | "virtual" | "sealed" | "override"
                  | "abstract" | "extern" .
IndexerDecltor  = Type ( InterfaceType "." )? "this"
                  "[" FormalParameterList "]" .
```

7.7 Nested Types

Types can be **nested** in order to localize and use abstractions within one type only. For example, a class can have nested declarations of classes, structures, interfaces, enumerations, and delegates, where each nested declaration has either public, protected, internal, protected internal, or private access. If the access is not specified, private is the default. Such localization may also be achieved by defining internal types within the same namespace and compiled separately.

The following example presents a class A in a namespace NT that uses nested types. This class processes internal work by creating and invoking instances of nested types. Although an instance of class A can be created outside NT, there is no access to any of its nested types:

```
namespace NT { // Using Nested Types
    public class A {
        public A() { DoInternalWork(); }
```

```
    // Internal methods:
    static void CallBack() {}
    void DoInternalWork() {
        new S().M();
        new C().M();
        new M(A.CallBack)();
    }

    // Internal nested types:
    internal interface I { void M();    }
    internal class  C : I { public void M() {} }
    internal struct S : I { public void M() {} }
    internal delegate void M();
  }
}
```

The next example presents an equivalent class A in a namespace IT that uses internal types instead. This class processes the same internal work by creating and invoking instances of its internal types. Again, although an instance of class A can be created outside IT, there is no access to any of its internal types:

```
namespace IT { // Using Internal Types
    public class A {
        public A() { DoInternalWork(); }

        // Internal methods:
        static void CallBack() {}
        void DoInternalWork() {
            new S().M();
            new C().M();
            new M(A.CallBack)();
        }
    }
    // Internal types:
    interface I { void M();    }
    class  C : I { public void M() {} }
    struct S : I { public void M() {} }
    delegate void M();
}
```

Consider the following main application (compiled separately), which attempts to use all the previous types. As expected, each attempted access to the internal and nested types generates the same compilation error stating that such type is inaccessible due to its protection level:

```
namespace TestNestedAndInternalTypes {
    using NT;
    using IT;

    public class MainTest {
        public static void Main() {
            new NT.A();
            new NT.A.S().M();            // Error: inaccessible.
            new NT.A.C().M();            // Error: inaccessible.
            new NT.A.M(NT.A.CallBack)(); // Error: inaccessible.

            new IT.A();
            new IT.S().M();              // Error: inaccessible.
            new IT.C().M();              // Error: inaccessible.
            new IT.M(IT.A.CallBack)();   // Error: inaccessible.
        }
    }
}
```

7.8 Other Modifiers

Other modifiers for type members include sealed, volatile, and extern. The sealed modifier means that a class cannot be extended or subclassed. System.String is an example of a sealed class that precludes any unwanted extensions. It can also used on virtual methods and properties to prevent further derived classes from overriding them. The volatile modifier denotes a member that can be modified asynchronously (hardware or thread) as in C/C++. The extern modifier specifies a method implemented in some other language, usually C or C++.

The new modifier, which was briefly introduced in Section 7.4.2, is used to break a polymorphic chain. If new is combined with the virtual modifier on the same member then a new polymorphic chain is started. Combining new with the override modifier, however, generates a compilation error.

In the following example, an existing Counter class has (unfortunately) not declared its GetCount method as virtual. In order to make it virtual without editing the existing file where the class is implemented, the GetCount method is inherited by a new class called NewCounter and redeclared as virtual with the help of the new modifier. Although the constructor of NewCounter also initializes a max bound, there is no need to use new with the method Tick. We need only override Tick to check with max instead of the predefined constant Int32.MaxValue:

```
public interface ICountable {
    bool Tick();
}
```

```
    public class Counter : ICountable {
        public                  Counter () { count = 0; }
        public          int     GetCount() { return count; }
        public override string ToString() { return count.ToString(); }
        protected       void    SetCount(int newCount) { count = newCount;}
        public virtual  bool    Tick()     { return ++count == Int32.MaxValue; }

        private         int   count;
    }
    public class NewCounter : Counter {
        public NewCounter(int max) : base() { this.max = max; }
        public new virtual int GetCount()   { return  base.GetCount(); }
        public override bool   Tick() {
            SetCount(base.GetCount()+1);
            if (base.GetCount() == GetMax()) {
                SetCount(0);
                return true;
            }
            return false;
        }
        public  int GetMax() { return max; }

        private int max;
    }
    public class TestNewModifier {
        public static void Main() {
            ICountable c  = new Counter();
            NewCounter c2 = new NewCounter(3);

            for (int n = 0; n < 9; n++) {
                System.Console.Write( c.ToString() );   c.Tick();
            }
            System.Console.WriteLine();

            for (int n = 0; n < 9; n++) {
                System.Console.Write( c2.ToString() ); c2.Tick();
            }
            System.Console.WriteLine();
        }
    }
```

Output:

012345678
012012012

As a final note, the new modifier is also helpful in controlling changes to a third-party class library used in current projects or applications. Consider the following method M declared in class A within the ThirdPartyLib class library namespace. Suppose also that class B inherits from class A and uses method M in the current OurLib namespace.

```
namespace ThirdPartyLib {
    public class A {
        public void M() { ... }
        ...
    }
}
namespace OurLib {
    public class B : A {
        public void My() {
            M();
            ...
        }
        ...
    }
}
```

If the manufacturer, say, releases a new version of the ThirdPartyLib class library and changes the name of method M to My, this change in their public interface forces the recompilation of our class B. The recompilation generates a warning message because class B.My now hides the inherited member A.My. This warning can be removed by adding the new keyword in front of the method B.My and by using the base prefix to call A.My as shown here:

```
namespace ThirdPartyLib {
    public class A {
        public void My() { ... }    // Change to the public interface of the
                                     // library class.
        ...
    }
}
namespace OurLib {
    public class B : A {
        public new void My() {      // Warning is removed.
            base.My();              // Access to the inherited method is still
                                    // possible.
            ...
        }
        ...
    }
}
```

Exercises

Exercise 7-1.   Write an object-oriented version of the Unix word count wc utility (see description in Exercise 6-3).

Exercise 7-2.   Implement the common behavior of the ICounter interface in an abstract Counter class. Hint: Only the process method (that compares each character read) stays abstract in order to be implemented in three concrete classes CharCounter, LineCounter, and WordCounter.

Exercise 7-3.   Extract the behavior of a counter in an ICounter interface. Hint: At least four methods are needed to count, process, reset, and get the counter value.

chapter **8**

Collections and Generics

The mathematical library of the FORTRAN programming language was and still is a fundamental strength of the language. Code that has been optimized and tested for decades continues to serve the needs of scientists and engineers worldwide. Newer programming languages, like Java and C#, are also supported by extensive libraries of reusable code, reducing software design in many cases to a question of finding the right class with the right behavior for the right job. This reuse of components is a practice of long standing in every engineering discipline. It is not surprising, therefore, that software reuse has gained much more prominence over the last two decades as designers have shied away from the risk of "reinventing the wheel" and embraced the security of reusing code that is more reliable, more portable, and more maintainable.

Object-oriented technology is a perfect catalyst for software reuse based on its three fundamental characteristics of classes, inheritance, and polymorphism. In this chapter, we examine in greater depth the Framework Class Library (FCL) of .NET first mentioned in Chapter 1. The FCL implements several traditional data structures, such as hash tables, queues, and stacks, that are modeled in an object-oriented way via classes and interfaces. Essentially, these classes and interfaces can be thought of as collections of objects that are accessible and organized in specific ways, but which share a similar common behavior. Although not part of the .NET Framework, generic classes naturally follow our discussion on collections. They offer better compile-time type checking and, hence, greater runtime efficiency over object collections.

8.1 Collections

As discussed in Section 4.7, an array is the simplest, and the only, data structure that is directly part of the System namespace. Each array in C# inherits from the System.Array abstract class and is a fixed size container of items with the same type. A **collection**, on the other hand, is a flexible and growable container that holds object references, meaning that every object removed from a C# collection must be cast back to the desired type as shown here:

```
Counter c = (Counter)myCollection.Remove(obj);
```

All collections in C# are part of the System.Collections namespace and offer a uniform and consistent behavior that is derived from several common interfaces, such as ICloneable, IList, ICollection, and IEnumerable, to name just a few. A number of concrete collections are already defined and are available for instantiation and use within the .NET Framework. These collections, along with their inherited interfaces, are listed here:

```
ArrayList  : IList, ICollection, IEnumerable, ICloneable
SortedList : IDictionary, ICollection, IEnumerable, ICloneable
Hashtable  : IDictionary, ICollection, IEnumerable,
             ISerializable, IDeserializationCallback, ICloneable
BitArray   : ICollection, IEnumerable, ICloneable
Queue      : ICollection, IEnumerable, ICloneable
Stack      : ICollection, IEnumerable, ICloneable
```

An ArrayList represents an unsorted sequence of objects that are accessible by an index. A SortedList, on the other hand, represents a collection of key/value pairs that are sorted by key and accessible by either key or index. The HashTable is also a collection of key/value pairs where objects are only accessible using the hash code of the key. A BitArray is identical to an ArrayList except that objects are restricted to those of type Boolean. Hence, BitArray is a compact array of bits. As expected, Queue and Stack are first-in, first-out (FIFO) and last-in, first-out (LIFO) collections of objects. Except for BitArray, the size of all collections may change dynamically.

The C# language also has three abstract collections from which other classes may inherit. These collections, listed below, are designed to be strongly typed and, hence, only contain objects of one type.

```
CollectionBase         : IList, ICollection, IEnumerable
DictionaryBase         : IDictionary, ICollection, IEnumerable
ReadOnlyCollectionBase : ICollection, IEnumerable
```

A CollectionBase is an indexed sequence of objects that, unlike the previous ArrayList, must all be of the same type. The DictionaryBase represents a collection of key/value pairs that are accessible by key only. Finally, ReadOnlyCollectionBase is an indexed "read-only" collection of objects and, therefore, objects cannot be added to or removed from the collection. Additional collections within the namespace System.Collections.Specialized are also available, but these specialized collections, such as StringCollection and NameValueCollection, are not covered.

For the sake of simplicity, the previous collections are divided into two broad categories: list-type and dictionary-type. Those collections that do not depend on the key values of its members for insertion, deletion, and other operations are classified as list-type collections. Otherwise, collections are considered as dictionary type.

8.1.1 Cloning Collections

Each concrete collection inherits from the ICloneable interface shown earlier. As mentioned in Chapter 7, the interface contains but a single method called Clone, which provides the cloning support for collections.

```
interface ICloneable {
    object Clone();
}
```

Although a typical Clone method returns either a deep or a shallow copy of the invoking object as illustrated in Section 4.6.3, the Clone method of each concrete collection given previously only returns a shallow copy of the invoking collection. Of course, a class may be derived from one of these collections and override the Clone method to perform a deep copy instead.

The abstract collections, on the other hand, do not inherit from ICloneable. Rather, that choice is left to the developer as shown in the two class definitions here:

```
class MyCloneableTypeCollection    : CollectionBase, ICloneable { ... }
class MyNonCloneableTypeCollection : CollectionBase { ... }
```

The main advantage however of implementing the ICloneable interface is to provide the ability to test whether or not an object (or any collection) is cloneable without exposing the type of the object at runtime.

```
if (thisObjectOrCollection is ICloneable) {
    object aCopy = thisObjectOrCollection.Clone();
    ...
}
```

8.1.2 Using List-Type Collections

In this section, we examine the iterators, constructors, and use of list-type collections, namely ArrayList, BitArray, Stack, Queue, and CollectionBase. It is important to note that the Array type also falls into this category. Both iterators and constructors are central to the understanding of the creation and manipulation of collection objects. They also serve to illustrate the common services inherited through the previous interfaces. A similar outline is followed in the next section on dictionary-type collections.

Iterators

All collections, both list-type and dictionary-type, inherit from the interface IEnumerable. The IEnumerable interface contains a single method called GetEnumerator, which creates and returns an enumerator of type IEnumerator.

```
public interface IEnumerable {
    IEnumerator GetEnumerator();
}
```

This enumerator, in turn, supports simple iteration over a collection. It hides how iteration is actually achieved and allows access to data without exposing the internal implementation of the collection. The enumerator is derived from the interface IEnumerator, which includes three abstract members as shown here:

```
interface IEnumerator {
    object  Current {get;}
    bool    MoveNext();
    void    Reset();
}
```

The Current property returns the reference of the current object in a collection. The MoveNext method advances to the "next" object in the collection and returns false when the enumerator moves beyond the last object. Finally, the Reset method reinitializes the enumerator by moving it back to just before the first object of the collection.

The enumerator itself is implemented as an internal class that is associated with a particular collection. Typically, the class is defined in the same namespace and file of the collection itself. Because the enumerator class inherits from IEnumerator, it is obliged to implement the two abstract methods, MoveNext and Reset, and the one property, Current, of the IEnumerator interface.

The GetEnumerator method, which creates and returns an enumerator for a given collection, may be invoked either explicitly or implicitly as shown next. Consider an instance of the ArrayList collection called list. Three names are added to list using its Add method. Once the names have been added, the method GetEnumerator is explicitly invoked. It returns a reference to the enumerator of list and assigns it to e.

```
ArrayList list = new ArrayList();

list.Add("Brian");
list.Add("Glen");
list.Add("Patrick");

IEnumerator e = list.GetEnumerator();   // Explicit invocation.
for ( ; e.MoveNext() ; )
    Console.WriteLine(e.Current);
```

Using the method MoveNext and the property Current implemented in the internal enumerator class associated with ArrayList, the enumerator e iterates through the collection list and outputs the three names.

If, on the other hand, a foreach loop associated with the collection is executed, the GetEnumerator method is invoked implicitly as shown here.

```
ArrayList list = new ArrayList();

list.Add("Brian");
list.Add("Glen");
list.Add("Patrick");

foreach (string s in list)              // Implicit invocation.
    Console.WriteLine(s);
```

Since GetEnumerator is invoked implicitly, the compiler automatically generates code "behind the scenes" that is similar to the for loop above. The end effect is the same.

In more generic terms, to iterate through any array or collection that stores objects of type T, the following code segment provides a useful template.

```
MyCollection c = new MyCollection();  // Creates a collection,
...                                    // uses it,
IEnumerator  e = c.GetEnumerator();   // creates an iterator,
while (e.MoveNext()) {                 // and iterates.
    T  item = (T)e.Current;
    Console.WriteLine(item);
}
```

Again, the same iteration may be achieved using the foreach statement, where the invocation of GetEnumerator and the cast to T are implicit.

```
MyCollection c = new MyCollection();  // Creates a collection,
...                                    // uses it,
foreach(T item in c)                   // and iterates.
    Console.WriteLine(item);
```

The implementation of a new iterator highlights, with a little more clarity, the mechanisms discussed previously. Consider an application where a special iterator is required for a collection SpecialList that is derived from ArrayList. This iterator is expected to print any instance of SpecialList in reverse order, starting from the last item down to the first. This task is easily achieved by encapsulating the new iterator in an internal class SpecialEnumerator that is associated with SpecialList. This class reimplements each of three methods of IEnumerator and is passed a reference to the current object upon creation. Note that GetEnumerator of the SpecialList collection overrides GetEnumerator of the ArrayList collection.

```
1   using System;
2   using System.Collections;
3
4   namespace T {
```

```
5     public class SpecialList : ArrayList {
6         public SpecialList(ICollection c) : base(c) { }
7         public override IEnumerator GetEnumerator() {
8             return new SpecialEnumerator(this);
9         }
10    }
11
12    internal class SpecialEnumerator : IEnumerator {
13        public SpecialEnumerator(ArrayList list) {
14            this.list = list;
15            Reset();
16        }
17        public bool    MoveNext() { return --index >= 0; }
18        public object Current    { get { return list[index]; } }
19        public void    Reset()    { index = list.Count; }
20
21        private ArrayList list;
22        private int        index;
23    }
24
25    public class TestNewIterator {
26        public static void Print(string name, IEnumerable list) {
27            Console.Write("{0,2}: ", name);
28            foreach (string s in list)
29                Console.Write("{0} ", s);
30            Console.WriteLine();
31        }
32        public static void Main() {
33            ArrayList al = new ArrayList();
34            al.Add("Michel");
35            al.Add("Brian");
36            al.Add("Glen");
37            al.Add("Patrick");
38
39            SpecialList sl = new SpecialList(al);
40
41            Print("al", al);
42            Print("sl", sl);
43        }
44    }
45 }
```

Four names are inserted into an instance of ArrayList called a1 (lines 34–37). Once inserted, an instance of SpecialList called s1 is created and initialized to a1 on line 39.

When the method Print is invoked on two occasions, first with a1 on line 41 and second with s1 on line 42, both instances are passed to the local parameter list of the parent type IEnumerable. In the case of a1, the GetEnumerator of ArrayList is implicitly invoked when the foreach loop is executed (lines 28–29). Likewise, in the case of s1, the GetEnumerator of SpecialList (lines 7–9) is invoked when the foreach is executed. The proper iterator associated with each type is therefore determined polymorphically and the expected results are printed out:

```
al: Michel Brian Glen Patrick
sl: Patrick Glen Brian Michel
```

Other Interfaces

Before discussing the constructors of list-type collections, we pause to introduce two additional interfaces called ICollection and IList. The ICollection interface, which is inherited by all collections, both list-type and dictionary-type, defines the size, the enumerators (from IEnumerable), and the synchronization and copy methods of a collection.

```
public interface ICollection : IEnumerable {
    int     Count           {get;}
    bool    IsSynchronized  {get;}
    object  SyncRoot        {get;}
    void    CopyTo (Array array, int index);
}
```

Three properties are defined in ICollection. The Count property returns the number of objects in the collection, the IsSynchronized property returns true if access to the collection is locked or thread-safe, and SyncRoot returns an object that is generally used to lock access to a collection. In addition, the CopyTo method copies the items of a collection into a one-dimensional array starting at a specified index.

The collections Array, ArrayList, and CollectionBase also derive from the interface IList, which allows objects contained in the collection to be accessed via an index. This interface also inherits from ICollection and IEnumerable and defines several members as shown here:

```
public interface IList : ICollection, IEnumerable {
    bool    IsFixedSize     {get;}
    bool    IsReadOnly      {get;}
    object this[int index] {get; set;}

    int  Add(object value);
    void Clear();
    bool Contains(object value);
    int  IndexOf(object value);
    void Insert(int index, object value);
```

```
        void Remove(object value);
        void RemoveAt(int index);
}
```

The property IsFixedSize returns true if a collection derived from IList has a fixed size.
Otherwise, it returns false. Similarly, the IsReadOnly property returns true if the collection is read-only. Otherwise, it returns false. The indexer this[int index] gets and
sets an item at a specified index. The methods Add, Clear, and Contains add an item to
the collection, remove all items from the collection, and determine whether the collection
contains a specific value. The method IndexOf simply returns the index of a specific item
in the collection whereas the method Insert places an item in the collection at a specified
location. Finally, the methods Remove and RemoveAt delete the first occurrence of a specific
value and delete the item at a specified index, respectively.

Constructors

Like all classes, instances of collections are created using constructors. Concrete collections have several constructors that typically fall into one of the following categories:
Without parameters (default), with a collection to be added, or with an initial capacity
of items. The constructors for the BitArray, ArrayList, Stack, and Queue collections are
given below. The constructors for Hashtable and SortedList follow in Section 8.1.3.

```
BitArray(int n, bool v)  // Constructor that initializes n bits,
                         // each to boolean value v.
BitArray(BitArray)       // Copy constructor from a specific BitArray.
BitArray(bool[])         // Copy constructor from a specific array of booleans.
BitArray(byte[])         // Copy constructor from a specific array of bytes.
BitArray(int[])          // Copy constructor from a specific array of integers.

ArrayList()              // Default constructor with initial capacity 16.
ArrayList(ICollection)   // Copy constructor from a specific collection.
ArrayList(int)           // Constructor with a specific initial capacity.

Stack()                  // Default constructor with initial capacity 10.
Stack(ICollection)       // Copy constructor from a specific collection.
Stack(int)               // Constructor with a specific initial capacity.

Queue()                  // Default constructor with initial capacity 32.
Queue(ICollection)       // Copy constructor from a specific collection.
Queue(int)               // Constructor with a specific initial capacity.
Queue(int, float)        // Constructor with a specific initial capacity
                         // and growth factor.
```

Aside from BitArray, the size of each collection is doubled when the collection reaches
its current capacity. In the case of Queue, the growth factor may be explicitly specified as

a parameter. A subset of the previous constructors is exercised in the following example. The methods, Push and Dequeue of the Stack and Queue collections, perform as expected by adding an object to the top of a stack and by removing and returning an object from the front of a queue. If the capacity of the Stack is reached when adding an object, then the size of the Stack is doubled. On the other hand, if the Queue is empty when a Dequeue operation is performed, then an InvalidOperationException is generated.

```
using System;
using System.Collections;

namespace T {
    public class TestBasicCollections {
        public static void Print(string name, ICollection c) {
            Console.Write("[{0,2} items] {1,2}: ", c.Count, name);
            foreach (bool b in c)
                Console.Write("{0} ", b ? "1" : "0");
            Console.WriteLine();
        }

        public static void Main() {
            byte[]    bytes = { 0x55, 0x0F };  // two bytes (16 bits)
            bool[]    bools = { true, false, true };
            Array     ba    = new bool[3];
            BitArray  b1    = new BitArray(8, true);
            BitArray  b2    = new BitArray(bytes);
            BitArray  b3    = new BitArray(bools);
            ArrayList a     = new ArrayList(bools);
            Stack     s     = new Stack(b3);
            Queue     q     = new Queue(b3);

            b3.CopyTo(ba, 0);
            s.Push(true);
            q.Dequeue();

            Print("b1", b1);
            Print("b2", b2);
            Print("b3", b3);
            Print("ba", ba);
            Print("a", a);
            Print("s", s);
            Print("q", q);
        }
    }
}
```

Notice that each list-type collection is passed from Main to the Print method via a local parameter c of the parent type ICollection. Hence, when the foreach statement is executed, the GetEnumerator method of the passed collection is polymorphically invoked to generate the following output:

```
[ 8 items] b1: 1 1 1 1 1 1 1 1
[16 items] b2: 1 0 1 0 1 0 1 0 1 1 1 1 0 0 0 0
[ 3 items] b3: 1 0 1
[ 3 items] ba: 1 0 1
[ 3 items]  a: 1 0 1
[ 4 items]  s: 1 1 0 1
[ 2 items]  q: 0 1
```

The next example exercises the ArrayList collection where the property Capacity is defined in ArrayList, and the properties Count and IsSynchronized are inherited from ICollection.

```
using System;
using System.Collections;

namespace T {
    public class TestBasicCollections {
        public static void Main() {
            ArrayList a = new ArrayList();

            a.Add("A"); a.Add("B"); a.Add("C");

            Console.WriteLine("Capacity: {0} items", a.Capacity);
            Console.WriteLine("Count:    {0} items", a.Count);
            Console.WriteLine("IsFixedSize?    {0}", a.IsFixedSize);
            Console.WriteLine("IsReadOnly?     {0}", a.IsReadOnly);
            Console.WriteLine("IsSynchronized? {0}", a.IsSynchronized);
            Console.WriteLine("a[0] = {0}", a[0]);
            Console.WriteLine("a[0] = {0}", a[0] = "a");
            Console.WriteLine("\"B\" found? = {0}", a.Contains("B"));
            Console.WriteLine("\"B\" index  = {0}", a.IndexOf("B"));
            a.RemoveAt(a.IndexOf("B"));
            a.Remove("C");

            foreach (string s in a)
                Console.Write("{0} ", s);
            Console.WriteLine();
        }
    }
}
```

Output:

```
Capacity: 4 items
Count:    3 items
IsFixedSize?    False
IsReadOnly?     False
IsSynchronized? False
a[0] = A
a[0] = a
"B" found? = True
"B" index  = 1
a
```

8.1.3 Using Dictionary-Type Collections

Dictionary-type collections, SortedList, Hashtable, and DictionaryBase, contain objects that are accessed, inserted, and deleted based on their key values. Hence, the iterators and constructors for dictionary-type collections require the support of other interfaces including IDictionary. The IDictionary interface, in particular, defines each entry in a collection as a key/value pair.

Iterators

As stated in the previous section, all collections inherit from the IEnumerable interface, which is used to create and return an enumerator that iterates through a collection. However, in order to iterate through and to access the items of any IDictionary collection, the enumerator interface for a dictionary-type collection inherits from IEnumerator and includes an additional three properties as shown here:

```
interface IDictionaryEnumerator : IEnumerator {
    DictionaryEntry  Entry {get;}
    object           Key   {get;}
    object           Value {get;}
}
```

The property Entry returns the key/value pair of the current item in the collection. Each key/value pair is represented by a DictionaryEntry structure that also includes separate properties for Key and Value:

```
struct DictionaryEntry {
    public DictionaryEntry(object key, object value) { ... }
    public object Key {get; set;}
    public object Value {get; set;}
    ...
}
```

Hence, the Key and Value properties of IDictionaryEnumerator access the Key and Value properties of DictionaryEntry.

Like list-type collections, the GetEnumerator method, which creates and returns an enumerator for a given dictionary-type collection, may be invoked either explicitly or implicitly. Consider an instance of the Hashtable collection called htable. Three names are added to htable using its Add method. Once the names, given as key/value pairs, have been added, the method GetEnumerator is explicitly invoked. It returns a reference to the enumerator of htable and assigns it to e:

```
Hashtable htable = new Hashtable();

htable.Add("Brian", "Brian G. Patrick");
htable.Add("Michel", "Michel de Champlain");
htable.Add("Helene", "Lessard");

IDictionaryEnumerator e = htable.GetEnumerator();  // Explicit invocation.
for ( ; e.MoveNext() ; )
    Console.WriteLine(e.Key);
```

Using the method MoveNext and the property Key (instead of Current), the enumerator e iterates through the collection htable and outputs the key values of each entry.

If, on the other hand, a foreach loop associated with the dictionary collection is executed, the GetEnumerator method is invoked implicitly as shown here.

```
Hashtable htable = new Hashtable();

htable.Add("Brian", "Brian G. Patrick");
htable.Add("Michel", "Michel de Champlain");
htable.Add("Helene", "Lessard");

foreach (DictionaryEntry s in htable)                // Implicit invocation.
    Console.WriteLine(s.Key);
```

As with list-type collections, the compiler automatically generates code "behind the scenes" to instantiate the enumerator.

Other Interfaces

Before presenting the constructors for SortedList and Hashtable, three additional interfaces must be introduced. The first interface called IComparer defines a Compare method that is used to order objects within a collection:

```
interface IComparer {
    int Compare(object x, object y)
}
```

An implementation of the Compare method may return a value indicating whether the first object is less than (−1), equal to (0), or greater than (+1) the second. By default, the IComparer interface is implemented by the Comparer class, which makes a case-sensitive comparison between strings. The CaseInsensitiveComparer class, on the other hand, performs case-insensitive string comparisons. In Section 7.3.1, a similar interface called IComparable was introduced. In this interface restated here, the method CompareTo compares the current object with its single parameter:

```
interface IComparable {
    int CompareTo(object o);
}
```

The second interface called IHashCodeProvider generates keys (integer hash codes) for objects used as entries in Hashtables. The hash code is supplied by a user implementation of a hash method called GetHashCode as shown here:

```
interface IHashCodeProvider {
    int GetHashCode(object o);
}
```

Finally, the third and largest interface called IDictionary is analogous to IList of the previous section. Dictionary-type collections, such as Hashtable, SortedList, and DictionaryBase, implement the IDictionary interface. This interface defines a collection on key/value pairs.

```
public interface IDictionary : ICollection, IEnumerable {
    bool    IsFixedSize     {get;}
    bool    IsReadOnly      {get;}
    object  this[object key] {get; set;}

    ICollection Keys    {get;}
    ICollection Values  {get;}

    int  Add(object value);
    void Clear();
    bool Contains(object value);
    void Remove(object value);
    IDictionaryEnumerator GetEnumerator();
}
```

The first two properties, IsFixedSize and IsReadOnly, as well as the methods Add, Clear, Contains, and Remove are the same as their corresponding members in IList. The indexer this[object key] gets and sets an item at a specified key (rather than index). The two additional properties, Keys and Values, return collections that contain the keys and values of a collection derived from IDictionary. Finally, the GetEnumerator method inherited from IEnumerable is redefined to return a IDictionaryEnumerator instead of IEnumerator.

Constructors

Many constructors are available for dictionary-like collections, especially for Hashtables. Unless otherwise specified by a given comparer, the objects within a SortedList collection are ordered according to an implementation of IComparable. This implementation defines how keys are compared. Only a subset of these constructors is provided here:

```
Hashtable()                  // With initial capacity 0.
Hashtable(IDictionary)       // From a specific dictionary.
Hashtable(int)               // With a specific initial capacity.
Hashtable(IDictionary, float) // From a specific dictionary and
                             // loading factor.
Hashtable(IHashCodeProvider, IComparer)
                             // With a specific hash code provider
                             // and comparer.

SortedList()                 // With initial capacity 0.
SortedList(IComparer)        // With a specific comparer.
SortedList(IDictionary)      // From a specific dictionary.
SortedList(int)              // With a specific initial capacity.
SortedList(IComparer, int)   // With a specific comparer and initial
                             // capacity.
SortedList(IDictionary, IComparer)
                             // From a specific dictionary using comparer.
```

The Hashtable collection represents buckets that contain items. Each bucket is associated with a hash code based on the key value of an item. Barring excessive collisions between items with identical hash codes, a hash table is designed for faster and easier retrieval than most collections. The SortedList collection, on the other hand, is a combination between a Hashtable, where an item is accessed by its key via the indexer [ ], and an Array, where an item is accessed by its index via the GetByIndex or SetByIndex methods. The items are sorted on keys using either an implementation of IComparer or an implementation of IComparable provided by the keys themselves. The index sequence is based on the sorted order, where the insertion and removal of items re-adjust the sequence automatically. Sorted lists, therefore, are generally less efficient than hash tables. For both hash tables and sorted lists, however, no duplicate keys are allowed.

The following example demonstrates the functionality of both Hashtable and SortedList. A class ReverseOrderComparer (lines 6–13) inherits and implements the IComparer interface to sort objects in reverse order. In addition, the class HashCodeGen (lines 15–20) inherits and implements the IHashCodeProvider interface to return on line 18 a hash code that is calculated as the sum of the first and last characters of an object (once cast to a string) and the length of the string itself.

```
1    using System;
2    using System.Collections;
```

```
3
4    namespace T {
5        // To sort in reverse alphabetical order
6        public class ReverseOrderComparer : IComparer {
7            public int Compare(object x, object y) {
8                string sx = x.ToString();
9                string sy = y.ToString();
10
11               return -sx.CompareTo(sy);
12           }
13       }
14       // To get a different hash code (first + last + length)
15       public class HashCodeGen : IHashCodeProvider {
16           public int GetHashCode(object o) {
17               string s = o.ToString();
18               return s[0] + s[s.Length-1] + s.Length;
19           }
20       }
21
22       public class TestDictionaries {
23           public static void Print(string name, IDictionary d) {
24               Console.Write("{0,2}: ", name);
25               foreach (DictionaryEntry e in d)
26                   Console.Write("{0} ", e.Key);
27               Console.WriteLine();
28           }
29           public static void Main() {
30               Hashtable h1 = new Hashtable();
31               h1.Add("Michel", "Michel de Champlain");
32               h1.Add("Brian",  "Brian G. Patrick");
33               h1.Add("Helene", "Helene Lessard");
34
35               SortedList s1 = new SortedList(h1);
36               SortedList s2 = new SortedList(h1, new ReverseOrderComparer());
37               Hashtable  h2 = new Hashtable(h1, new HashCodeGen(),
38                                                 new ReverseOrderComparer() );
39
40               Print("h1", h1);
41               Print("s1", s1);
42               Print("s2", s2);
43               Print("h2", h2);
44               h2.Add("Be",  "Be Sharp");
45               Print("h2", h2);
46               h1.Add("Be",  "Be Sharp");
```

```
47                      Print("h1", h1);
48             }
49       }
50  }
```

Given these supporting methods, an instance h1 of Hashtable is created using its default constructor on line 30. The same three names are inserted as key/value pairs (lines 31–33). Two instances of SortedList, s1 and s2, are then created and initialized to h1 on lines 35 and 36, respectively. In the case of s2, the comparer ReverseOrderComparer is also passed as the second parameter. Finally, a second instance h2 of Hashtable is created on line 37 and implemented to use HashCodeGen and ReverseComparer. The output is as follows:

```
h1: Helene Michel Brian
s1: Brian Helene Michel
s2: Michel Helene Brian
h2: Brian Michel Helene
h2: Brian Michel Helene Be
h1: Helene Be Michel Brian
```

8.1.4   Using Iterator Blocks and yield Statements

Iterating through arrays and collections is neatly handled using the foreach loop, as shown here on a simple array of integers:

```
int[] numbers = {1, 2, 3, 4, 5, 6, 7, 8, 9};

foreach (int n in numbers)
    System.Console.WriteLine("{0}", n);
```

Any collection implicitly creates an iterator associated with a foreach statement as long as two interfaces, IEnumerable and IEnumerator, are implemented. The following example shows a typical implementation of two classes that implement IEnumerable and IEnumerator, respectively. The first class called IntCollection implements the single method GetEnumerator declared in IEnumerable. The second class called IntEnumerator implements the three members (Current, MoveNext, and Reset) declared in IEnumerator. The IntEnumerator class also encapsulates the internal state of a collection defined by its reference, its index, and possibly other information.

```
1   using System.Collections;
2
3   public class IntCollection : IEnumerable {
4       public IntCollection(int[] numbers) {
5           this.numbers = numbers;
6       }
7       public virtual IEnumerator GetEnumerator() {
8           return new IntEnumerator(numbers);
```

```
9           }
10          // ...
11          private int[]  numbers;
12  }
13
14  class IntEnumerator : IEnumerator {
15          public  IntEnumerator(int[] list) {
16              this.list = list; Reset();
17          }
18          public object Current {
19              get { return list[index]; }
20          }
21          public bool MoveNext() {
22              return ++index < list.Length;
23          }
24          public void Reset() {
25              index = -1;
26          }
27          private int[]  list;
28          private int    index;
29  }
30
31  class TestIntCollection {
32          public static void Main() {
33              IntCollection ic = new IntCollection(new int[]
34                                             {1, 2, 3, 4, 5, 6, 7, 8, 9});
35              IEnumerator   e  = ic.GetEnumerator();
36
37              foreach (int n in ic)
38                  System.Console.WriteLine("{0}", n);
39          }
40  }
```

Using the yield statement, the previous code can be significantly reduced as shown here: C# 2.0

```
1   using System.Collections;
2
3   public class IntCollection : IEnumerable {
4           public IntCollection(int[] numbers) {
5               this.numbers = numbers;
6           }
7           public virtual IEnumerator GetEnumerator() {
8               for (int n = 0; n < numbers.Length; n++)
9                   yield return numbers[n];
10          }
```

```
11     // ...
12     private int[] numbers;
13  }
```

Any block statement that contains at least one yield statement is called an **iterator block**. In the previous example, the block statement from lines 7 to 10 defines an iterator block and produces an ordered sequence of values. The identifier yield is not a keyword itself, but rather has a contextual meaning when immediately preceding a return or break keyword. On one hand, the yield return generates the next iteration value, and on the other hand, a yield break immediately ends an iteration.

By using a yield return statement on line 9, the GetEnumerator method returns an object reference each time the foreach statement calls the iterator. Traversing the collection is simply a matter of stepping through the collection using a loop in an iterator block and yielding the next object reference upon every iteration. In another example, which follows, the iterator block iterates through an array list and returns even values until either the list is exhausted or a value greater than 9 is reached. In the latter case, a yield break is invoked to end the iteration.

```
public IEnumerator GetEnumerator() {
    for (int n = 0; n < numbers.Length; n++) {
        if (numbers[n]   >= 10)  yield break;
        if (numbers[n]%2 == 0 )  yield return numbers[n];
    }
}
```

8.2 Generics

C# 2.0

Generics, also called templates, allow classes, structures, interfaces, delegates, and methods to be parameterized by the data types they represent. In addition to providing stronger compile-time type checking, generics are an improvement over heterogeneous collections by eliminating explicit conversions, boxing/unboxing operations, and runtime checks on data types.

Many object-oriented core libraries provide data structures or collections, such as stacks, queues, linked lists, hash tables, and so on. One of the main advantages of these collections is their heterogeneity. Because the input and return parameters of collection methods are of root type object, collections may be composed of any data type. The following is a typical example of a Queue class, where objects are inserted at the tail using the Enqueue method and retrieved from the head using the Dequeue method:

```
public class Queue {
    ...
    public void    Enqueue(object n) { ... }
    public object Dequeue()         { ... }
    ...
}
```

These heterogeneous collections also have many disadvantages. First, the flexibility of adding and removing data of any type comes with an overhead. Each time a value type is passed to the Enqueue method and returned by the Dequeue method, the value is implicitly boxed and explicitly unboxed as shown here:

```
Queue q = new Queue();
...
q.Enqueue(23);          // The integer 23 is implicitly boxed.
int i = (int)q.Dequeue(); // The object (23) must be cast back (unboxed)
                          // to an int.
```

These implicit and explicit operations involve both memory allocations and runtime type checks. Although boxing/unboxing operations are not applicable with reference types, the data retrieved must still be explicitly cast back to the proper type as shown here:

```
Queue q = new Queue();
...
q.Enqueue("C#");                 // The string "C#" reference is passed
                                 // (no boxing).
string s = (string)q.Dequeue();  // The object reference ("C#") must be
                                 // cast back to a string (no unboxing).
```

In the previous example, performance is compromised, even though there are no boxing/unboxing operations. In other words, the runtime system must perform type checking on the object that is cast back to ensure that the object retrieved is really of type string as specified by the explicit cast. In any case, there is always a risk that the user of a queue will wrongly cast an object as shown here.

```
q.Enqueue("C#");
...
int i = (int)q.Dequeue();        // Generates an InvalidCastException.
```

Because any type of object can be inserted into a queue, this logical error cannot be picked up at compile-time. Hence, an InvalidCastException is generated at runtime. In the next section, we show how generics provide the capability to define homogeneous collections, in other words, collections that only store items of the same type. Consequently, type verification is done at compile-time and runtime performance is improved.

8.2.1 Defining Generics

Generics are another incarnation of templates or parameterized classes found in other languages, such as C++ and Java 1.5 Tiger. The type parameters are enclosed within angle brackets following the name of the class, interface, delegate, or method. For example, the heterogeneous collection Queue given previously is redeclared as a generic Queue class with a type parameter T as shown here:

```
public class Queue<T> {
    ...
    public void  Enqueue(T n) { ... }
    public T     Dequeue()    { ... }
    ...
}
```

Hence, any instance of Queue, created with a particular type T, may only store objects of type T and, thereby, avoid castings and runtime type checks. As another example, consider the class BoundedQueue, which is dedicated for integer items:

```
    public class BoundedQueue {
        public BoundedQueue(int capacity) {
            items = new int[capacity];
            ...
        }
        public  void  Enqueue(int item) { ... }
        public  int   Dequeue()         { ... }
        ...
        private int[] items;
        private int   head;
        private int   tail;
        private int   capacity;
    }
```

The corresponding generic class for BoundedQueue parameterizes its item type as T:

```
    public class BoundedQueue<T> {
        public BoundedQueue(int capacity) {
            items = new T[capacity];
            ...
        }
        public  void Enqueue(T item) {...}
        public  T    Dequeue()       {...}
        ...
        private T[]  items;
        private int  head;
        private int  tail;
        private int  capacity;
    }
```

8.2.2   Declaring Generic Objects

Using the previous definition of the generic class Queue, an instance for integers and a second instance for strings are instantiated next. In both cases, the respective type, either int or string, is passed as a type argument within angle brackets.

```
BoundedQueue<int>    qi = new BoundedQueue<int>(12);
BoundedQueue<string> qs = new BoundedQueue<string>(15);
```

These queues are now restricted to their own types and compile-time checking is done easily:

```
qi.Enqueue(3);              // OK.
qi.Enqueue(5);              // OK.
qs.Enqueue("Hello");        // OK.
int head = qi.Dequeue();    // OK.
string first = qs.Dequeue(); // OK.
first = qi.Dequeue();       // Compile-time error: type mismatch.
```

When declaring a generic instance, the type parameter(s) can be of any type. However, it may be required on occasion to restrict the type parameter(s) to a specific behavior. For example, a type parameter may need to implement the Clone method defined in the ICloneable interface as shown here:

```
public class MyClass<T, V> {
    public void Process(T obj, V value) {
        ...
        T  t = (T)((System.ICloneable)obj).Clone();
        ...
    }
}
```

In this case, the obj of type T is cast to ICloneable. Unfortunately, the explicit cast incurs the overhead of a runtime type check and failing that, an InvalidCastException is raised when T is not derived from the ICloneable interface. To remove the burden of a runtime check, an optional list of constraints can be placed on the type parameter(s). These type constraints are appended after the keyword where in the header of the class definition.

C# 2.0

```
public class MyClass<T, V> where T : System.ICloneable {
    public void Process(T obj, V value) {
        ...
        T  t = (T)obj.Clone();
        ...
    }
}
```

Hence, it is only required at compile-time to determine if T is derived from the ICloneable interface.

Exercises

Exercise 8-1. Write a generic anonymous delegate and class for the DiscountRule delegate of the class Discount (see Section 7.1.1) in order to instantiate three types: float, double, and decimal.

Exercise 8-2. Write a generic collection to enter and list contacts using SortedDictionary<Key, Value> in the System.Collections.Generic namespace.

Exercise 8-3. Write a DomainObject class that implements the following IUniqueId interface:

```
public interface IUniqueId {
    String  GetId();
}
```

Then complete the implementation of the following abstract class Contact, which inherits from the DomainObject class and the IContact interface, and uses hash tables to store names and addresses.

```
public interface IContact : IUniqueId {
    String  GetName();
    String  GetName(String key);
    void    SetName(String key, String value);
    String  GetAddress(String key);
    void    SetAddress(String key, IAddress value);
}

public abstract class Contact : DomainObject, IContact {
    public Contact()                                          { init(); }
    public Contact(String id) : base(id)                      { init(); }
    protected virtual void Init()                             { ... }
    public String GetName(String key)                         { ... }
    public void    SetName(String key, String value)         { ... }
    public String GetAddress(String key)                      { ... }
    public void    SetAddress(String key, IAddress value) { ... }

    public abstract String  GetName();

    private Hashtable  addresses;
    private Hashtable  names;
}
```

Note that the GetName method stays abstract in order to be defined in subclasses such as Person and Organization.

chapter **9**

Resource Disposal, Input/Output, and Threads

The .NET Framework provides a number of tools that support resource disposal, input/output, and multi-threading. Although the disposal of managed resources is handled automatically by the garbage collector in C#, the disposal of unmanaged resources, such as Internet and database connections, still requires the definition of an explicit destructor as outlined in Chapter 3. In this chapter, we present how a destructor is translated into an equivalent Finalize method and how the implementation of the Dispose method from the IDisposable interface ensures that resources, both managed and unmanaged, are gracefully handled without duplicate effort.

Input/output is a broad topic, and therefore, our discussion is limited to reading/writing binary, byte, and character streams as provided by the System.IO namespace. A short discussion on reading XML documents from streams is also included.

To enable concurrent programming, the C# language supports the notion of lightweight processes or threads. Of principal importance, however, is the synchronization of threads and the disciplined access to critical regions. Based on the primitives in the Monitor class of the .NET Framework, the lock statement provides a serializing mechanism to ensure that only one thread at a time is active in a critical region. It is a challenging topic and, hence, we present several examples to carefully illustrate the various concepts.

9.1 Resource Disposal

In Section 3.1.4, it was pointed out that an object may acquire resources that are unknown to the garbage collector. These resources are considered unmanaged and are not handled by the .NET Framework. Responsibility for the disposal of unmanaged resources, therefore, rests with the object itself and is encapsulated in a destructor as shown here:

```
public class ClassWithResources {
    ~ClassWithResources() {
        // Release resources
    }
    ...
}
```

Although the destructor is typically concerned with the release of unmanaged resources, it may also release (or flag) managed resources by setting object references to null. When a destructor is explicitly defined, it is translated automatically into a virtual Finalize method:

```
public class ClassWithResources {
    virtual void Finalize() {
        try {
            // Release resources
        }
        finally {
            base.Finalize();    // Base class chaining.
        }
    }
    ...
}
```

The finally clause chains back the disposal of resources to the parent object, its parent, and so on until remaining resources are released by the root object.

Because the invocation of the destructor (or Finalize method) is triggered by the garbage collector, its execution cannot be predicted. In order to ensure the release of resources not managed by the garbage collector, the Close or Dispose method, inherited from IDisposable, can be invoked explicitly. The IDisposable interface given here provides a uniform way to explicitly release resources, both managed and unmanaged.

```
interface IDisposable {
    void Dispose();
}
```

Whenever the Dispose method is invoked explicitly, the GC.SuppressFinalize should also be called to inform the garbage collector not to invoke the destructor (or Finalize method) of the object. This avoids the duplicate disposal of managed resources.

To achieve this goal, two Dispose methods are generally required: one with no parameters as inherited from IDisposable and one with a boolean parameter. The following code skeleton presents a typical strategy to dispose both managed and unmanaged resources without duplicate effort.

```
public class ClassWithResources : IDisposable {
    ClassWithResources() {
        // Initialize resources
        disposed = false;
    }

    ~ClassWithResources() { // Translated as Finalize()
        Dispose(false);
    }

    public void Dispose() {
        Dispose(true);
        GC.SuppressFinalize(this);
    }

    protected virtual void Dispose(bool disposeManaged) {
        if (!disposed) {
            if (disposeManaged) {
                // Code to dispose managed resources.
            }
            // Code to dispose unmanaged resources.
            disposed = true;
        }
    }
    ...
    private bool disposed;
}
```

If the Dispose method (without parameters) is not invoked, the destructor calls Dispose(false) via the garbage collector. Only unmanaged resources in this case are released since managed resources are automatically handled by the garbage collector. If the Dispose method is invoked explicitly to release both managed and unmanaged resources, it also advises the garbage collector not to invoke Finalize. Hence, managed resources are not released twice. It is worth noting that the second Dispose method (with the boolean parameter) is protected to allow overriding by the derived classes and to avoid being called directly by clients.

The using statement shown here can also be used as a clean way to automatically release all resources associated with any object that has implemented the Dispose method.

```
using ( anObjectWithResources ) {
    // Use object and its resources.
}
```

In fact, the using statement is shorter but equivalent to the following try/finally block:

```
try {
    // Use object and its resources.
}
finally {
    if ( anObjectWithResources != null ) anObjectWithResources.Dispose();
}
```

The following example shows a common application of the using statement when opening a text file:

```
using ( StreamReader sr = new StreamReader("file.txt") ) {
    ...
}
```

9.2 Input/Output

Thus far, our discussion on input/output has been limited to standard output streams using the System.Console class. In this section, we examine how the .NET Framework defines the functionality of input/output (I/O) via the System.IO namespace. This namespace encapsulates classes that support read/write activities for binary, byte, and character streams. The complete hierarchy of the System.IO namespace is given here:

```
System.Object
    BinaryReader              (Binary I/O Streams)
    BinaryWriter
    MarshallByRefObject
        Stream                (Byte I/O Streams)
            BufferedStream
            FileStream
            MemoryStream
        TextReader            (Character I/O Streams)
        TextWriter
            StreamReader
            StringReader
            StreamWriter
            StringWriter
```

Each type of stream is discussed in the sections that follow.

9.2.1 Using Binary Streams

The binary I/O streams, BinaryReader and BinaryWriter, are most efficient in terms of space but at the price of being system-dependent in terms of data format. These streams read/write simple data types such as byte, sbyte, char, ushort, short, and so on. In the following example, an unsigned integer magicNumber and four unsigned short integers stored in array data are first written to a binary file called file.bin and then read back and output to a console.

```
1   using System.IO;
2
3   namespace BinaryStream {
4       class TestBinaryStream {
5           static void Main() {
6               uint magicNumber = 0xDECAF;
7
8               ushort[] data = { 0x0123, 0x4567, 0x89AB, 0xCDEF };
9
10              FileStream   fs = new FileStream("file.bin", FileMode.Create);
11              BinaryWriter bw = new BinaryWriter(fs);
12
13              bw.Write(magicNumber);
14              foreach (ushort u in data)
15                  bw.Write(u);
16
17              bw.Close();
18
19              fs = new FileStream("file.bin", FileMode.Open);
20              BinaryReader br = new BinaryReader(fs);
21
22              System.Console.WriteLine("{0:X8}", br.ReadUInt32() );
23              for (int n = 0; n < data.Length; n++)
24                  System.Console.WriteLine("{0:X4}", br.ReadUInt16() );
25
26              br.Close();
27          }
28      }
29  }
```

Once the array data is created and initialized on line 8, an instance of FileStream called fs is instantiated on line 10 and logically bound to the physical file file.bin. The FileStream class is actually a subclass of Stream, which is described in the next subsection. Next, an instance of BinaryWriter called bw is created and associated with fs. It is used to write the values from magicNumber and data to file.bin (lines 13–15). After bw is closed, the program reads back the values from fs using an instance of BinaryReader called br, which is created and associated with fs on line 20. The first value is read back as UInt32 (line 22), and the remaining four are read back as UInt16 (lines 23–24). Each time, the integers are output in their original hexadecimal format.

9.2.2 Using Byte Streams

The Stream abstract class given next defines all basic read/write methods in terms of bytes. A stream is opened by creating an instance of a subclass of Stream chained with its protected default constructor. The stream is then closed by explicitly invoking the Close method. This method flushes and releases any associated resources, such as network connections or file handlers, before closing the stream. The Flush method can also be invoked explicitly in order to write all memory buffers to the stream.

```
    abstract class Stream : MarshalByRefObject, IDisposable {
                    Stream();  // Opens the stream.
        virtual  void Close();   // Flushes and releases any resources.
        abstract void Flush();
        abstract int  Read (byte[] buffer, int offset, int count);
        abstract void Write(byte[] buffer, int offset, int count);
        virtual  int  ReadByte();
        virtual  void WriteByte(byte value);

        abstract bool CanRead  {get;} // True if the current stream
                                      // supports reading.
        abstract bool CanSeek  {get;} // True if the current stream
                                      // supports seeking.
        abstract bool CanWrite {get;} // True if the current stream
                                      // supports writing.

        abstract long Length   {get;}    // The length of the stream in bytes.
        abstract long Position {get; set;}// The position within the current
                                          // stream.
        ...
    }
```

The Stream class supports both synchronous and asynchronous reads/writes on the same opened stream. Synchronous I/O means that the main (thread) application is blocked and must wait until the I/O operation is complete in order to return from the read/write method. On the other hand, with asynchronous I/O, the main application can call the sequence BeginRead/EndRead or BeginWrite/EndWrite in such a way that it can keep up with its own work (timeslice).

The Stream class inherits from one class and one interface. The MarshalByRefObject class provides the ability for stream objects to be marshaled by reference. Hence, when an object is transmitted to another application domain (AppDomain), a proxy of that object with the same public interface is automatically created on the remote machine and serves as an intermediary between it and the original object.

The Stream abstract class is the base class for three byte I/O streams: BufferedStream, FileStream, and MemoryStream. The BufferedStream class offers buffered I/O and, hence, reduces the number of disk accesses. The FileStream class binds I/O streams with a specific file. And the MemoryStream class emulates I/O streams from disk or remote connection by allowing direct read/write access in memory. The following example illustrates the use of both BufferedStream and FileStream to read a file as a sequence of bytes until the end of stream is reached:

```
using System.IO;

namespace ByteStream {
    class TestByteStream {
        static void Main() {
            FileStream     fs = new FileStream("ByteStream.cs", FileMode.Open);
            BufferedStream bs = new BufferedStream(fs);

            int c;

            while ( (c = bs.ReadByte()) != -1 )
                System.Console.Write((char)c);

            bs.Close();
        }
    }
}
```

This well-known programming idiom reads a byte within the while loop where it is assigned to an integer c and compared to end-of-stream (-1). Although bytes are read, it is important to store each character into a meta-character c that is larger than 16-bits (Unicode), in our case, an int of 32-bits. If not, the possibility of reading non-printable characters such as 0xFFFF (-1 on a 16-bit signed) from a binary or text file will have the effect of exiting the loop before reaching the end-of-stream.

9.2.3 Using Character Streams

Analogous to the Stream abstract class, the character I/O streams, TextReader and TextWriter, are abstract base classes for reading and writing an array of characters or a string. The concrete classes, StreamReader and StreamWriter, implement TextReader and TextWriter, respectively, in order to read/write characters from/to a byte stream in a particular encoding. Similarly, the concrete classes, StringReader and StringWriter, implement TextReader and TextWriter in order to read/write strings stored in an underlying StringBuilder. The following program copies the text file src to the text file dst using instances of StreamReader and StreamWriter to read from and write to their respective files. In the first version, the copying is done character by character.

```
1    using System.IO;
2
3    namespace CharacterStream {
```

```
4      class Copy {
5          static void Main(string[] args) {
6              if (args.Length != 2) {
7                  System.Console.WriteLine("Usage: cp <src> <dst>");
8                  return;
9              }
10             FileStream   src       = new FileStream(args[0], FileMode.Open);
11             FileStream   dst       = new FileStream(args[1], FileMode.Create);
12             StreamReader srcReader = new StreamReader(src);
13             StreamWriter dstWriter = new StreamWriter(dst);
14
15             for (int c; (c = srcReader.Read()) != -1; )
16                 dstWriter.Write((char)c);
17
18             srcReader.Close();
19             dstWriter.Close();
20         }
21     }
22 }
```

When lines 15 and 16 are replaced with those below, copying from the source to destination files is done line by line.

```
for (string s; (s = srcReader.ReadLine()) != null; )
    dstWriter.WriteLine(s);
```

9.2.4   Reading XML Documents from Streams

As demonstrated in the previous three sections, streams are powerful and flexible pipelines. Although a discussion of XML is well beyond the scope of this book, it is interesting, nonetheless, to briefly illustrate how XML files can be read from different Stream–based sources: files, strings, and so on.

The class XmlTextReader is one class that provides support, such as node-based navigation for reading XML files. In the first example, an instance of FileStream pipes data from the file file.xml on disk to an instance of XmlTextReader:

```
new System.Xml.XmlTextReader( new FileStream("file.xml", FileMode.Open) )
```

In this second example, an instance of StringReader pipes data from the string xml in memory to an instance of XmlTextReader:

```
new System.Xml.XmlTextReader( new StringReader( xml ) )
```

9.3 Threads

Many years ago, operating systems introduced the notion of a process in order to execute multiple programs on the same processor. This gave the user the impression that programs were executing "simultaneously," albeit on a single central processing unit. Each program, represented as a process, was isolated in an individual workspace for protection. Because of these protections, using processes for client/server applications gave rise to two performance issues. First, the context switch to reschedule a process (save the running process and restore the next ready one) was quite slow. And second, I/O activities could force context switches that were simply unacceptable, for example, blocking a process for I/O and preventing the completion of its execution time slice.

Today, all commercial operating systems offer a more efficient solution known as the lightweight process or **thread**. The traditional process now behaves like a small operating system where a thread scheduler selects and appoints threads (of execution) within its own workspace. Although a thread may be blocked for I/O, several other threads within a process can be rescheduled in order to complete the time slice. The average throughput of an application then becomes more efficient. Multi-threaded applications are very useful to service multiple clients and perform multiple simultaneous access to I/O, databases, networks, and so on. In this way, overall performance is improved, but sharing resources still requires mechanisms for synchronization and mutual exclusion. In this section, we present the System.Threading namespace containing all classes needed to achieve multi-threaded or concurrent programming in C# on the .NET Framework.

9.3.1 Examining the Thread Class and Thread States

Each thread is an instance of the System.Threading.Thread class and can be in one of several states defined in the enumeration called ThreadState as shown in Figure 9.1. When created, a thread goes into the Unstarted or ready state. By invoking the Start method, a thread is placed into a ready queue where it is eligible for selection as the next running thread. When a thread begins its execution, it enters into the Running state. When a thread has finished running and ends normally, it moves into the StopRequested state and is later transferred to the Stopped or terminated state when garbage collection has been safely performed. A running thread enters the WaitSleepJoin state if one of three invocations is done: Wait, Sleep, or Join. In each case, the thread resumes execution when the blocking is done. A running thread can also be suspended via a call to the Suspend method. An invocation of Resume places the thread back into the Running state. Finally, a thread may enter into the AbortRequested state and is later transferred to the Aborted or terminated state when garbage collection has been safely performed.

All threads are created with the same priority by the scheduler. If priorities are not modified, all user threads are run in a round-robin fashion. It is possible, however, to change the priority of a thread, but care should be exercised. A higher-priority thread may never relinquish control, and a lower-priority thread may never execute. In C#, there are five possible priorities: Lowest, BelowNormal, Normal, AboveNormal, and Highest. The default priority is Normal.

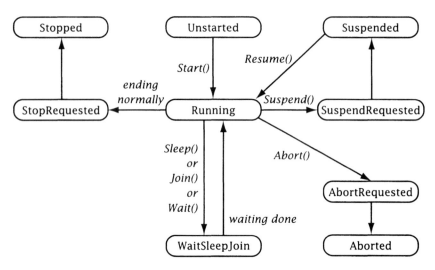

Figure 9.1: Thread states and transitions.

9.3.2   Creating and Starting Threads

Tip A thread executes a code section that is encapsulated within a method. It is good practice to define such a method as private, to name it as void Run() {...}, and to include an infinite loop that periodically or aperiodically sends/receives information to/from other threads. This method is the execution entry point specified as a parameterless delegate called ThreadStart:

```
delegate void ThreadStart();
```

In the following example, the constructor of the class MyThread creates a thread on line 6 using the previous delegate as a parameter, initializes number to the given parameter on line 7, and places the thread in the ready queue on line 8. Two threads, t1 and t2, are instantiated on lines 21 and 22 with 1 and 2 as parameters.

```
1    using System.Threading;
2
3    namespace BasicDotNet {
4        public class MyThread {
5            public MyThread(int number) {
6                t = new Thread(new ThreadStart(this.Run));
7                this.number = number;
8                t.Start();
9            }
10           private void Run() {
11               while (true)
12                   System.Console.Write("{0}", number);
13           }
```

```
14          private Thread   t;
15          private int      number;
16      }
17
18      public class MainThread {
19          public static void Main() {
20              System.Console.WriteLine("Main Started.");
21              MyThread t1 = new MyThread(1);
22              MyThread t2 = new MyThread(2);
23              System.Console.WriteLine("Main: done.");
24          }
25      }
26  }
```

Each thread prints its own number until its timeslice expires. Upon expiration, the sched-uler picks the next ready thread for execution. Notice that the MainThread ends normally after starting both threads t1 and t2 as shown in the following output:

```
Main Started.
Main: done.
11111111111111111111111111111111111111111111111111111111111111111111111111
11111111111111111111111111111122222222222222222222222222222222222222222222
22222222222222222222222222222222222222222222222222222222222222222222222222
22222222222222222222222222222221111111111111111111111111111111111111111111
11111111111111111111111111111111111111111111111111111111111111111111111111
11111111111111111111111111111122222222222222222222222222222222222222222222
222222222222222222222222222222222222222222222222222222222222222222222...
```

On line 6, a delegate inference may also be used to assign the method name this.Run to the Thread constructor as follows:

```
t = new Thread(this.Run);
```

In this case, the explicit creation of a ThreadStart delegate is avoided.

9.3.3 Rescheduling and Pausing Threads

The Thread.Sleep method pauses the current thread for a specified time in milliseconds. If the time is zero (0), then the current thread simply relinquishes control to the scheduler and is immediately placed in the ready queue, allowing other waiting threads to run. For example, if the following Run method is used within the MyThread class, the values 1 and 2 are alternatively output as each thread is immediately paused after writing its number:

```
private void Run() {
    while (true) {
        Thread.Sleep(0);
```

```
                    System.Console.Write("{0}", number);
                }
        }
```

Output:

```
Main Started.
Main: done.
1212121212121212121...
```

In another example, each thread is paused for a length of time proportional to its own thread number, one and two seconds, respectively. Hence, the thread with number equal to 1 is able to print on average twice the number of values as the thread with number equal to 2.

```
        private void Run() {
            while (true) {
                Thread.Sleep(number * 1000);
                System.Console.Write("{0}", number);
            }
        }
```

Output:

```
Main Started.
Main: done.
12112112112112112111...
```

9.3.4   Suspending, Resuming, and Stopping Threads

In the following example, the Main thread creates two threads, t1 and t2, on lines 35 and 36. Note that both threads are started within the constructor of MyThread. When not suspended or stopped, the threads run for a timeslice of 10 seconds while the Main thread sleeps. During the first timeslice on line 38, both threads print their respective numbers. When the Main thread awakens, it immediately suspends t1 (line 39) and puts itself to sleep once again for ten seconds (line 40). In the meantime, the second thread t2 continues to print out its number every two seconds. When the Main thread awakens for the second time, thread t1 is resumed and both threads execute for a timeslice of another ten seconds. Finally, thread t1 is stopped on line 43 and ten seconds later, thread t2 is stopped on line 45 before the Main thread ends itself normally.

```
1    using System.Threading;
2
3    namespace BasicDotNet {
```

```
4    public class MyThread {
5        public MyThread(int number) {
6            t = new Thread(Run);
7            this.number = number;
8            t.Start();
9        }
10       private void Run() {
11           while (true) {
12               Thread.Sleep(number * 1000);
13               System.Console.Write("{0}", number);
14           }
15       }
16       public void Suspend() {
17           System.Console.WriteLine("\nThread {0} suspended", number);
18           t.Suspend();
19       }
20       public void Resume() {
21           System.Console.WriteLine("\nThread {0} resumed", number);
22           t.Resume();
23       }
24       public void Stop() {
25           System.Console.WriteLine("\nThread {0} stopped", number);
26           t.Abort();
27       }
28       private Thread  t;
29       private int     number;
30   }
31
32   public class MainThread {
33       public static void Main() {
34           System.Console.WriteLine("Main Started.");
35           MyThread t1 = new MyThread(1);
36           MyThread t2 = new MyThread(2);
37
38           Thread.Sleep(10 * 1000);
39           t1.Suspend();
40           Thread.Sleep(10 * 1000);
41           t1.Resume();
42           Thread.Sleep(10 * 1000);
43           t1.Stop();
44           Thread.Sleep(10 * 1000);
45           t2.Stop();
46
47           System.Console.WriteLine("Main: done.");
```

```
48          }
49       }
50   }
```

Output:

```
Main Started.
1211211211211
Thread 1 suspended
22222
Thread 1 resumed
121121121121121
Thread 1 stopped
22222
Thread 2 stopped
Main: done.
```

It is worth noting that when a thread is aborted, the runtime system throws a ThreadAbortException that cannot be caught. However, it does execute all finally blocks before the thread terminates. Also, an exception is thrown if a Suspend invocation is made on a thread that is already suspended or if a Resume invocation is made on a thread that is not suspended. Because code that uses the Suspend and Resume methods is deadlock-prone, both methods have been deprecated (made obsolete) in the latest version of the .NET Framework.

9.3.5   Joining and Determining Alive Threads

A thread is **alive** once it is moved from the Unstarted state and has yet to be aborted or terminated normally. If a thread is alive, then the method IsAlive returns true. Otherwise, it returns false. A thread may also block itself until another thread has terminated. Hence, the thread that invokes the method <specifiedThread>.Join waits until the specified thread ends its execution. The overloaded Join method may also be invoked with a TimeSpan parameter that sets the maximum time delay for the specified thread to terminate. Finally, if the specified thread has not been started, then a ThreadStateException is thrown.

In the following example, the Main thread spawns two other threads, t1 and t2, on lines 11 and 12. In addition, the current thread (in this case Main) is assigned to me on line 13 using the read-only property CurrentThread. On lines 14 to 19, the status of the three threads, either alive or unstarted, is output based on the return value of IsAlive. The main thread then starts t1 and t2 on lines 20 and 21, making them alive to print their respective numbers 1 and 2. Thereafter, the main thread waits on t1 and t2 by invoking the Join method with the appropriate thread on lines 27 and 32, respectively. To verify that threads t1 and t2 are indeed terminated, an output message is generated on lines 29 and 34.

```
1    using System.Threading;
2
3    namespace BasicDotNet {
4        public class MainThread {
5            private static void One() { System.Console.WriteLine("1");
6                                        Thread.Sleep(1000); }
7            private static void Two() { System.Console.WriteLine("2");
8                                        Thread.Sleep(2000); }
9
10           public static void Main() {
11               Thread  t1 = new Thread(One);
12               Thread  t2 = new Thread(Two);
13               Thread  me = Thread.CurrentThread;
14               System.Console.WriteLine("Main [{0}].", me.IsAlive ? "Alive" :
15                                        "Unstarted");
16               System.Console.WriteLine("One  [{0}].", t1.IsAlive ? "Alive" :
17                                        "Unstarted");
18               System.Console.WriteLine("Two  [{0}].", t2.IsAlive ? "Alive" :
19                                        "Unstarted");
20               t1.Start();
21               t2.Start();
22               System.Console.WriteLine("One  [{0}].", t1.IsAlive ? "Alive" :
23                                        "Unstarted");
24               System.Console.WriteLine("Two  [{0}].", t2.IsAlive ? "Alive" :
25                                        "Unstarted");
26
27               t1.Join();
28               System.Console.WriteLine("One joined.");
29               System.Console.WriteLine("One  [{0}].", t1.IsAlive ? "Alive" :
30                                        "Ended");
31
32               t2.Join();
33               System.Console.WriteLine("Two joined.");
34               System.Console.WriteLine("Two  [{0}].", t2.IsAlive ? "Alive" :
35                                        "Ended");
36               System.Console.WriteLine("Main ending...");
37           }
38       }
39   }
```

Output:

```
Main [Alive].
One  [Unstarted].
Two  [Unstarted].
```

```
One   [Alive].
Two   [Alive].
1
2
One joined.
One   [Ended].
Two joined.
Two   [Ended].
Main ending...
```

9.3.6 Synchronizing Threads

In order to allow multiple threads to access a shared resource or **critical section** in a safe and predictable way, some synchronization mechanism is required. Otherwise, access is chaotic. Such synchronization is achieved by serializing threads and thereby ensuring that only one thread at a time is able to execute within a critical section. In C#, the mechanism to ensure mutual exclusion to a critical section is based on the notion of **locks**.

Using the lock Statement

A lock statement in C# is associated with any class or object, including this. A thread that wishes to enter a critical section is first placed in a ready queue associated with the lock (not to be confused with the ready queue of the threading system). Once a lock becomes available, a thread is chosen from the ready queue to acquire the lock and enter the critical section that it wishes to execute. Upon completion of the critical section, the thread releases the lock, enabling another thread from the ready queue to obtain the lock and enter a critical section associated with the lock. Until the critical section is exited and the lock is released, no other thread may access the critical section of the object or class. The syntax of the lock statement is shown here. In this example, a lock is associated with an object called obj.

```
lock ( obj ) {        // Acquire (an object) lock and enter critical section.
    ...               // Execute critical section.
}                     // Exit critical section and release the (object) lock.
```

Any thread that is currently executing the critical section prevents other threads from entering any code section protected by lock(obj) for the same object obj. In another example, a lock is associated with a class called C.

```
lock ( typeof(C) ) {  // Refer to the meta-class of C and lock its class.
    ...               // Execute critical section.
}
```

Here, any thread that is currently executing the critical section prevents other threads from entering any code section protected by lock(typeof(C)) for the same class C. The following example illustrates the use of the System.Type object of the SharedFunctions class as the lock for the Add and Remove static methods here:

```
class SharedFunctions {
    public static void Add(object x) {
        lock ( typeof(SharedFunctions) ) {
            // Critical section
        }
    }
    public static void Remove(object x) {
        lock ( typeof(SharedFunctions) ) {
            // Critical section
        }
    }
}
```

It is good programming practice to only lock private or internal objects and classes. $\boxed{\text{Tip}}$
Because external threads have no access to private or internal lock objects or classes,
the possibility of external threads creating deadlocks is precluded.

Once inside a critical section, a thread may block itself. In this case, the thread is
placed in a waiting queue and releases the lock. The waiting queue, like the ready queue,
is associated with the lock. The thread remains in the waiting queue until another thread,
currently executing in the critical section, signals to one or more threads in the waiting
queue to move back to the ready queue. Once a thread is moved back to the ready queue, it
is eligible to re-acquire the lock on the critical section. However, once acquired, the execution of the thread within the critical section recommences at the point where it originally
blocked itself.

Using the Monitor Class
The implementation of the lock statement in C# is based on the synchronization primitives
defined here in the Monitor class of the .NET Framework.

```
public sealed class Monitor {
    public static void Enter(object);
    public static void Exit(object);
    public static void Pulse(object);
    public static void PulseAll(object);
    public static bool TryEnter(object);
    public static bool TryEnter(object, int);
    public static bool TryEnter(object, TimeSpan);
    public static bool Wait(object);
    ...
}
```

All methods in the Monitor class are static. Also, because the class Monitor is sealed, no other class is able to derive from it. The methods Enter and Exit acquire and release an exclusive lock on a specific object or class. These methods are used for surrounding a critical section in order to achieve thread synchronization. A thread that invokes Enter remains in the ready queue (waits) if another thread currently holds the lock to the critical section it wishes to enter. Otherwise, it is able to obtain the lock and continue execution within the critical section. An invocation of Exit, on the other hand, releases the lock, enabling another thread (if any) from the ready queue to acquire the lock and enter a critical section associated with the lock. The lock statement, therefore, is equivalent to the following statements:

```
Monitor.Enter( obj );
try {
    // Critical section
} finally {
    Monitor.Exit( obj );
}
```

If a thread wishes to "peek" at a critical section and avoid being blocked, it can invoke the method TryEnter that returns false if the critical section is busy. The two additional TryEnter methods wait for a maximum of int milliseconds or a specific TimeSpan to acquire the lock on the given object.

The Wait method invoked by a thread *within* a critical section releases the lock of the critical section, blocks the calling thread and places it on the waiting queue, and enables another thread to enter a critical section associated with the lock. Conversely, when a thread invokes the Pulse or PulseAll method *within* a critical section, one or all threads who were previously blocked using the Wait method on the same object are moved from the waiting queue back to the ready queue. It is important to emphasize once again that once a thread re-acquires a lock and re-enters a critical section, its execution recommences at the point where it originally blocked itself.

As an example of synchronization, consider a multiplexer that combines two serial data streams into a single parallel output stream as shown in Figure 9.2. If characters arrive at either serial input port, maximum throughput is achieved when the application

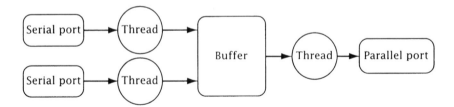

Figure 9.2: Thread synchronization in accessing a buffer.

is able to process input from both serial ports simultaneously and to provide output to the parallel port. A multi-threaded application of the multiplexer uses three threads and is implemented as follows.

```
1   using System;
2   using System.Threading;
3
4   class Buffer {
5       private readonly int Max;
6
7       public Buffer(int max) {
8           Max = max;
9           head = tail = count = 0;
10          buffer = new char[Max];
11          full = false;
12          empty = true;
13      }
14      public void put(char c) {
15          lock (this) {      // Critical section access to buffer using lock.
16              while (full) Monitor.Wait(this);  // Blocks if buffer full.
17
18              buffer[tail] = c;
19              if (++count == Max) full = true;
20              empty = false;
21              tail = (tail + 1) % Max;
22              Monitor.Pulse(this);               // Notifies the parallel port.
23          }
24      }
25      public char get() {
26          char c;
27       // lock (this) {
28          Monitor.Enter(this); // Critical section access to buffer using Monitor.
29          try {
30              while (empty) Monitor.Wait(this); // Blocks if buffer empty.
31
32              c = buffer[head];
33              if (--count == 0) empty = true;
34              full = false;
35              head = (head + 1) % Max;
36              Monitor.PulseAll(this);            // Notifies all serial ports.
37          } finally {
38              Monitor.Exit(this);
39          }
```

```
40          // }
41              return c;
42          }
43      private char[] buffer;
44      private bool    full, empty;
45      private int     head, tail, count;
46  }
47
48  class SerialPortThread {
49      public SerialPortThread(Buffer buffer, int num) {
50          this.buffer = buffer;
51          this.num = num;
52      }
53      private static char inputFromSerial() {
54          Thread.Sleep(500); // Waits 0.5 sec (to emulate communication latency).
55          return c++;
56      }
57      public void run() {
58          while (true) {
59              char c = inputFromSerial();
60              Console.WriteLine("sp{0}  {1}", num, c);
61              buffer.put(c);
62          }
63      }
64      private static char   c = 'a'; // Shared by all serial ports.
65      private         int     num;
66      private         Buffer  buffer;
67  }
68
69  class ParallelPortThread {
70      public ParallelPortThread(Buffer buffer) {
71          this.buffer = buffer;
72      }
73      public void run() {
74          while (true) {
75              char c = buffer.get();
76              Console.WriteLine("          pp  {0}", c);
77              Thread.Sleep(100); // Waits 0.1 sec (to emulate printing latency).
78          }
79      }
80      private Buffer  buffer;
81  }
82
83  class Multiplexer {
```

```
84      public static void Main() {                    // Main thread entry.
85          Buffer          buf = new Buffer(4);
86          SerialPortThread    sp1 = new SerialPortThread(buf, 1);
87          SerialPortThread    sp2 = new SerialPortThread(buf, 2);
88          ParallelPortThread pp  = new ParallelPortThread(buf);
89
90          // Creates all threads passing on their run entry points.
91          Thread s1 = new Thread(new ThreadStart(sp1.run));
92          Thread s2 = new Thread(new ThreadStart(sp2.run));
93          Thread p  = new Thread(new ThreadStart(pp.run));
94
95          Console.WriteLine("    in      out");
96
97          s1.Start();    // Starts first serial port.
98          s2.Start();    // Starts second serial port.
99          p.Start();     // Starts parallel port.
100     }
101 }
```

On line 85, a buffer buf of size four is instantiated. Two serial ports, sp1 and sp2, and one parallel port, pp, are instantiated on lines 86–88 with a reference to the same buffer buf. Three threads, created on lines 91–93 with their corresponding run entry points, begin execution on lines 97–99. Although the main thread completes execution, the three threads continue to run "forever."

In the SerialPortThread class, the run method entry point contains an infinite loop (lines 58–62) that inputs a character from a serial port and places it in the shared buffer. On the other hand, in the ParallelPortThread class, the run method entry also contains an infinite loop (lines 74–78) that reads from the shared buffer and prints the character that is read.

To synchronize access to the shared buffer, the methods put and get must contain critical sections. When the parallel port thread attempts to get a character, verification on line 30 checks if the buffer is empty. If so, the thread is blocked until one of the two serial threads puts a character in the shared buffer. Conversely, when a serial port thread attempts to put a character into the shared buffer, verification on line 16 checks if the buffer is full. If so, the thread is blocked until the parallel thread gets a character from the shared buffer. A serial port notifies the parallel port on line 22 using the Pulse method that the buffer is no longer empty, whereas the parallel port on line 36 uses the PulseAll method to inform all serial ports that the buffer is no longer full. It is worth noting that the lock mechanism for the put method uses the lock statement, and that the lock mechanism for the get method defines the equivalent lock using the methods of Monitor. The following sample output illustrates that no characters are lost and that all threads are well synchronized without concern for their relative speed or starting order.

```
        in       out
sp1    a
               pp   a
sp2    b
               pp   b
sp1    c
sp2    d
               pp   c
               pp   d
sp1    e
               pp   e
sp2    f
sp1    g
               pp   f
               pp   g
sp2    h
               pp   h
sp1    i
               pp   i
...
```

In the .NET Framework, most collection classes are not thread safe by default. They can become thread safe by implementing a synchronized method or by using the lock statement (or Monitor methods) via the SyncRoot property.

As a final note, the .NET Framework System.Threading namespace provides a class called ThreadPool that facilitates the handling of multiple threads often used in socket connections, wait operations from ports or I/O, and so on. This class allows one to create, start, and manage many individual concurrent activities without having to set properties for each thread. Another useful class in this namespace is the Timer class that periodically executes a method at specified intervals on a separate thread. A thread timer may be used to signal back-ups for files and databases.

Exercises

Exercise 9-1. The previous object-oriented version of the Unix word count wc utility supports standard input only. Improve this utility by allowing a developer to count from optional specified files as shown here:

```
WcCommandLine = "wc" Options? Files? .
```

Exercise 9-2. Write a class TestContact that contains a method LoadFile that loads and creates contact objects from a text file using a try/catch/finally block. The text file is formatted as follows:

```
de Champlain;Michel;mdec@DeepObjectKnowledge.com
Patrick;Brian;bpatrick@trentu.ca
```

Hint: Reuse the class StringTokenizer suggested in Exercise 4-2.

Exercise 9-3.   The singleton implementation on pages 33–34 is not thread safe. Write one that is thread safe.

Exercise 9-4.   In order to complete a TUI to enter organizations, use the following abstract class as a foundation to implement an application called eOrg.exe:

```
namespace eCard.Presentation.TUI {
    public abstract class AbstractShell {
        public AbstractShell(string version, string copyright) {
            this.version = version;
            this.copyright = copyright;

            // Display the application's banner
            About();
        }
        protected virtual string Version   { get { return version; } }
        protected virtual string Copyright { get { return copyright; } }
        protected virtual void   About() {
            Console.WriteLine("\n"+Version+"\nCopyright (c)"+Copyright+"\n");
        }
        protected abstract void  New();
        protected abstract void  Edit();
        protected abstract void  Delete();
        public    abstract void  Run(string[] args);

        private string    version;
        private string    copyright;
    }
}
```

This application loads organizations from an orgs.org file and allows a user to enter, edit, and remove them, as shown in the following sample execution:

```
eOrg v1.0

Loading organizations...
0 organizations loaded.

N)ew  E)dit  D)elete  L)ist  S)ave As..  Q)uit and save   Enter your choice: N
```

```
      Name: DeepObjectKnowledge Inc.
DomainName: DeepObjectKnowledge.com

 1) First.Last  2) Last.First  3) F.Last      4) Last.F       5) F+Last
 6) Last+F       7) F.L         8) L.F          9) F+L         10) L+F
11) First+Last 12) Last+First 13) F_L          14) L_F         15) F_Last
16) Last_F      17) First_Last 18) Last_First 19) Other.
EmailFormat: 19


N)ew  E)dit  D)elete  L)ist  S)ave As..  Q)uit and save    Enter your choice: L

No   Domain                     Name                      EmailFormat

1    DeepObjectKnowledge.com  DeepObjectKnowledge Inc.    Other.

N)ew  E)dit  D)elete  L)ist  S)ave As..  Q)uit and save    Enter your choice: N

       Name: University of Trent
Domain Name: trentu.ca

 1) First.Last  2) Last.First  3) F.Last      4) Last.F       5) F+Last
 6) Last+F       7) F.L         8) L.F          9) F+L         10) L+F
11) First+Last 12) Last+First 13) F_L          14) L_F         15) F_Last
16) Last_F      17) First_Last 18) Last_First 19) Other.
EmailFormat: 5

N)ew  E)dit  D)elete  L)ist  S)ave As..  Q)uit and save    Enter your choice: E
No: 2
       Name: University of Trent
 DomainName: trentu.ca
EmailFormat: F+Last

N)ame  D)omainName  E)mailFormat  O)K    Enter your choice: N

Name: Trent University

       Name: Trent University
 DomainName: trentu.ca
EmailFormat: F+Last

N)ame  D)omainName  E)mailFormat  O)K    Enter your choice: O

N)ew  E)dit  D)elete  L)ist  S)ave As..  Q)uit and save    Enter your choice: L
```

```
No  Domain                     Name                      EmailFormat

1   DeepObjectKnowledge.com    DeepObjectKnowledge Inc.  Other.
2   trentu.ca                  Trent University          F+Last

N)ew  E)dit  D)elete  L)ist  S)ave As..  Q)uit and save   Enter your choice: Q

Saving 2 organizations in 'orgs.org'
```

Hint: Reuse the classes StringTokenizer (from Exercise 4-2), EmailFormat (from Exercise 6-2), and Input (from Exercise 6-4). Backups can be done using the "Save As..." option.

chapter **10**

Reflection and Attributes

Applications in older programming languages provided little data about themselves other than lines of code, required memory, and other basic tidbits of information. But as software applications become more complex and rely more heavily on growing libraries of reusable code, there is an increasing burden on software management. The extraction of information about an application is called reflection and makes extensive use of metadata that is gathered from the compilation process.

Attributes are one type of metadata and are used to annotate code. These attributes may be pre- or user-defined and help guide the developer toward those modules or classes that satisfy certain requirements. Reflection, in this sense, is analogous to searching on keywords except that attributes are derived classes and are replete with their own methods. Certain attributes, such as Obsolete, inform developers when code is replaced and must be updated. It is an issue of vital importance when applications rely on different versions of code in order to compile and execute correctly. In this chapter, we introduce the process of reflection and the creation and use of metadata using attributes.

10.1 Reflection

Reflection is the ability to look into and access information or **metadata** about an application itself. Applications such as debuggers, builders, and integrated development environments that extract and rely on this information are called **meta-applications**. For example, the *IntelliSense* feature of Visual Studio .NET presents to the user a list of available public members whenever a dot (.) is typed after a class name or an object reference.

In the .NET Framework, reflection or meta-programming is supported by the System.Reflection namespace. In the sections that follow, we examine the reflection

211

hierarchy and describe how metadata about assemblies, modules, classes, and members is defined and accessed.

10.1.1   Examining the Reflection Hierarchy

As mentioned early on in Chapter 1, an assembly is the logical unit of deployment in .NET applications, where an assembly is either an application (.exe) or a library (.dll). Not surprisingly, the reflection hierarchy of C# is anchored at the assembly, as shown here:

```
Object
    Assembly
    Module
    MemberInfo
        Type
        EventInfo
        PropertyInfo
        FieldInfo
        MethodBase
            ConstructorInfo
            MethodInfo
```

The Assembly class encapsulates a manifest of one or more modules and an optional set of resources. The Module class represents a .dll or .exe file, where each file contains one or more Types in possibly different namespaces. Types include interfaces, classes, delegates, and so on. The two classes, MemberInfo and MethodBase, are abstract and define common members for their derived concrete classes Type, EventInfo, PropertyInfo, FieldInfo, ConstructorInfo, and MethodInfo. Covering all methods available in these classes, however, is beyond the scope of this book, but a representative sample is presented in the sections that follow.

10.1.2   Accessing Assemblies

All information concerning assemblies, modules, and types are described as metadata and are mainly generated by the compiler. To retrieve this information at runtime, objects of type Assembly, Module, or Type, to name a few from the hierarchy, are created and assigned a meta-class object that contains information about the assembly, module, or type, respectively. For example, the meta-class object of System.Int32 can be retrieved via the GetType method of Type using the class name as a parameter:

```
Type t = Type.GetType("System.Int32");
```

The same meta-class object can also be retrieved using an instance of int, in this case i, to invoke GetType:

```
int  i = 6;
Type t = i.GetType();
```

At the top level, accessing information in a reflective application interrogates an assembly and retrieves information about its modules via a GetModules method. In turn, information about all types within a module is available via the GetTypes method. As shown previously, the GetType method retrieves the meta-object for a single type. Finally, information on the constructors, methods, fields, events, properties, and nested types of each type are extracted using the methods GetConstructors, GetMethods, GetFields, GetEvents, GetProperties, and GetNestedTypes, respectively. In the first example that follows, information (or metadata) on the object, bool, and ClassAndMembers types is extracted and output:

```
using System;
using System.Reflection;

namespace TestReflection {
    public class ClassAndMembers {
        public static void Print(Type t) {
            Console.WriteLine("\n{0}", t);

            MemberInfo[] members = t.GetMembers();

            foreach(MemberInfo m in members)
                Console.WriteLine("\t{0,-11}  {1,-11}", m.MemberType, m.Name);
        }
        public static void Main() {
            Print(typeof(object));
            Print(typeof(bool));
            Print(typeof(ClassAndMembers));
        }
    }
}
```

Output:

```
System.Object
    Method       GetType
    Method       ToString
    Method       Equals
    Method       Equals
    Method       ReferenceEquals
    Method       GetHashCode
    Constructor  .ctor

System.Boolean
    Method       GetHashCode
    Method       ToString
```

```
Method       ToString
Method       Equals
Method       Equals
Method       CompareTo
Method       CompareTo
Method       Parse
Method       TryParse
Method       GetTypeCode
Method       GetType
Field        TrueString
Field        FalseString

TestReflection.ClassAndMembers
Method       Print
Method       Main
Method       GetType
Method       ToString
Method       Equals
Method       GetHashCode
Constructor  .ctor
```

In the second example, information on various classes, interfaces, and structures is extracted using a number of Boolean methods of the System.Type class.

```csharp
using System;
using System.Reflection;

interface      MyInterface { }
abstract class MyAbstractClass { }
public class   MyBaseClass { }
sealed class   MyDerivedClass : MyBaseClass { }
struct         MyStruct { }

class TypesInfo {
    private const string FORMAT =
        "{0,-16} {1,-8} {2,-5} {3,-9} {4,-9} {5,-6} {6,-6} {7,-9}";
    public static void GetTypeInfo(string typeName) {
        Type t = Type.GetType(typeName);

        Console.WriteLine(
            String.Format(FORMAT, t.FullName,    t.IsAbstract, t.IsClass,
                                  t.IsInterface, t.IsPrimitive, t.IsPublic,
                                  t.IsSealed, t.IsValueType)
        );
    }
```

```
public static void Main() {
    Console.WriteLine(String.Format(FORMAT+"\n", "Type", "Abstract",
                                    "Class", "Interface", "Primitive",
                                    "Public", "Sealed", "ValueType")
    );
    GetTypeInfo("System.Int32");
    GetTypeInfo("System.Type");
    GetTypeInfo("MyInterface");
    GetTypeInfo("MyAbstractClass");
    GetTypeInfo("MyBaseClass");
    GetTypeInfo("MyDerivedClass");
    GetTypeInfo("MyStruct");
}
}
```

Output:

Type	Abstract	Class	Interface	Primitive	Public	Sealed	ValueType
System.Int32	False	False	False	True	True	True	True
System.Type	True	True	False	False	True	False	False
MyInterface	True	False	True	False	False	False	False
MyAbstractClass	True	True	False	False	False	False	False
MyBaseClass	False	True	False	False	True	False	False
MyDerivedClass	False	True	False	False	False	True	False
MyStruct	False	False	False	False	False	True	True

10.2 Attributes

An **attribute** is an annotation that can be applied to global targets, including assemblies or .NET modules as well as other targets including classes, methods, fields, parameters, properties, return types, and events. It is a way to extend the metadata stored in an assembly or module with user-defined custom metadata. Each attribute, therefore, tells the compiler to gather metadata about a particular target at compile-time. This metadata can be later retrieved at runtime by an application via reflection. An attribute specifies an optional global target, either an executable assembly or a .NET module, followed by optional input arguments, all within square brackets. The EBNF definition is given here:

EBNF

```
Attributes       = AttributeSections .
AttributeSection = "[" AttributeTargetSpecifier? AttributeList ", "? "]" .
AttributeTargetSpecifier = AttributeTarget ":" .
Attribute               = AttributeName AttributeArguments? .
```

```
AttributeArguments        = ( "(" PositionalArgumentList? ")" )
                          | ( "(" PositionalArgumentList   ","
                                  NamedArgumentList ")" )
                          | ( "("  NamedArgumentList    ")" ) .
```

Each attribute is implicitly defined by a class that inherits from the abstract class `Attribute` under the `System` namespace. The suffix `Attribute` is typically added by convention to all derived classes. For example, a class `Portable` that is compliant with the CLS in an application can be specified as follows:

```
using System.Attribute;

[CLSCompliant]              // or [CLSCompliantAttribute]
public class Portable { ... }
```

where the `CLSCompliant` attribute is predefined in the `System.Attribute` namespace as:

```
public sealed class CLSCompliantAttribute : Attribute { ... }
```

There are many predefined attribute classes in the .NET Framework, but three attributes are particularly useful for developers: Serializable, Conditional, and Obsolete. These three attributes are covered in greater detail in the following three subsections.

10.2.1   Using Attributes for Exception Serialization

Serialization is the process of storing the state of an object to a storage medium in order to make it transportable from one machine to another. Serialization is therefore useful for data storage and for passing objects across application domains. To meet this objective, the state of an object represented by its class name, its public and private fields, and its assembly is converted to a stream of bytes.

Tip

The attribute [Serializable] is used to make objects serializable. For example, it is important to serialize all exception classes so that exceptions may be sent across different machines. The following user-defined class exception enables serialization by adding the [Serializable] attribute to the class as shown here:

```
using System;
using System.Runtime.Serialization;

[Serializable]
public class UserException: Exception, ISerializable {

    // Three basic constructors.
    public UserException() {}
    public UserException(string msg) : base(msg) {}
    public UserException(string msg, Exception inner) : base(msg, inner) {}
```

```
       // Deserialization constructor.
       public UserException(SerializationInfo info,
                            StreamingContext  context) : base(info, context){}
   }
```

This exception class implements the ISerializable interface, the three basic constructors already discussed in Section 6.4, and a deserialization constructor to create an object from previously serialized data.

10.2.2 Using Attributes for Conditional Compilation

In C/C++, developers use assertions as preconditions in order to control conditional compilation:

```
   void Require(bool expr) { ... }

   void Fct(int n) {
   #if PRECONDITION
       Require(n > 0);
   #endif
       ...
   }
```

Although C/C++ preprocessing directives are supported in C#, similar control in C# can also be achieved with the aid of attributes. In order to do so, the System.Diagnostics namespace must be imported (line 1). The equivalent C# version of the C/C++ program above is given below where the attribute Conditional has a single argument called "PRECONDITION" on line 4:

```
1    using System.Diagnostics;
2
3    public class TestConditional {
4        [Conditional("PRECONDITION")]
5        public static void Require(bool expr) { ... }
6
7        public static void Fct(int n) {
8            Require(n > 0);
9            ...
10       }
11   }
```

The conditional attribute works differently than conditional compilation via #if/#endif. A method adorned with this attribute is always compiled into the assembly. The conditional attribute is used by the C# compiler to eliminate call sites to that method if the associated conditional is defined. For example, by compiling the previous class with or without /define:PRECONDITION, the code for the static method Require on line 5 is always generated by the compiler. However, without the /define:PRECONDITION, the call to Require on line 8 is removed.

10.2.3 Using Attributes for Obsolete Code

Suppose now that the Abs method has been improved and renamed as Absolute. To tell developers to use Absolute instead of Abs, the attribute Obsolete provides a warning when an older version of a member, in this case a method, is used. An informative message promoting the use of the newer method is generated at compile-time.

```
using System;

public class Math {
    [Obsolete ("Use Math.Absolute() instead.")]
    public static int Abs(int n) { return (n < 0) ? -n : n; }
}
```

Therefore, upon compiling TestAbs and AbsObsolete as shown here:

```
csc TestAbs.cs AbsObsolete.cs
```

the following warning message is generated:

```
TestAbs.cs(3,51): warning CS0612: 'Math.Abs(int)' is obsolete:
'Use Math.Absolute() instead.'
```

Even with a warning, an executable is still generated. However, after some period of time, developers may wish to force their users to update their code by replacing an older version of a class member with a newer one, for example, replacing Abs with Absolute. By adding a true parameter to the Obsolete attribute, an error message instead of a warning message is generated. Since the default value of the second parameter is false, only a warning message is generated when the parameter is omitted as shown here. However, unlike a warning, no executable is generated if the second parameter of Obsolete is true and obsolete code, such as Abs, remains part of the application.

```
using System;

public class Math {
    [Obsolete ("Use Math.Absolute() instead.", true)]
    public static int Abs(int n) { return (n < 0) ? -n : n; }
}
```

Hence, the compilation of the previous code using Abs generates the following error message:

```
TestAbs.cs(3,51): error CS0619: 'Math.Abs(int)' is obsolete:
'Use Math.Absolute() instead.'
```

10.2.4 Defining User-Defined Attributes

When a class library or framework contains hundreds if not thousands of classes, it is very useful to "tag" classes with user-defined attributes. These tags are then used to later search for those classes that satisfy specific attributes. As mentioned earlier, an attribute class derives from System.Attribute with an optional Attribute suffix to its name. The context of the new attribute is specified by AttributeUsage using System.AttributeTargets. The latter is an enumeration that provides all possible targets, such as module, class, method, and so on. For example, if invariant (protected) methods that check the bounds of private fields have been implemented for many critical classes of an application, it is convenient to define a invariant attribute that tags these specific methods as targets using AttributeTargets.Method as shown here:

```
using System.Attribute;

[AttributeUsage(AttributeTargets.Method)]
public class InvariantAttribute : Attribute {
    public InvariantAttribute() {}
}
```

This new attribute can now be used to tag methods in the following manner:

```
using System.Attribute;

public class Critical {
    ...
    [Invariant]
    protected void InvariantMethod() { ... }
}
```

If an invariant method has been or will be tested by a quality assurance team, adding a Test enum parameter to the Attributes namespace is helpful. The following modification includes both a default constructor that initializes status to NotDone, and a second constructor that initializes status, defined as a Status property, to a Test parameter.

```
using System;

namespace Attributes {
    public enum Test { NotDone, Failed, InProgress, Passed }

    [AttributeUsage(AttributeTargets.Method)]
    public class InvariantAttribute : Attribute {
        public InvariantAttribute() {
            status = Test.NotDone;
        }
        public InvariantAttribute(Test status) {
            Status = status;
        }
        public Test Status {
            get { return status; }
```

```
            set { status = value; }
        }
        private Test status;
    }
}
```

10.2.5   Using User-Defined Attributes

Assuming that the previous user-defined attribute Invariant is in the file Attributes.cs, the component Attributes.dll is generated as follows:

```
    csc /t:library Attributes.cs
```

To use the Invariant attribute within an application, the Attributes component must be imported as shown next. In this case, four classes (A, B, C, and D) are encapsulated in MyNamespace and stored in a file called UsingAttributes.cs. Each class, except D, is preceded by an invariant attribute that denotes its current testing status.

```
using System;
using System.Reflection;
using Attributes;

namespace MyNamespace {
    public class A {
        [Invariant]
        protected void InvariantMethod() { }
        // Other methods...
    }
    public class B {
        [Invariant(Test.Failed)]
        protected void InvariantMethod() { }
        // Other methods...
    }
    public class C {
        [Invariant(Status = Test.InProgress)]
        protected void InvariantMethod() { }
        // Other methods...
    }
    public class D { }
    // And many other classes...
}
```

In order to compile the previous file, the compiler command must refer to the Attributes.dll component as follows:

```
    csc /t:library /r:Attributes.dll UsingAttributes.cs
```

10.2.6 Extracting Attributes Using Reflection

As mentioned previously, reflection is used to search and find all attributes associated with an assembly (.exe or .dll), its modules, and other members. Using the UsingAttributes.dll component, the following example illustrates how the assembly file[1] is first loaded on line 8 by invoking Assembly.Load. Using the GetModule method on line 9, the component UsingAttributes.dll is retrieved and assigned to module. All classes contained in module are then extracted and stored in an array types on line 11. From this point forward, the next program does the following:

- Prints all classes found in UsingAttributes.dll (lines 13–16).

- Prints for each class a list of all public methods (lines 18–21). Note that the GetMethods method retrieves only public methods by default.

- Prints for each class a list of all non-public instance methods (lines 23–27). In this case, it is necessary to specify the kind of methods. Since invariants are protected instance methods, a bit filter called BindingFlags is set to flag those methods that are both instance and non-public (i.e., private and protected).

- Prints all classes that have invariant attributes (lines 29–36) using the same filter.

```
1   using System;
2   using System.Reflection;
3   using Attributes;
4
5   namespace MyNamespace {
6       class TypesWithInvariants {
7           public static void Main() {
8               Assembly assembly = Assembly.Load("UsingAttributes");
9               Module   module   = assembly.GetModule("UsingAttributes.dll");
10
11              Type[] types = module.FindTypes(Module.FilterTypeName, "*");
12
13              Console.WriteLine("Types found in 'UsingAttributes.dll': ");
14              foreach(Type t in types)
15                  Console.Write("{0} ", t.Name);
16              Console.WriteLine();
17
18              Console.WriteLine("\nFor every type, list all public methods:");
19              foreach(Type t in types)
20                  foreach (MethodInfo m in t.GetMethods())
21                      Console.WriteLine("{0} has {1}", t, m.Name);
22
```

---

[1] Based on the Common Object File Format (COFF).

```
23              Console.WriteLine("\nFor every type, list all non-public instance methods:");
24              foreach(Type t in types)
25                  foreach (MethodInfo m in t.GetMethods(BindingFlags.Instance |
26                                                        BindingFlags.NonPublic))
27                      Console.WriteLine("{0} has {1}", t, m.Name);
28
29              Console.WriteLine("\nTypes that have invariant attributes:");
30              foreach (Type t in types)
31                  foreach (MethodInfo m in t.GetMethods(BindingFlags.Instance |
32                                                        BindingFlags.NonPublic))
33                      foreach (Attribute attrib in m.GetCustomAttributes(true)) {
34                          if (attrib is InvariantAttribute)
35                              Console.WriteLine("{0} has {1}", t, m.Name);
36                      }
37          }
38      }
39  }
```

The output of the preceding program is generated next. It is important to recall that all classes derive from the root class and, therefore, include all public and protected methods of object.

```
Types found in 'UsingAttributes.dll':
A B C D

For every type, list all public methods:
MyNamespace.A has GetType
MyNamespace.A has ToString
MyNamespace.A has Equals
MyNamespace.A has GetHashCode
MyNamespace.B has GetType
MyNamespace.B has ToString
MyNamespace.B has Equals
MyNamespace.B has GetHashCode
MyNamespace.C has GetType
MyNamespace.C has ToString
MyNamespace.C has Equals
MyNamespace.C has GetHashCode
MyNamespace.D has GetType
MyNamespace.D has ToString
MyNamespace.D has Equals
MyNamespace.D has GetHashCode
```

```
For every type, list all non-public instance methods:
MyNamespace.A has InvariantMethod
MyNamespace.A has MemberwiseClone
MyNamespace.A has Finalize
MyNamespace.B has InvariantMethod
MyNamespace.B has MemberwiseClone
MyNamespace.B has Finalize
MyNamespace.C has InvariantMethod
MyNamespace.C has MemberwiseClone
MyNamespace.C has Finalize
MyNamespace.D has MemberwiseClone
MyNamespace.D has Finalize

Types that have invariant attributes:
MyNamespace.A has InvariantMethod
MyNamespace.B has InvariantMethod
MyNamespace.C has InvariantMethod
```

10.3 Where to Go from Here

One of the worst things that can happen in any software-development environment is *not* knowing that a solution, either a class or namespace in our object-oriented context, already exists. The danger, of course, is that the "wheel is reinvented" by re-designing and re-implementing a similar solution without the benefit of extensive testing in the public domain. Although we will never have enough days in our lives to be proficient with every class in the .NET Framework, our duty as developers is to be aware that such abstractions exist and to exploit their use in our applications whenever possible.

The .NET Framework is a huge library, and although it was not the mandate of this short book to cover the .NET Framework in detail, it is useful nonetheless to end with a quick roadmap of the core namespaces contained in this framework. All core classes and namespaces encapsulated by the System namespace are listed here in alphabetical order with a brief description of their main purpose.

```
Name:                        Main purpose:

System                       Fundamental Base Classes
  CodeDom                    Code Document Object Model for XML documents
  Collections                List-type and dictionary-type classes and interfaces
  ComponentModel             Component (design- and runtime) behavior
  Configuration              Access and manipulation of .CONFIG files
  Configuration.Assemblies   Access and manipulation of .DLL and .EXE files
  Configuration.Install      Base class for all component installers
  Data                       Data access via ADO.NET
```

Data.Common	Data providers
Data.OleDb	OLE DB and ODBC providers
Data.SqlClient	SQL server data provider
Data.SqlTypes	SQL server native data types
Diagnostics	Application debugging and code execution tracing
Diagnostics.SymbolStore	Read, write, debug symbolic information from MSIL maps
DirectoryServices	Access active directory service providers such as IIS, LDAP, etc.
Drawing	Graphical Drawing Interface (GDI+)
EntrepriseServices	Server-based support for transactions and message queuing
Globalization	Culture-specific support (languages, calendars, currency, etc.)
IO	Input/Output (Streams, Readers, Writers)
Management	Windows Management Instrumentation (disk space and CPU utilization)
Messaging	Message queuing on the network
Net	Networking (HTTP protocol, authentication, etc.)
Net.Sockets	Implementation of the Windows Sockets interface
Reflection	Extraction of metadata to mirror assemblies, types, etc.
Reflection.Emit	Emission and execution using metadata and MSIL
Resources	Resource Management of culture-specific objects and strings
Runtime.CompilerServices	Specification/modification of CLR's metadata for compiler writers
Runtime.InteropServices	COM interoperability
Runtime.Remoting	Distributed applications in using/publishing remote objects
Runtime.Serialization	Serialization and deserialization of objects
Security	Security manager and permissions classes
Security.Cryptography	Secure coding and decoding of data
ServiceProcess	Windows services to be installed and run without a user interface
Text	Text Manipulation (ASCII, Unicode, UTF-7, and UTF-8)
Text.RegularExpressions	Regular expression engine
Threading	Multi-thread programming (synchronization, grouping, etc.)
Timer	Server-based timer component for multi-threaded applications
Web	Browser/server communication services using the HTTP protocol
Web.Services	Development and use of web services

Web.UI	User interface development of controls and pages in a web application
Windows.Forms	User interface development Windows forms in a Windows-based application
Xml	Processing of XML (schemas, serialization, parsing, etc.)

Exercises

Exercise 10-1. Enumerations in C# provide more information than their equivalent in C++ since their corresponding names (string values) are stored in the assembly as metadata. Extract the names of an enumeration via the GetNames method and use them to extend a new enumeration type at runtime with System.Reflection.Emit.

Exercise 10-2. Write a class Assertion that uses conditional attributes with two overloaded static methods, Require and Ensure, that throw PreconditionException and PostconditionException, respectively, if the evaluation of their boolean expressions is not true.

```
public class PreconditionException : Exception { ... }
public class PostconditionException : Exception { ... }

public class Assertion {
    [Conditional("Precondition")]
    public static void Require(bool expr)  { ... }

    [Conditional("Precondition")]
    public static void Require(bool expr, string msg)  { ... }

    [Conditional("Postcondition")]
    public static void Ensure(bool expr) { ... }

    [Conditional("Postcondition")]
    public static void Ensure(bool expr, string msg) { ... }
}
```

appendix **A**

C# 2.0 Grammar

This appendix contains the grammatical summary of the C# 2.0 programming language. Its syntax is described in a concise fashion using the EBNF notation as summarized once again in Table A.1.

The grammar productions are logically grouped into two main grammars: lexical and syntactic. The lexical grammar defines tokens extracted by the lexical analyzer or scanner, and the syntactic grammar is used by the parser to specify how the tokens are organized to produce valid C# programs.

Notation	Meaning
A*	Repetition—zero or more occurrences of A
A+	Repetition—one or more occurrences of A
A?	Option—zero or one occurrence of A
A B	Sequence—A followed by B
A | B	Alternative—A or B
"0".."9"	Alternative—one character between 0 and 9 inclusively
(A B)	Grouping—of an A B sequence

Table A.1: Notation for Extended Backus–Naur Form.

A.1 Lexical Grammar

```
Input           = InputSection? .
InputSection    = InputSectionPart+ .
InputSectionPart = (InputElements? NewLine) | PpDirective .
InputElement    = Whitespace | Comment | Token .
```

A.1.1 Line Terminators

All line terminators are represented by the Newline production. A Newline is either a carriage return (CR) as the \u000D or '\r' character, a line feed (LF) as the \u000A or '\n' character, a (CR) followed by (LF), a line separator (LS) as the \u2028 character, or a paragraph separator (PS) as the \u2029 character.

```
NewLine = CR | LF | CRLF | LS | PS .
```

A.1.2 White Space

A white space is any character with Unicode Class Zs, a horizontal tab (HT) as the \u0009 or '\t' character, a vertical tab (VT) as the \u000B or '\v' character, or a form feed (FF) as the \u000C or '\f' character.

```
Whitespace = AnyCharacterWithUnicodeClassZs | HT | VT | FF .
```

A.1.3 Comments

```
Comment                   = SingleLineComment | DelimitedComment .
SingleLineComment         = "//" InputCharacters? .
InputCharacter            = AnyUnicodeCharacterExceptANewLine .
DelimitedComment          = "/*" DelimitedCommentCharacters?  "*/" .
DelimitedCommentCharacter = NotAsterisk | ("*" NotSlash) .
NotAsterisk               = AnyUnicodeCharacterExcept "*" .
NotSlash                  = AnyUnicodeCharacterExcept "/" .
```

A.1.4 Tokens

```
Token = Identifier | Keyword | Literal | OperatorOrPunctuator .
```

Note: null, true, and false are keywords as well as literals.

A.1.5 Unicode Character Escape Sequences

```
UnicodeEscapeSequence = ("\u" FourHexDigits) | ("\U" FourHexDigits FourHexDigits) .
FourHexDigits         = HexDigit  HexDigit  HexDigit  HexDigit .
```

A.1.6 Identifiers

```
Identifier              = AvailableIdentifier | ("@" IdentifierOrKeyword) .
AvailableIdentifier     = An IdentifierOrKeyword that is not a Keyword .
IdentifierOrKeyword     = IdentifierStartCharacter  IdentifierPartCharacters? .
IdentifierStartCharacter = LetterChar | "_" .
IdentifierPartCharacter = LetterChar   | DecimalDigitChar | ConnectingChar
                        | CombiningChar | FormattingChar .
```

A LetterChar is either a Unicode character of classes Lu, Ll, Lt, Lm, Lo, or Nl; or a Unicode-character-escape-sequence representing a character of classes Lu, Ll, Lt, Lm, Lo, or Nl. A CombiningChar is either a Unicode character of classes Mn or Mc; or a Unicode-character-escape-sequence representing a character of classes Mn or Mc. A DecimalDigitChar is either a Unicode character of the class Nd, or a Unicode-character-escape-sequence representing a character of the class Nd. A ConnectingChar is either a Unicode character of the class Pc, or a Unicode-character-escape-sequence representing a character of the class Pc. A FormattingChar is either a Unicode character of the class Cf, or a Unicode-character-escape-sequence representing a character of the class Cf.

A.1.7 Keywords

abstract	as	base	bool	break
byte	case	catch	char	checked
class	const	continue	decimal	default
delegate	do	double	else	enum
event	explicit	extern	false	finally
fixed	float	for	foreach	goto
if	implicit	in	int	interface
internal	is	lock	long	namespace
new	null	object	operator	out
override	params	private	protected	public
readonly	ref	return	sbyte	sealed
short	sizeof	stackalloc	static	string
struct	switch	this	throw	true
try	typeof	uint	ulong	unchecked
unsafe	ushort	using	virtual	void
volatile	while			

A.1.8 Literals

```
Literal            = BooleanLiteral   | IntegerLiteral | RealLiteral
                   | CharacterLiteral | StringLiteral  | NullLiteral .
BooleanLiteral     = "true" | "false" .
IntegerLiteral     = DecimalIntLiteral | HexIntLiteral .
DecimalIntLiteral  = DecimalDigits  IntegerTypeSuffix? .
DecimalDigit       = "0".."9" .
IntegerTypeSuffix  = "U" | "u" | "L" | "l" | "Ul" | "ul" | "Lu" | "lu" | "UL" | "uL" | "LU" | "lU" .
HexIntegerLiteral  = ("0x" | "0X") HexDigits  IntegerTypeSuffix? .
HexDigit           = "0..9" | "A".."F" | "a".."f" .
RealLiteral        = ( DecimalDigits  "."  DecimalDigits  ExponentPart?  RealTypeSuffix? )
                   | (               "."  DecimalDigits  ExponentPart?  RealTypeSuffix? )
                   | (                    DecimalDigits  ExponentPart   RealTypeSuffix? )
                   | (                    DecimalDigits                 RealTypeSuffix  ) .
```

```
ExponentPart         = ("e" | "E") Sign? DecimalDigits .
Sign                 = "+" | "-" .
RealTypeSuffix       = "F" | "f" | "D" | "d" | "M" | "m" .
CharacterLiteral     = "'" Character "'" .
Character            = SingleCharacter | SimpleEscapeSequence | HexEscapeSequence | UnicodeEscapeSequence .
SingleCharacter      = Any Character Except Quote, Escape, and NewLine .
SimpleEscapeSequence = "\'" | "\\" | "\0" | "\a" | "\b" | "\f" | "\n" | "\r" | "\t" | "\v" | DQuote .
DQuote               = "\"" (\u0022) .
Quote                = "'" (\u0027) .
Escape               = "\\" (\u005C) .
HexEscapeSequence    = "\x" HexDigit HexDigit? HexDigit? HexDigit? .
StringLiteral        = RegularStringLiteral | VerbatimStringLiteral .
RegularStringLiteral          = " RegularStringLiteralCharacters? " .
RegularStringLiteralCharacter = SingleRegularStringLiteralCharacter | SimpleEscapeSequence
                              | HexadecimalEscapeSequence | UnicodeEscapeSequence .
SingleRegularStringLiteralCharacter = Any Character Except DQuote, Escape, and NewLine .
VerbatimStringLiteral               = "@" DQuote VerbatimStringLiteralCharacters? DQuote .
VerbatimStringLiteralCharacter      = SingleVerbatimStringLiteralCharacter | QuoteEscapeSequence .
SingleVerbatimStringLiteralCharacter = Any Character Except DQuote .
QuoteEscapeSequence                 = "\'" .
NullLiteral                         = "null" .
```

A.1.9 Operators and Punctuators

```
{       }       [       ]       (       )       .       ,       =       ;
+       -       *       /       %       &       |       ^       !       ~
=       <       >       ?       ::      ++      --      &&      ||      ->
==      !=      <=      >=      +=      -=      *=      /=      %=      &=
|=      ^=      <<=     <<      > >     > >=
```

A.1.10 Preprocessing Directives

```
PpDirective     = PpDeclaration | PpConditional | PpLine | PpDiagnostic | PpRegion | PpPragma .
PpNewLine       = Whitespace? SingleLineComment? NewLine .
ConditionalSymbol = Any IdentifierOrKeyword Except "true" or "false" .
PpExpr          = Whitespace? PpOrExpr Whitespace? .
PpOrExpr        = PpAndExpr (Whitespace? "||" Whitespace? PpAndExpr)* .
PpAndExpr       = PpEqualityExpr (Whitespace? "&&" Whitespace? PpEqualityExpr)* .
PpEqualityExpr  = PpUnaryExpr (Whitespace? ("==" | "!=") Whitespace? PpUnaryExpr)* .
PpUnaryExpr     = ("!" Whitespace? PpPrimaryExpr)* .
PpPrimaryExpr   = "true" | "false" | ConditionalSymbol | "(" Whitespace? PpExpr Whitespace? ")" .

PpDeclaration = Whitespace? "#" Whitespace? ("define"|"undef") Whitespace ConditionalSymbol PpNewLine .
PpConditional = PpIfSection   PpElifSections?   PpElseSection?   PpEndif .
```

```
PpIfSection   = Whitespace? "#" Whitespace? "if" Whitespace PpExpr PpNewLine ConditionalSection? .
PpElifSection = Whitespace? "#" Whitespace? "elif" Whitespace PpExpr PpNewLine ConditionalSection? .
PpElseSection = Whitespace? "#" Whitespace? "else"  PpNewLine ConditionalSection? .
PpEndifLine   = Whitespace? "#" Whitespace? "endif" PpNewLine .

ConditionalSection = InputSection | SkippedSection .
SkippedSection     = SkippedSectionPart+ .
SkippedSectionPart = (SkippedCharacters? NewLine) | PpDirective .
SkippedCharacters  = Whitespace?  NotNumberSign  InputCharacters? .
NotNumberSign      = Any InputCharacter Except "#" .
PpLine             = Whitespace? "#" Whitespace? "line" Whitespace LineIndicator PpNewLine .
LineIndicator      = (DecimalDigits Whitespace FileName) | DecimalDigits | "default" .
FileName           = "\"" FileNameCharacters "\"" .
FileNameCharacter  = Any InputCharacter Except "\"" .

PpDiagnostic       = Whitespace?  "#"  Whitespace? ("error" | "warning")  PpMessage .
PpMessage          = NewLine | (Whitespace  InputCharacters?  NewLine) .
PpRegion           = PpStartRegion  ConditionalSection?  PpEndRegion .
PpStartRegion      = Whitespace?  "#"  Whitespace?  "region"    PpMessage .
PpEndRegion        = Whitespace?  "#"  Whitespace?  "endregion"  PpMessage .
PpPragma           = Whitespace?  "#"  Whitespace?  "pragma"      PragmaBody PpNewLine .
PragmaBody         = PragmaWarningBody .
PragmaWarningBody  = "warning" Whitespace WarningAction ( Whitespace WarningList )? .
WarningAction      = "disable" | "restore" .
WarningList        = DecimalDigits ( Whitespace? "," Whitespace? DecimalDigits )* .
```

A.2 Syntactic Grammar

A.2.1 Namespace, Type, and Simple Names

```
NamespaceName       = NamespaceOrTypeName .
TypeName            = NamespaceOrTypeName .
NamespaceOrTypeName = ( Identifier TypeArgumentList? )
                    | ( "." Identifier TypeArgumentList? )*
                    | QualifiedAliasMember .
SimpleName          = Identifier TypeArgumentList? .
QualifiedAliasMember = Identifier "::" Identifier TypeArgumentList? .
```

A.2.2 Types

```
Type       = ValueType | ReferenceType | TypeParameter .
ValueType  = StructType | EnumType | NullableType .
StructType = TypeName | SimpleType .
```

```
SimpleType    = NumericType | "bool" .
NumericType   = IntegralType | RealType | "decimal" | "char" .
IntegralType  = "sbyte" | "short" | "int" | "long" | "byte" | "ushort" | "uint" | "ulong" .
RealType      = "float" | "double" .
EnumType      = TypeName .
NullableType  = ValueType "?" .
ReferenceType = ClassType | InterfaceType | ArrayType | DelegateType .
ClassType     = TypeName | "object" | "string" .
InterfaceType = TypeName .
ArrayType     = NonArrayType RankSpecifiers .
NonArrayType  = Type .
RankSpecifier = "[" DimSeparators? "]" .
DimSeparators = ","+ .
DelegateType  = TypeName .
```

A.2.3 Variables

```
VariableReference = Expr .
```

A.2.4 Expressions

```
Argument    = Expr | ("ref" | "out") VariableReference .
PrimaryExpr = PrimaryNoArrayCreationExpr | ArrayCreationExpr .
PrimaryNoArrayCreationExpr = Literal | SimpleName | ParenthesizedExpr | MemberAccess
            | InvocationExpr | ElementAccess | ThisAccess | BaseAccess | PostIncrementExpr
            | PostDecrementExpr | ObjectCreationExpr | DelegateCreationExpr | TypeofExpr
            | SizeofExpr | CheckedExpr | UncheckedExpr | DefaultValueExpr |
            | AnonymousMethodExpr .

ParenthesizedExpr    = "(" Expr ")" .
MemberAccess         = ( PrimaryExpr "." Identifier TypeArgumentList? )
                     | ( PredefinedType "." Identifier TypeArgumentList? )
                     | ( QualifiedAliasMember "." Identifier ) .
InvocationExpr       = PrimaryExpr "(" ArgumentList? ")" .
ElementAccess        = PrimaryNoArrayCreationExpr  "[" ExprList "]" .
ThisAccess           = "this" .
BaseAccess           = "base" ( "." Identifier ) | ( "[" ExprList "]" ) .
PostIncrementExpr    = PrimaryExpr "++" .
PostDecrementExpr    = PrimaryExpr "--" .
ObjectCreationExpr   = "new" Type "(" ArgumentList? ")" .
DelegateCreationExpr = "new" DelegateType "(" Expr ")" .
TypeofExpr           = "typeof" "(" Type | "void" ")" .
CheckedExpr          = "checked" "(" Expr ")" .
UncheckedExpr        = "unchecked" "(" Expr ")" .
```

```
DefaultValueExpr      = "default" "(" Type ")".
AnonymousMethodExpr   = "delegate" AnonymousMethodSignature? Block .


PredefinedType       = "bool" | "byte" | "char" | "decimal" | "double" | "float" | "int" | "long"
                      | "object" | "sbyte" | "short" | "string" | "uint" | "ulong" | "ushort" .
ArrayCreationExpr    = ( "new" NonArrayType "[" ExprList "]" RankSpecifiers? ArrayInitializer? )
                      | ( "new" ArrayType   ArrayInitializer ) .
UnaryExpr            = PreIncExpr | PreDecExpr | CastExpr | ( ("+"|"-"|"!"|"~"|"*")? PrimaryExpr ) .
PreIncExpr           = "++" UnaryExpr .
PreDecExpr           = "--" UnaryExpr .
CastExpr             = "(" Type ")" UnaryExpr .
MultiplicativeExpr   = UnaryExpr (MulOp UnaryExpr)* .
AdditiveExpr         = MultiplicativeExpr (AddOp MultiplicativeExpr)* .
ShiftExpr            = AdditiveExpr (ShiftOp AdditiveExpr)* .
RelationalExpr       = ShiftExpr ( (RelOp ShiftExpr) | (TypeTestingOp Type) )* .
EqualityExpr         = RelationalExpr (EquOp RelationalExpr)* .
AndExpr              = EqualityExpr ("&" EqualityExpr)* .
ExclusiveOrExpr      = AndExpr ("^" AndExpr)* .
InclusiveOrExpr      = ExclusiveOrExpr ("|" ExclusiveOrExpr)* .
ConditionalAndExpr   = InclusiveOrExpr ("&&" InclusiveOrExpr)* .
ConditionalOrExpr    = ConditionalAndExpr ("||" ConditionalAndExpr)* .
NullCoalescingExpr   = ConditionalOrExpr ("??" ConditionalOrExpr)* .
ConditionalExpr      = NullCoalescingExpr | ( NullCoalescingExpr "?" Expr ":" Expr) .
Assignment           = UnaryExpr  AssignmentOp  Expr
AssignmentOp         = "=" | "+=" | "-=" | "*=" | "/=" | "%=" | "&=" | "|=" | "^=" | "<<=" | ">>=" .
MulOp                = "*" | "/" | "%" .
AddOp                = "+" | "-" .
ShiftOp              = "<<" | ">>" .
RelOp                = "<" | ">" | "<=" | ">=" .
TypeTestingOp        = "is" | "as" .
EquOp                = "==" | "!=" .
Expr                 = ConditionalExpr | Assignment .
ConstantExpr         = Expr .
BooleanExpr          = Expr .
```

A.2.5 Statements

```
Stmt         = EmbeddedStmt | LabeledStmt | DeclStmt .
EmbeddedStmt = ExprStmt | EmptyStmt | Block | SelectionStmt | IterationStmt
             | JumpStmt | TryStmt | CheckedStmt | UncheckedStmt | LockStmt
             | UsingStmt | YieldStmt .
ExprStmt     = StmtExpr ";" .
StmtExpr     = InvocationExpr | ObjectCreationExpr | Assignment
             | PostIncExpr | PostDecExpr | PreIncExpr | PreDecExpr .
```

```
EmptyStmt     = ";" .
Block         = "{" Stmts? "}" .

SelectionStmt = IfStmt | SwitchStmt .
IfStmt        = "if" "(" BooleanExpr ")" EmbeddedStmt ( "else" EmbeddedStmt )? .
BooleanExpr   = Expr .
SwitchStmt    = "switch" "(" Expr ")"  SwitchBlock .
SwitchBlock   = "{" SwitchSections? "}" .
SwitchSection = SwitchLabels Stmts .
SwitchLabel   = ( "case" ConstantExpr ":" ) | ( "default"  ":" ) .

IterationStmt = WhileStmt | DoStmt | ForStmt | ForeachStmt .
WhileStmt     = "while" "(" BooleanExpr ")" EmbeddedStmt .
DoStmt        = "do" EmbeddedStmt "while" "(" BooleanExpr ")" ";" .
ForStmt       = "for" "(" ForInitializer? ";" ForCondition? ";" ForIterator? ")" EmbeddedStmt .
ForInitializer = LocalVariableDecl | StmtExprList .
ForCondition  = BooleanExpr .
ForIterator   = StmtExprList .
ForeachStmt   = "foreach" "(" Type Identifier "in" Expr ")" EmbeddedStmt .

JumpStmt      = BreakStmt | ContinueStmt | GotoStmt | ReturnStmt | ThrowStmt .
BreakStmt     = "break" ";" .
ContinueStmt  = "continue" ";" .
GotoStmt      = "goto" ( Identifier | ("case" ConstantExpr) | Default ) ";" .
ReturnStmt    = "return" Expr? ";" .
ThrowStmt     = "throw" Expr? ";" .
TryStmt       = "try" Block ( CatchClauses | FinallyClause )? | ( CatchClauses FinallyClause )? .
CatchClauses  = ( SpecificCatchClauses  GeneralCatchClause? )
                | ( SpecificCatchClauses? GeneralCatchClause  ) .

SpecificCatchClauses    = SpecificCatchClause+ .
SpecificCatchClause     = "catch" "(" ClassType Identifier? ")" Block .
GeneralCatchClause      = "catch" Block .
FinallyClause           = "finally" Block .
CheckedStmt             = "checked" Block .
UncheckedStmt           = "unchecked" Block .
LockStmt                = "lock" "(" Expr ")" EmbeddedStmt .
UsingStmt               = "using" "(" ResourceAcquisition ")" EmbeddedStmt .
YieldStmt               = ("yield" "return" Expr) | ("yield" "break") .

ResourceAcquisition     = LocalVariableDecl | Expr .
LabeledStmt             = Identifier ":" Stmt .
DeclStmt                = ( LocalVariableDecl | LocalConstantDecl ) ";" .
LocalVariableDecl       = Type LocalVariableDecltorList .
```

```
LocalVariableDecltor     = Identifier ( "=" LocalVariableInitializer )? .
LocalVariableInitializer = Expr | ArrayInitializer .
LocalConstantDecl        = "const" Type ConstantDecltorList .
ConstantDecltor          = Identifier "=" ConstantExpr .
```

A.2.6 Namespaces

```
CompilationUnit     = ExternAliasDirectives? UsingDirectives? GlobalAttributes? NamespaceMemberDecls? .
NamespaceDecl       = "namespace" QualifiedIdentifier NamespaceBody ";"? .
QualifiedIdentifier = Identifier ( "." Identifier )* .
NamespaceBody       = "{" ExternAliasDirectives? UsingDirectives? NamespaceMemberDecls? "}" .
UsingDirective      = "using" ( UsingAliasDirective | NamespaceName ) ";" .
UsingAliasDirective = Identifier "=" NamespaceOrTypeName .
ExternAliasDirective = "extern" "alias" Identifier ";" .
NamespaceMemberDecl = NamespaceDecl | TypeDecl .
TypeDecl            = ClassDecl | StructDecl | InterfaceDecl | EnumDecl | DelegateDecl .
```

A.2.7 Classes

```
ClassDecl        = Attributes? ClassModifiers? "partial"? "class" Identifier
                   TypeParameterList? ClassBase? TypeParameterConstraintsClauses? ClassBody ";"? .
ClassModifier    = "new" | "public" | "protected" | "internal" | "private"
                   | "abstract" | "sealed" | "static" .
ClassBase        = ":" (ClassType | InterfaceTypeList | (ClassType "," InterfaceTypeList)) .
ClassBody        = "{" ClassMemberDecls? "}" .
ClassMemberDecl  = ConstantDecl | FieldDecl | MethodDecl | PropertyDecl | EventDecl
                   | IndexerDecl | OperatorDecl | ConstructorDecl | DestructorDecl
                   | StaticConstructorDecl | TypeDecl | GenericMethodDecl .
ConstantDecl     = Attributes? ConstantModifiers? "const" Type ConstantDecltorList ";" .
ConstantModifier = "new" | "public" | "protected" | "internal" | "private" .
ConstantDecltor  = Identifier "=" ConstantExpr .
FieldDecl        = Attributes? FieldModifiers? Type VariableDecltors ";" .
FieldModifier    = "new" | "public" | "protected" | "internal" | "private"
                   | "static" | "readonly" | "volatile" .
VariableDecltor  = Identifier ( "=" VariableInitializer )? .
VariableInitializer = Expression | ArrayInitializer .
MethodDecl       = MethodHeader MethodBody .
MethodHeader     = Attributes? MethodModifiers? ReturnType MemberName "(" FormalParameterList? ")" .
MethodModifier   = "new" | "public" | "protected" | "internal" | "private" | "static"
                   | "virtual" | "sealed" | "override" | "abstract" | "extern" .
ReturnType       = Type | "void" .
MemberName       = Identifier | (InterfaceType "." Identifier) .
MethodBody       = Block | ";" .
FormalParameterList = FixedParameterList | (FixedParameterList "," ParameterArray) | ParameterArray .
```

```
FixedParameter      = Attributes? ParameterModifier? Type Identifier .
ParameterModifier   = "ref" | "out" .
ParameterArray      = Attributes? "params" ArrayType Identifier .
PropertyDecl        = Attributes? PropertyModifiers? Type MemberName "{" AccessorDecls "}" .
PropertyModifier    = "new" | "public" | "protected" | "internal" | "private" | "static"
                      | "virtual" | "sealed" | "override" | "abstract" | "extern" .
AccessorDecls       = ( GetAccessorDecl SetAccessorDecl? ) | ( SetAccessorDecl GetAccessorDecl? ) .
GetAccessorDecl     = Attributes? AccessorModifier? "get" AccessorBody .
SetAccessorDecl     = Attributes? AccessorModifier? "set" AccessorBody .
AccessorModifier    = "protected | "internal" | "private"
                      | ("protected" "internal") | ("internal" "protected") .
AccessorBody        = Block | ";" .
EventDecl           = Attributes? EventModifiers? Event Type (VariableDecltors ";")
                      | (MemberName "{" EventAccessorDecls "}") .
EventModifier       = "new" | "public" | "protected" | "internal" | "private" | "static"
                      | "virtual" | "sealed" | "override" | "abstract" | "extern" .
EventAccessorDecls  = (AddAccessorDecl RemoveAccessorDecl) | (RemoveAccessorDecl AddAccessorDecl) .
AddAccessorDecl     = Attributes? "add" Block .
RemoveAccessorDecl  = Attributes? "remove" Block .
IndexerDecl         = Attributes? IndexerModifiers? IndexerDecltor "{" AccessorDecls "}" .
IndexerModifier     = "new" | "public" | "protected" | "internal" | "private" | "static"
                      | "virtual" | "sealed" | "override" | "abstract" | "extern" .
IndexerDecltor      = Type ( InterfaceType "." )? "this" "[" FormalParameterList "]" .
OperatorDecl        = Attributes? OperatorModifiers OperatorDecltor OperatorBody .
OperatorModifier    = "public" | "static" | "extern" .
OperatorDecltor     = UnaryOpDecltor | BinaryOpDecltor | ConversionOpDecltor .

UnaryOpDecltor          = Type "operator" OverloadableUnaryOp "(" Type Identifier ")" .
OverloadableUnaryOp     = "+" | "-" | "!" | "˜" | "++" | "--" | "true" | "false" .
BinaryOpDecltor         = Type "operator" OverloadableBinaryOp
                          "(" Type Identifier "," Type Identifier ")" .
OverloadableBinaryOp    = "+" | "-" | "*" | "/" | "%" | "&" | "|" | "^" | "<<"
                          | ">>" | "==" | "!=" | ">" | "<" | ">=" | "<=" .
ConversionOpDecltor     = ( Implicit | Explicit )? "operator" Type "(" Type Identifier ")" .
OperatorBody            = Block | ";" .
ConstructorDecl         = Attributes? ConstructorModifiers? ConstructorDecltor ConstructorBody .
ConstructorModifier     = "public" | "protected" | "internal" | "private" | "extern" .
ConstructorDecltor      = Identifier "(" FormalParameterList? ")" ConstructorInitializer? .
ConstructorInitializer  = ":" ( "base" | "this" )? "(" ArgumentList? ")" .
ConstructorBody         = Block | ";" .
StaticConstructorDecl   = Attributes? StaticConstructorModifiers
                          Identifier "(" ")" StaticConstructorBody .
StaticConstructorModifiers = ( "extern"? "static" ) | ( "static" "extern"? ) .
StaticConstructorBody   = Block | ";" .
```

```
DestructorDecl          = Attributes? "extern"? "~" Identifier "(" ")" DestructorBody .
DestructorBody          = Block | ";" .
```

A.2.8 Structs

```
StructDecl       = Attributes? StructModifiers? "partial"? "struct" Identifier
                   TypeParameterList? StructInterfaces? TypeParameterConstraintsClauses?
                   StructBody ";"? .
StructModifier   = "new" | "public" | "protected" | "internal" | "private" .
StructInterfaces = ":" InterfaceTypeList .
StructBody       = "{" StructMemberDecls? "}" .
StructMemberDecl = ConstantDecl | FieldDecl | MethodDecl | PropertyDecl | EventDecl
                 | IndexerDecl | OperatorDecl | ConstructorDecl | StaticConstructorDecl
                 | TypeDecl | GenericMethodDecl .
```

A.2.9 Arrays

```
ArrayType          = NonArrayType RankSpecifiers .
NonArrayType       = Type .
RankSpecifier      = "[" DimSeparators? "]" .
DimSeparator       = "," .
ArrayInitializer   = ( "{" VariableInitializerList?     "}" )
                   | ( "{" VariableInitializerList ","  "}" ) .
VariableInitializer = Expression | ArrayInitializer .
```

A.2.10 Interfaces

```
InterfaceDecl         = Attributes? InterfaceModifiers? "partial"? "interface" Identifier
                        TypeParameterList? InterfaceBase? TypeParameterConstraintsClauses?
                        InterfaceBody ";"? .
InterfaceModifier     = "new" | "public" | "protected" | "internal" | "private" .
InterfaceBase         = ":" InterfaceTypeList .
Interface-body        = "{" InterfaceMemberDecls? "}" .
InterfaceMemberDecl   = InterfaceMethodDecl | InterfacePropertyDecl | InterfaceEventDecl
                      | InterfaceIndexerDecl | InterfaceGenericMethodDecl .
InterfaceMethodDecl   = Attributes? "new"? ReturnType Identifier "(" FormalParameterList? ")" ";" .
interfacePropertyDecl = Attributes? "new"? Type Identifier "{" InterfaceAccessors "}" .
InterfaceAccessors    = ( Attributes? "get" ";" ) | ( Attributes? "set" ";" )
                      | ( Attributes? "get" ";"        Attributes? "set" ";" )
                      | ( Attributes? "set" ";"        Attributes? "get" ";" ) .
InterfaceEventDecl    = Attributes? "new"? Event Type Identifier ";" .
InterfaceIndexerDecl  = Attributes? "new"? Type "this" "[" FormalParameterList "]"
                        "{" InterfaceAccessors "}" .
```

A.2.11   Enums

```
EnumDecl       = Attributes? EnumModifiers? "enum" Identifier EnumBase? EnumBody ";"? .
EnumBase       = ":" IntegralType .
EnumBody       = ( "{" EnumMemberDeclList? "}" ) | ( "{" EnumMemberDeclList ","  "}" ) .
EnumModifier   = "new" | "public" | "protected" | "internal" | "private" .
EnumMemberDecl = Attributes? Identifier ( "=" ConstantExpression )? .
```

A.2.12   Delegates

```
DelegateDecl     = Attributes? DelegateModifiers? "delegate" ReturnType Identifier
                   TypeParameterList? "(" FormalParameterList? ")"
                   TypeParameterConstraintsClauses ";" .
DelegateModifier = "new" | "public" | "protected" | "internal" | "private" .


AnonymousMethodSignature = "(" AnonymousMethodParameterList? ")" .
AnonymousMethodParameter = ParameterModifier? Type Identifier .
```

A.2.13   Attributes

```
GlobalAttributes              = GlobalAttributeSections .
GlobalAttributeSection        = "[" GlobalAttributeTargetSpecifier AttributeList ","? "]" .
GlobalAttributeTargetSpecifier = GlobalAttributeTarget ":" .
GlobalAttributeTarget         = "assembly" | "module" .
Attributes                    = AttributeSections .
AttributeSection              = "[" AttributeTargetSpecifier? AttributeList ","? "]" .
AttributeTargetSpecifier      = AttributeTarget ":" .
AttributeTarget               = "field"    | "event"  | "method" | "param"
                              | "property" | "return" | "type" .
Attribute                     = AttributeName AttributeArguments? .
AttributeName                 = TypeName .
AttributeArguments            = ( "(" PositionalArgumentList? ")" )
                              | ( "(" PositionalArgumentList  "," NamedArgumentList ")" )
                              | ( "(" NamedArgumentList       ")" ) .
PositionalArgument            = AttributeArgumentExpr .
NamedArgument                 = Identifier "=" AttributeArgumentExpr .
AttributeArgumentExpr         = Expr .
```

A.3   Generics

```
TypeParameterList   = "<" TypeParameters ">" .
TypeParameters      = Attributes? TypeParameter ( "," Attributes? TypeParameter )* .
```

```
TypeParameter         = Identifier .
TypeArgumentList      = ActualTypeArgumentList | AritySpecifier .
ActualTypeArgumentList = "<" TypeArguments ">" .
TypeArgument          = Type .
AritySpecifier        = "<" ","* ">" .


GenericMethodDecl     = GenericMethodHeader MethodBody .
GenericMethodHeader   = Attributes? MethodModifiers? ReturnType MemberName TypeParameterList?
                        "(" FormalParameterList? ")" TypeParameterConstraintsClauses? .


InterfaceGenericMethodDecl = Attributes? "new"? ReturnType Identifier TypeParameterList?
                        "(" FormalParameterList? ")" TypeParameterConstraintsClauses? .


TypeParameterConstraintsClause = "where" TypeParameter ":" TypeParameterConstraints .


TypeParameterConstraints = PrimaryConstraint | SecondaryConstraints | ConstructorConstraint
                        | (PrimaryConstraint "," SecondaryConstraints)
                        | (PrimaryConstraint "," ConstructorConstraint)
                        | (SecondaryConstraints "," ConstructorConstraint)
                        | (PrimaryConstraint "," SecondaryConstraints "," ConstructorConstraint) .
PrimaryConstraint     = ClassType | "class" | "struct" .
SecondaryConstraints  = InterfaceType | TypeParameter | ( "," InterfaceType )*
                        | ( "," TypeParameter )* .
ConstructorConstraint = "new" "(" ")" .
```

appendix **B**

Predefined XML Tags for Documentation Comments

This appendix presents a subset of the predefined XML tags that are most useful for C# program documentation. All tags must be preceded by the /// comment.

XML Tag	Meaning and Example
<c>	Describes a line of code.
	<c>int i = 10;</c>
<code>	Describes multiple lines of code.
	<code> *CodeSample* </code>
<example>	Describes the code sample.
	<example> *Description* </example>
<exception>	Describes which exceptions a class can throw.
	<exception cref="type"> *Description* </exception>
	<exception cref="System.Exception"> Thrown when... </exception>
<include>	Includes comments from another documentation file.
	<include file='filename' path='tagpath[@name="id"'/>
	<include file='Class.doc' path='Doc/Prj[@name="Class"]/*'/>

Table B.1: Predefined XML tags for documentation comments.

XML Tag	Meaning and Example

<list>	Inserts a list into the documentation.
	`<list type="bullet" | "number" | "table">`
	    `<listheader>`
	        `<term>` *Name* `</term>`
	        `<description>` *Description* `</description>`
	    `</listheader>`
	    `<item>`
	        `<term>` *Name* `</term>`
	        `<description>` *Description* `</description>`
	    `</item>`
	`</list>`

<para>	Sets off the text as a paragraph. `<para>` *Text* `</para>`

<param>	Describes a given parameter.
	`<param name="name">` *Description* `</param>`
	`<param name="n">` *The specified integer value.* `</param>`

<paramref>	Associates a given XML tag with a specified parameter. `<paramref name="name"/>` The `<paramref name="n"/>` parameter specifies an integer value.

<permission>	Describes the access permission of a member.
	`<permission cref="type">` *Description* `</permission>`
	`<permission cref="MyClass.MyMethod">` Public access.`</permission>`

<remarks>	Describes the type of a given member. `<remarks>` *Description* `</remarks>`
<returns>	Describes the return value. `<returns>` *Description* `</returns>`

<see>	Provides a cross-reference to related elements available to the current compilation environment.
	`<see cref="element"/>`
	`<see cref="MyClass.MyMethod"/>`

<seealso>	Same as the `<see>` tag except it emits a separate "see also" section.
<summary>	Describes a given class or member. `<summary>` *Description* `</summary>`
<value>	Describes a given property. `<value>` *Description* `</value>`

Table B.1: *(continued)*

References

References on C#, XML, and .NET Specifications

ECMA-334 *C# Language Specification* (First Edition), `http://www.ecma-international.org`, December 2001.

ECMA-334 *C# Language Specification* (Second Edition), `http://www.ecma-international.org`, December 2002.

ECMA/TC39-TG2 *C# Language Specification* (Working Draft 2.7), `http://www.ecma-international.org`, June 2004.

Microsoft *C# Version 1.2 Language Specification*, Microsoft Corporation, June 2003.

Microsoft *C# Version 2.0 Language Specification*, Microsoft Corporation, May 2004.

ECMA-335 *Common Language Infrastructure* (First Edition), `http://www.ecma-international.org`, December 2001.

W3C *Extensible Markup Language (XML) 1.0*, `http://www.w3.org/XML`, February 2004.

Microsoft *.NET Framework Standard Library Annotated Reference*, Volume 1: Base Class Library and Extended Numerics Library, Microsoft .NET Development Series, Addison-Wesley Professional, June 2004.

References on Object-Oriented Design

Martin Fowler, *Refactoring: Improving the Design of Existing Code*, Addison-Wesley, 1999.

Erich Gamma, Richard Helm, Ralph Johnson, John Vlissides, *Design Patterns: Elements of Reusable Object-Oriented Software*, Addison-Wesley, 1995.

Bertrand Meyer, *Object-Oriented Software Construction* (2nd Edition), Prentice-Hall, 1997.

John Vlissides, *Pattern Hatching: Design Patterns Applied*, Addison-Wesley, 1998.

Related Web Sites

http://www.ecma-international.org/publications/standards/Ecma-334.htm
   The official ECMA C# language specification site.

http://msdn.microsoft.com/net
   The official Microsoft .NET developers site.

http://msdn.microsoft.com/vcsharp/team/language
   The official Microsoft Visual C# language site.

http://www.gotdotnet.com
   The Microsoft .NET Framework community support site.

Index

Lightning Source UK Ltd.
Milton Keynes UK
01 October 2009

144382UK00001B/172/P